CMS Made Simple 1.6
Beginner's Guide

Create a fully functional and professional website using CMS Made Simple

Sofia Hauschildt

[PACKT]
PUBLISHING

BIRMINGHAM - MUMBAI

CMS Made Simple 1.6

Beginner's Guide

Copyright © 2010 Packt Publishing

First published: March 2010

Production Reference: 1250210

Published by Packt Publishing Ltd.
32 Lincoln Road
Olton
Birmingham, B27 6PA, UK.

ISBN 978-1-847198-20-4

www.packtpub.com

Cover Image by Vinayak Chittar (vinayak.chittar@gmail.com)

Credits

Author

Sofia Hauschildt

Reviewers

Jeremy Bass

Yury V. Zaytsev

Acquisition Editor

Sarah Cullington

Development Editor

Chaitanya Apte

Technical Editors

Gauri Iyer

Smita Solanki

Copy Editor

Leonard D'Silva

Indexer

Hemangini Bari

Editorial Team Leader

Aanchal Kumar

Project Team Leader

Lata Basantani

Project Coordinator

Srimoyee Ghoshal

Proofreader

Lesley Harrison

Graphics

Geetanjali Sawant

Production Coordinator

Shantanu Zagade

Cover Work

Shantanu Zagade

About the Author

Sofia Hauschildt is a web mastering and web development tutor, who started designing and developing professional websites in 1995 just before her graduation in Computer Science. With experience as a data warehouse developer and ERP consultant, she became a self-employed tutor. During her career, she has been contracted by IT and management academies, the German army, several city administrations, and international companies such as Siemens. Her work as a tutor is always focused on practical training combined with a theoretical background in order to get fast and handy results.

I would like to express my gratitude to all those who gave me the possibility to complete this book. I want to thank my husband Jens for investing a huge amount of time in the first reviews of this book and his patient love. Furthermore, I have to thank Yury V. Zaytsev for his stimulating support and interesting discussions.

A special thanks goes to my parents who encouraged me to go ahead with this book and gave me incredible mental support.

About the Reviewers

Jeremy Bass began learning web construction at the age of 12 using the "view source" on sites such as the young Yahoo and the late GeoCities. Armed with a computer and a talent for the fine arts, he has been in computer-based graphics ever since. A few of the high points are stents at an international telescope (Gemini in Hawaii) and winning a Telly award for 3D animation. Currently, Jeremy works with Digital Barn Productions in Idaho, and Defined Clarity in Philadelphia along with freelancing and participation in the CMSMS community.

> I would like to thank my wife, Aimee, for understanding I work long hours not just to grow, but for her and the kids. This was fun.

Yury V. Zaytsev has an advanced degree in physics from the Nizhny Novgorod State University, Russia, and is currently working towards his doctorate in Computational Neuroscience at the University of Freiburg, Germany. Yury's primary interests concern scientific computing, modeling, and simulation, particularly of the complex dynamics of large populations of neurons.

Yury's first contact with computers was at the age of 6 when he programmed his first text-based role-playing game in BASIC on a historical 80386 machine. This inspired a never ending passion for programming, which also led to a brief career at the age of 17 in freelance web development for companies in Russia, Europe, and overseas.

Having successfully implemented many commercial and hobby projects with CMS Made Simple, Yury is happy to contribute to the widespread adoption of CMSMS for the benefit of both users and developers.

Table of Contents

Preface	**1**
Chapter 1: Building Websites with CMS Made Simple	**7**
What is a CMS?	**8**
A CMS versus a website builder	9
Why CMS Made Simple?	**9**
Case study website	**10**
Functional specifications	10
Preparing for installation	**11**
Browser	11
FTP browser	12
File archiver	12
Uploading CMS Made Simple's files	12
Summary	**18**
Chapter 2: Getting Started	**19**
Installing CMS Made Simple step-by-step	**20**
Choosing a language	20
Step 1: Validating file integrity (optional)	21
Step 2: Checking requirements	22
Step 3: Testing file creation mask (optional)	25
Step 4: Admin account information	26
Step 5: Database information	27
Sample content and templates	28
Step 6: Creating tables	28
Step 7: Installation is complete	29
Understanding the admin console	**29**
Finishing the installation	33
Sending e-mails with CMS	**33**
Known issues	35
Summary	**36**

Chapter 3: Creating Pages and Navigation   37

Creating pages	**39**
Time for action – adding a new page to the website	**39**
Editing pages	**42**
Time for action – editing existing pages	**42**
Previewing changes	43
Changing the page alias	43
Deleting pages	43
Formatting page content	43
Configuring TinyMCE	45
Time for action – activating search and replace function	**48**
Adding meta tags	50
Time for action – adding meta tags to pages	**50**
Adding global meta tags	52
Understanding page hierarchy	**52**
Time for action – adding subpages to a website	**52**
Breadcrumbs	54
Search engine friendly URLs	54
Time for action – creating search engine friendly URLs	**55**
Getting more success from hierarchy	56
Controlling the navigation of the website	**57**
Time for action – preventing pages from displaying in the navigation	**57**
What is your start page?	58
More navigation control with content types	59
Efficient work with pages	**60**
Creating a new page as a copy of existing one	60
Changing multiple pages at once	60
Creating pages and navigation	**63**
Summary	**64**

Chapter 4: Design and Layout   65

Working with existing templates	**66**
Time for action – importing a ready-made template	**66**
Creating a new template	**67**
Time for action – creating a new template	**68**
Adding dynamic parts to templates	69
Time for action – adding Smarty tags to a template	**70**
Having control over the output	72
Time for action – adding Smarty parameters to the template	**72**
Using plugins in content	74
Adding stylesheets to the template	**74**
Creating a new stylesheet	75

Time for action – creating the stylesheet   **75**

Media types for stylesheets   78

Creating navigation for the website   **78**

Time for action – adding navigation to the template   **79**

Designing navigation—the pure CSS way   80

Time for action – design navigation with pure CSS   **80**

Adding sidebar navigation   83

Porting a HTML template   **84**

Time for action – porting a HTML template to CMS Made Simple   **85**

Learning Smarty basics   **91**

Working with Smarty variables   91

Time for action – getting Smarty variables   **91**

Controlling output with the IF function   94

Time for action – displaying tags in dependence of the page   **94**

Creating navigation template with Smarty loop   96

Time for action – creating a menu template   **97**

Exporting templates   **101**

Time for action – displaying tags in dependence of the page   **101**

Summary   **104**

Chapter 5: Using Core Modules   **107**

Understanding global content blocks   **108**

Time for action – adding a global content block to the website   **108**

Managing news articles with module News   **110**

Displaying news on the website   111

Time for action – displaying news on the page   **111**

Adding news   112

Time for action – adding news items   **112**

News categories   114

Time for action – creating news categories   **114**

Customizing news templates   116

Time for action – creating a new summary template   **117**

Adding custom fields to the module News   119

Time for action – adding custom fields   **120**

Using the news title as the page title   122

Using the search function with the module Search   **122**

Time for action – adding a search form   **123**

Browsing files with File Manager   **125**

Using Image Manager   **126**

Time for action – using the image editor   **126**

Using images in template and content   128

Using Menu Manager in content   130
Time for action – creating a sitemap   130
Printing pages   133
Time for action – adding a print link   133
   Adding media type to stylesheets   135
   Generating a PDF version of the page   136
Adding more modules to your website   136
   Using the Module Manager   136
   Installing additional modules   137
Time for action – module installation   137
   Installing modules with XML file   139
   Available upgrades   140
   How to find the best CMS Made Simple module for your purpose   140
   Uninstalling and removing modules   140
Summary   142

Chapter 6: Users and Permissions   **145**
Understanding users and their roles   146
Time for action – creating a new user   146
Time for action – assigning a user to a group   148
Content permissions   150
Time for action – creating an editor account   150
   Additional editors   152
   Creating new pages   153
Time for action – adding page permissions   153
Designer permissions   155
Time for action – creating a test area for the designer   156
Viewing the admin log   157
Archiving changes and restoring them   158
Time for action – restoring changes made by an editor   159
Overview of all default permissions   160
   Module permissions   162
User notifications   163
Summary   165

Chapter 7: Using Third-party Modules   **167**
Creating a photo gallery   168
Time for action – creating the first gallery   168
   Adding albums to a gallery   170
   Using the gallery on other pages   170
Time for action – adding random images to the template   170
   Creating your own gallery template   172

Adding forms with the module Form Builder — **174**
Time for action – adding a contact form to the website — **174**
Customizing the contact form — 176
Adding new fields to the forms — 178
Adding salutation as a radio button group — 178
Adding department as a pulldown field — 180
Adding multiple choice selection with the checkbox group — 181
Adding a Captcha to the forms — 182
Sending out newsletters — **183**
Time for action – sending mails to registered customers — **184**
Displaying videos — **188**
Adding your own player — 190
Summary — **194**

Chapter 8: Creating Your Own Functionality — **195**
Creating a product catalog — **195**
Creating a new catalog-like module — 196
Step 1: Basic information about the module — 197
Step 2: Creating levels — 198
Step 3: Finishing creation and module installation — 207
Configuring the new Products Catalogue module — 208
Creating the product list template — 209
Time for action – creating a new list template — **209**
Implementing service desk functionality — **211**
Managing visitors' logins — 211
Time for action – creating the first user account — **212**
Useful settings for module FrontEndUsers — 214
Templates for the FrontEndUsers module — 215
Creating protected pages — 216
Time for action – protecting the service desk — **217**
Creating user area for support requests — 218
Adding answer fields to the tickets — 222
Time for action – creating new fields — **222**
Templates for ticket list and ticket detail view — 223
Time for action – customizing list of tickets — **223**
Enabling dialog within tickets — 226
Summary — **230**

Chapter 9: E-commerce Workshop — **231**
Module Products — **232**
Time for action – adding the first product — **233**
Creating custom fields — 234
Define your own fields — 235
Creating a product hierarchy — 236

Customizing product templates	237
Creating detail view for product	244
Module Cart	**245**
Time for action – connecting products and cart	**245**
Module Orders	**247**
Time for action – adding the checkout step	**248**
Integrating the login screen	250
Integrating customer registration	252
Module Paypal Gateway	**255**
Time for action – creating test accounts	**256**
Configuring PayPal's seller account	258
Payment Receiving Preferences	258
Instant Payment Notification	259
Language encoding	260
Optional modules for the e-commerce suite	**261**
Summary	**263**
Chapter 10: Advanced Use of CMS Made Simple	**265**
Localization and translation	**265**
Configuring dates	266
Making multilingual websites	267
Editing language entries	269
The hierarchy solution	270
Adding flags as the language menu	270
Separate news articles by language	271
CMS Made Simple translation center	272
Translating modules in your installation	273
Time for action – custom translation of the module	**274**
Additional content and controls for editors	**274**
Additional content blocks	275
Time for action – adding a content block for subtitles	**275**
Extra page attribute	276
Time for action – using extra page attributes	**276**
Search engine optimization (SEO)	**277**
Title of your website	277
Meta tags	279
Meta tag keywords	280
Using SEO markup in templates	281
Using SEO markup in pages	282
Using keywords in page alias and image files	283
Search engine friendly URLs	284
Time for action – turning on search engine friendly URLs	**284**
Avoiding duplicate content	286

Consequently use domain with www or without www 286
Avoid publishing of print versions of your pages 287
Use tag for canonical URLs 288
Creating XML sitemaps for search engines 288
Visitor statistics 289
User-defined tags **289**
How to make a user-defined tag 290
Time for action – creating your own user-defined tag **290**
Parameters for tags 291
How to get the page information in UDT 292
Understanding events **293**
Time for action – sending mails after page update **293**
Integrating jQuery in navigation **294**
Time for action – integrating jQuery in navigation **295**
Summary **298**
Chapter 11: Administration and Troubleshooting **299**
Getting system information **300**
Backing up your website **303**
Backing up website files 304
Time for action – creating a backup with the module **304**
Backing up database 306
Time for action – creating a database backup **306**
Manual backup 307
Backing up database with phpMyAdmin 307
Time for action – creating a backup with phpMyAdmin **308**
Move CMS Made Simple to another web hosting **309**
Step 1 310
Step 2 310
Step 3 310
Step 4 310
Step 5 311
Upgrading CMS Made Simple **311**
Optimizing (performance tuning) **314**
Compression 314
Persistent connections 315
CSS in global settings and static CSS 315
How to secure your installation **316**
System verification 317
Usernames and passwords 319
Hiding admin directory 320
File permissions 320

CMS Made Simple and server version 322
Troubleshooting **323**
CMS Made Simple Wiki 323
Help for modules 324
Built-in help 324
What does this do? 324
How do I use it? 324
Parameters 324
Forge (bugs and feature request) 325
How to get a quick answer in the forum 325
Using search 325
Finding the right board 326
Topic subject 327
Provide as much information as possible 327
Describe the problem step-by-step 328
Help others if you have been helped 328
Commercial support 329
Support contracts 329
Software development 330
What about larger projects? 330
Is the development team a corporation or company? 330
How do I contact you? 331
Summary **333**
Appendix: Pop Quiz Answers **335**
Chapter 3 **335**
Creating Pages and Navigation 335
Chapter 4 **336**
Design and Layout 336
Chapter 5 **336**
Using Core Modules 336
Chapter 6 **337**
Users and Permissions 337
Chapter 7 **337**
Using Third-party Modules 337
Chapter 8 **337**
Creating Your Own Functionality 337
Chapter 9 **338**
E-commerce Workshop 338
Chapter 10 **338**
Advanced Use of CMS Made Simple 338
Chapter 11 **338**
Administration and Troubleshooting 338
Index **339**

Preface

CMS Made Simple is an open source content management system that allows rapid website development in a fraction of the normal time, while avoiding hours of coding by providing modules and third-party add-ons. With this book in hand, you will be able to harness the power of this modular and extensible content management system at your fingertips.

This guide for CMS Made Simple is based on practical and working solutions allowing you to understand how this powerful and simple application can support you in your daily work. The workshop helps you to create engaging, effective, and easy-to-use CMS websites for businesses, clubs, and organizations.

This is a step-by-step case study, aimed at helping you to build a complete professional website with CMS Made Simple. You can take a ready-to-use template or implement your own custom design, enrich the website with features such as a photo gallery, an e-commerce solution with a PayPal checkout, and forms of any complexity or popular jQuery effects, and finish it off by optimizing it for search engines. The useful HTML and CSS code snippets are optimized and can be easily adapted for your own projects. Chapter-by-chapter, you will put yourself into the role of a web designer, developer, administrator, and business manager, thus learning every aspect needed for building rich websites that are very simple to manage.

What this book covers

Chapter 1, Building Websites with CMS Made Simple introduces the case study website with its functional requirements.

Chapter 2, Getting Started explains how to install CMS Made Simple, how its admin console is organized, and how to configure CMS Made Simple for sending out e-mails.

Chapter 3, Creating Pages and Navigation focuses on creating, editing, and organizing pages. It introduces the page hierachy and search engine friendly URLs. At the end of this chapter, you will have the complete page structure for the case study website.

Chapter 4, Design and Layout explains how to create a new template and how to port a ready HTML/CSS design to CMS Made Simple. At the end of this chapter, you will be able to implement an individual design for a website.

Chapter 5, Using Core Modules covers standard modules of CMS Made Simple, such as News, Search, Image and File Manager, and Printing (including built-in PDF output), and shows you how to install additional modules such as FAQ.

Chapter 6, Users and Permissions explains how the permissions of different users can be organized in the admin console.

Chapter 7, Using Third-party Modules explains how to implement a photo gallery with an individual design, add a contact form with custom fields, install Captcha functionality, manage newsletters, and implement YouTube videos on the website.

Chapter 8, Creating Your Own functionality introduces two approaches to creating your own functionality. In the first part, you learn how to use the module maker to create a product catalog. In the second part, you learn how to create a service desk functionality using a module.

Chapter 9, E-commerce Workshop covers a step-by-step workshop to see how an e-commerce shop with a PayPal checkout can be realized with the e-commerce suite.

Chapter 10, Advanced Use of CMS Made Simple explains how to create multilingual websites, make search engine optimizations, and use jQuery plugins in the navigation of the website. The integration of a visitor statistic and some advanced techniques enrich the functionality of the case study website.

Chapter 11, Administration and Troubleshooting explains how to keep your website up-to-date and secure and how to do some performance tuning. At the end of the chapter, you will get an answer to the question "How can I get quick help in the forum?"

Appendix, Pop Quiz Answers contains the answers to the pop quizzes throughout the book.

What you need for this book

CMS Made Simple is a PHP application that uses a MySQL database. This means that you need a web hosting with PHP and MySQL to run CMS Made Simple. You can install a web server on your local PC for testing environments and/or on the remote web hosting for live websites. The requirements for CMS Made Simple are as follows:

- Web server on Linux/Unix or Windows 2000/XP/ME/2003 or OS X
- PHP 5.2.x (NOT PHP 5.3)
    - o `safe_mode` should be off
    - o At least 16 MB of available memory for PHP

- o   PHP tokenizer support enabled
- o   At least one of ImageMagick or GDlib enabled
- MySQL 4.1+ or PostgreSQL 7+
- Enough access to your server to upload files and change some permissions

Who this book is for

This book is perfect for newcomers as well as webmasters who are looking for an introduction to building powerful and professional websites with a content management system. Basic knowledge of HTML and CSS is the only requirement. The workshop covers all aspects of web publishing and is aimed for web designers, web developers, editors, and web managers.

Conventions

In this book, you will find several headings appearing frequently.

To give clear instructions of how to complete a procedure or task, we use:

Time for action – heading

1. Action 1
2. Action 2
3. Action 3

Instructions often need some extra explanation so that they make sense, so they are followed with:

What just happened?

This heading explains the working of tasks or instructions that you have just completed.

You will also find some other learning aids in the book, including:

Pop quiz – heading

These are short multiple choice questions intended to help you test your own understanding.

Have a go hero – heading

These set practical challenges and give you ideas for experimenting with what you have learned.

You will also find a number of styles of text that distinguish between different kinds of information. Here are some examples of these styles, and an explanation of their meaning.

Code words in text are shown as follows: "Your root directory can be `public_html` (or `wwwroot` or `htdocs`), please ask your provider if you are not sure where to upload the files."

A block of code is set as follows:

```
#top-navi ul
{
        height: 22px;
        padding: 0px;
        margin: 10px 0;
        border-top: 1px solid #e5e4e2;
        border-bottom: 1px solid #e5e4e2;
}
```

When we wish to draw your attention to a particular part of a code block, the relevant lines or items are set in bold:

```
{foreach from=$nodelist item=node}
  <a href="{$node->url}">
    <img src="uploads/design/{$node->alias}.jpg"
        alt="{$node->menutext}" border="0" />
  </a>
{/foreach}
```

New terms and **important words** are shown in bold. Words that you see on the screen, in menus or dialog boxes for example, appear in the text like this: "Open **My First Style Sheet** from the list of stylesheets (**Layout | Stylesheets**) for edit."

Warnings or important notes appear in a box like this.

Tips and tricks appear like this.

Reader feedback

Feedback from our readers is always welcome. Let us know what you think about this book—what you liked or may have disliked. Reader feedback is important for us to develop titles that you really get the most out of.

To send us general feedback, simply send an e-mail to feedback@packtpub.com, and mention the book title via the subject of your message.

If there is a book that you need and would like to see us publish, please send us a note in the **SUGGEST A TITLE** form on www.packtpub.com or e-mail suggest@packtpub.com. If there is a topic that you have expertise in and you are interested in either writing or contributing to a book on, see our author guide on www.packtpub.com/authors.

Customer support

Now that you are the proud owner of a Packt book, we have a number of things to help you to get the most from your purchase.

Downloading the example code for the book

Visit http://www.packtpub.com/files/code/8204_Code.zip to directly download the example code.

The downloadable files contain instructions on how to use them.

In this book, you may occasionally come across a single line of code appearing on two different lines. Please note that this has been done only for the purpose of indentation due to space constraints. When using such code make sure it's on one line in your script file.

Errata

Although we have taken every care to ensure the accuracy of our content, mistakes do happen. If you find a mistake in one of our books—maybe a mistake in the text or the code—we would be grateful if you would report this to us. By doing so, you can save other readers from frustration and help us improve subsequent versions of this book. If you find any errata, please report them by visiting http://www.packtpub.com/support, selecting your book, clicking on the **let us know** link, and entering the details of your errata. Once your errata are verified, your submission will be accepted and the errata will be uploaded on our website, or added to any list of existing errata, under the Errata section of that title. Any existing errata can be viewed by selecting your title from http://www.packtpub.com/support.

Piracy

Piracy of copyright material on the Internet is an ongoing problem across all media. At Packt, we take the protection of our copyright and licenses very seriously. If you come across any illegal copies of our works, in any form, on the Internet, please provide us with the location address or website name immediately so that we can pursue a remedy.

Please contact us at copyright@packtpub.com with a link to the suspected pirated material.

We appreciate your help in protecting our authors, and our ability to bring you valuable content.

Questions

You can contact us at questions@packtpub.com if you are having a problem with any aspect of the book, and we will do our best to address it.

1

Building Websites with CMS Made Simple

You already have some experience in creating websites with HTML and CSS and you know that you do not need any special software to create websites. However, if the website starts growing or your customers have more and more changes for the existing homepage, you wish you could automate some tasks like adding a new page to the website or slight changes in the design without having to edit every HTML file. CMS helps you to apply any change throughout the website with minimal efforts. It saves your time and reduces repeating tasks.

If you're holding this book in your hand, then it means that you are going to build a website with a CMS. A CMS is a complex application that works in the background and helps to separate different tasks while creating and running websites. Those tasks can include:

- ◆ Designing and laying out the website
- ◆ Implementing different website functionalities
- ◆ Writing and publishing content
- ◆ Analyzing and promoting the website

When creating websites with pure HTML and CSS, you usually mix logic, presentation, and content within the same code. However, this is time consuming and inflexible. For example, after adding additional navigation items or changing the year of copyright in the footer section of the page, you have to synchronize the changes made in every HTML file. Your customers may not be able to manage the content of their websites by themselves, as they would need HTML knowledge to do it. The solution to all the issues listed is a step towards content management system.

So let's get started with it...

What is a CMS?

CMS is an abbreviation for **content management system**. Generally, it is an application that helps to create a website structure and manage its content. By content, we mean any type of documents such as pages, images, structured data as products or users, and so on.

The most important goal of any CMS is the strict separation of content, design, and programming. You do not need to understand how a CMS is programmed when you write and publish the content. You do not need to be a web designer to create new pages and organize them into the navigation of the website. A programmer creates functionalities. A designer creates a layout without knowing how the program code is written and what exactly the content of every page will be. The editor uses the functions supplied by the programmer. The written content is automatically pasted into the layout created by the designer. That's it! Everyone does the job he/she can do best.

Typically, a CMS is used to offer the ability to manage the content of the website without any programming knowledge. The webmaster uses the CMS to create websites for customers who would like to manage their content by themselves. Once the design is made and the functionality is implemented, the customer can start entering his/her content. He/she does not care about anything else. He/she uses a graphical user interface to manage the content that is wrapped into the design.

A CMS consists of files and, in the case of CMS Made Simple, a database. Files provide functions that can retrieve any data from the database: content, design, features, and so on. The data retrieved is then wrapped as HTML and sent to the client (browser), because your visitors do not care how your website is made.

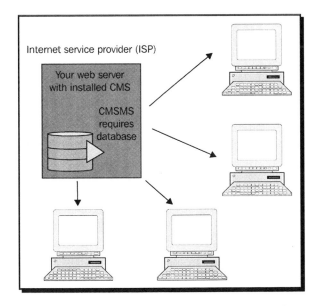

In the last image, you see a client-server structure. The server is your web space where the CMS is installed along with the database. Clients are visitors to your website. This means that to run a CMS, especially CMS Made Simple, you need some web space where you can create a new database and install CMS Made Simple. We will install CMS Made Simple step-by-step in the next chapter.

A CMS versus a website builder

A CMS is not a website builder. A website builder is used by people who would like to build websites without learning the technical aspects of web page production. They use ready-made design templates and select from the limited functions that the website builder offers. This kind of website production is inflexible and is often used to build private pages. A CMS caters to professional webmasters who create an individual website's layout and integrate any features that a customer needs.

Why CMS Made Simple?

You have decided to build a website with CMS Made Simple. Good choice! CMS Made Simple has several advantages:

- It's free for personal and commercial use.
- It's simple. You won't need more than half an hour to introduce your customer to the usage of the CMS. It is mostly intuitive.
- It's flexible in design. Any design that is created in HTML and CSS can be ported to CMS Made Simple. There are no restrictions.
- It's modular. The basic functionality of CMS Made Simple can be extended by installing over 100 additional modules that are offered for free on the official website.
- It's popular. You are not alone. A large international community helps you to solve your individual issues. Thousands of websites are already built using CMS Made Simple, so you are not going to be alone.
- It's open source. You can create your own functionality the way you need.

You can avoid provider lock-in to a certain proprietary closed source CMS solution. If a provider of proprietary software decides to charge you more, goes out of business, or does not want to incorporate desired new functionalities, then there's nothing you can do. With an Open Source CMS, if you face a problem that you can't solve on your own, you can at least hire a programmer who will solve it for you.

Case study website

In this book, we will work on a case study website that will be completed at the end of Chapter 8, *Creating Your Own Functionality*, and can be filled with content and published at this point. Imagine that you have to create a business website for the company *businessWorld* from scratch. *businessWorld* is a company that needs a website based on a CMS, as the content of the website will be managed by the staff of the company. Our task is to create a basic website structure, implement the custom layout delivered in HTML and CSS, and provide the functionalities that the company describes in the functional specifications.

Functional specifications

The total number of pages is not mentioned. The staff will add any required pages in the course of time. The new pages should automatically be added to the navigation of the website. The layout will be delivered as an HTML or CSS template and must be ported to CMS Made Simple.

Besides the ordinary content pages, the website should also include the following:

- A news section, where news articles are created, categorized, and published to the website at the given date
- A search function for content pages and news articles
- A printing ability as PDF for all pages
- A FAQ section that can be consequently extended with new questions and answers
- A photo gallery, where products images and photos of the team members can be organized in albums
- A product catalog with custom fields and product hierarchy
- A contact form to avoid direct e-mail communication and reduce spam
- A newsletter with self-subscription by the website visitor
- A service desk for registered customers

Different editor permissions are required for each section of the website. There will be some staff members who are allowed to manage only news articles. Others will be responsible for the products catalog, but will not have access to the news area, and so on. The website should be optimized for search engines. During the lifetime of the website, the webmaster is required to regularly update the website if new releases of the modules or of core CMS Made Simple are published. Now that we know the specifications, let's move on to preparing our system for installation.

Preparing for installation

First of all, gather the details required for the installation of CMS Made Simple. You will need to know the following:

Data	Your value
Domain (website address)	http://
FTP host	
FTP user	
FTP password	
Database host address	
Database port (optional)	
Database name*	
Database username	
Database password	

*You have to create an empty database before you start the installation. It depends on your hosting as to how the new database can be created. Generally, a database can be created in the admin panel of your web hosting. Ask your provider for help if you face any difficulties.

All the information listed in the table should be available before you start the installation. Missing any of this information will make the installation of CMS Made Simple impossible. The information requested can be obtained from your hosting's support. Figure out and write down all the required access data now. You will need it during the setup and configuration process.

To start with the setup of CMS Made Simple on your web hosting, your domain should be registered and connected. Test it now. Open your browser, and give your domain name in the address bar. OK? If not, your domain provider will help you to solve any issues.

Browser

You can use any browser to manage CMS Made Simple, except Internet Explorer 6. This browser is pretty old. It was released in August, 2001 and does not meet the requirements of the modern Internet. Nevertheless, visitors of your website who use Internet Explorer 6 will not have any difficulties viewing your pages. This restriction is valid only for you as the webmaster of the website.

FTP browser

You will need FTP access to your website. This kind of access is available on almost every web hosting. With the FTP connection data (see the previous table), you can connect to the hosting and upload all files that are required for installing and running CMS Made Simple.

There are many free FTP browsers that you can use. If you do not have an FTP browser, then I recommend the open source software **FileZilla** that is distributed free of charge on `http://filezilla-project.org/`. Download and install FileZilla right now.

 You need only **FileZilla Client**, not FileZilla Server!

File archiver

A file archiver is a program that you can use to extract the files of CMS Made Simple onto your local disk. As the files of CMS Made Simple are distributed as archives, the program should be able to handle `tar.gz` files. If you do not have a file archiver, then you can use the open source application **7-Zip** that can be freely downloaded from `http://www.7-zip.org`.

Now that we have all the access information and required software, we can start with the installation.

Uploading CMS Made Simple's files

The CMS Made Simple files can be downloaded from the official website of CMS Made Simple. Open `http://cmsmadesimple.org`, and click on **Downloads | CMSMS Releases** in the top main navigation. You will see the list of files that are available for download, but you do not need all of them.

Stable Releases

1.6.6 Released On: 2009-10-03 18:18 | Changelog

    cmsmadesimple-1.6.6-base-checksum.dat
    cmsmadesimple-1.6.6-base.tar.gz
    cmsmadesimple-1.6.6-checksums.dat
    cmsmadesimple-1.6.6-full-checksum.dat
    cmsmadesimple-1.6.6-full.tar.gz
    cmsmadesimple-base-diff-1.6.4-1.6.6.tar.gz
    cmsmadesimple-base-diff-1.6.5-1.6.6.tar.gz
    cmsmadesimple-full-diff-1.6.4-1.6.6.tar.gz
    cmsmadesimple-full-diff-1.6.5-1.6.6.tar.gz

For every release, there is a bunch of files. The newest release is placed at the very top of the list. There are two different versions of CMS Made Simple—**full version** and **base version**. There is no difference in the functionality or features, just in the included languages. The base version includes only English for the administration console of CMS Made Simple, whereas the full version includes all translations of the admin console (over twenty languages). So, when you need only the English language in the administration console of your website, you can take the base version. It is a bit smaller than the full version.

Find the file named `cmsmadesimple-X.X.X-full.tar.gz` or `cmsmadesimple-X.X.X-base.tar.gz` (depending on the version you need). Here, `X.X.X` stands for the number of the release. For example, for release 1.6.6 (displayed in the last screenshot), you will have to download the file `cmsmadesimple-1.6.6-full.tar.gz` or `cmsmadesimple-1.6.6-base.tar.gz`.

Click on the file to save it to your local disk. Then, using 7-Zip or any other file archiver of your choice, extract it onto your local disk, so that you can see what is inside. To extract using 7-Zip, right-click on the file, and select **7-Zip | Extract Here**, as shown in the following screenshot:

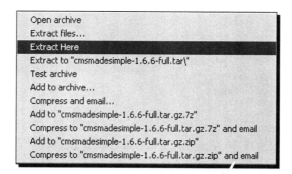

This will create a new file called `cmsmadesimple.1.6.6-full.tar`. The numbers in the filename depends on the version and release number of CMS Made Simple that you have downloaded. Right-click on this new file again, and select **7-Zip | Extract to "cmsmadesimple-1.6.6-full\"**, as shown in the next screenshot:

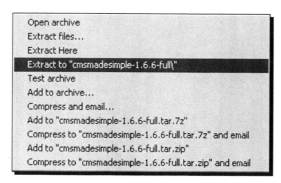

This action will create a new folder called `cmsmadesimple-1.6.6-full` on your local disk (or similar depending on the version and release number). This folder contains all files that you need to install CMS Made Simple. You have to upload them to your web space now.

Open FileZilla or an FTP browser of your choice. You have to connect to your web hosting to upload the files. In FileZilla, click on **File | Site Manager**. In **Site Manager**, click the **New Site** button. You should see a dialog window, as shown in the following screenshot:

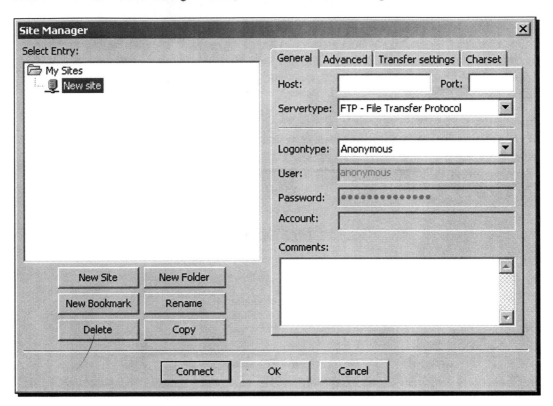

Enter your FTP host in the field **Host** on the right-hand side. Then click on the field **Logontype** and select **Normal** from the list. Now, you can enter your FTP **User** and FTP **Password** in the respective fields below. Your FTP login details should have been provided by your hosting company. Contact your hosting company's support if you encounter any issues. Click on **Connect**. The connection should be established, and you will see a screen similar to the following:

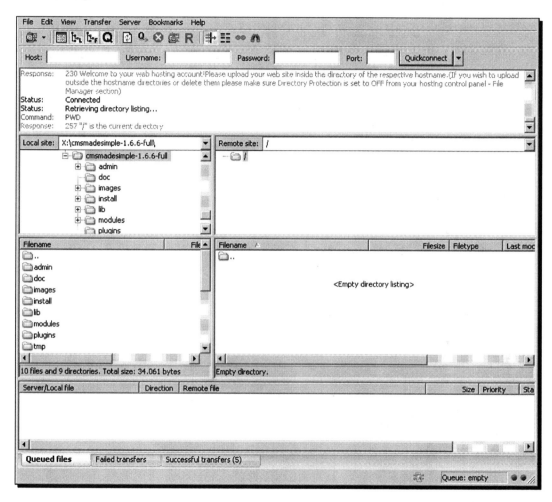

On the left-hand side of the screen, you can see your local disk. Navigate to the folder where you have extracted the installation files of CMS Made Simple. On the right-hand side, you see the remote folder of your web hosting.

You have to upload all files and folders from the local disk with exactly the same folder structure to the root or to a subdirectory on the web space. Your root directory can be `public_html` (or `wwwroot` or `htdocs`), please ask your provider if you are not sure where to upload the files. Locating the files in the root directory will make your site available to the users at `http://www.yourdomain.com`. If you create a subdirectory below the root directory, for example, `public_html/somename`, then your website will be available only in the subdirectory as `http://www.yourdomain.com/somename`. I recommend uploading the files to the root directory, unless you have already installed other applications there.

To upload all folders and files of CMS Made Simple, select everything on the left-hand (local) side, right-click, and select **Upload**.

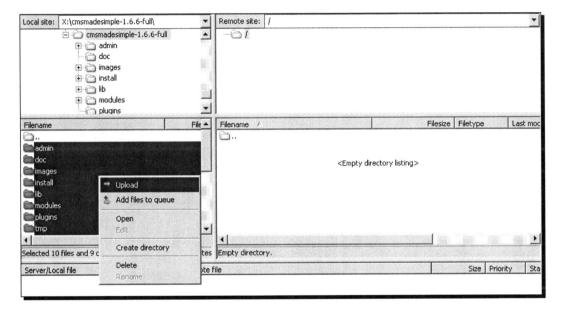

Depending on your connection, it may take more than fifteen minutes to upload the files. As the FTP browser creates some connections to the server, it may happen that some files are already being copied with other connections. In this case, you will see a window similar to the following:

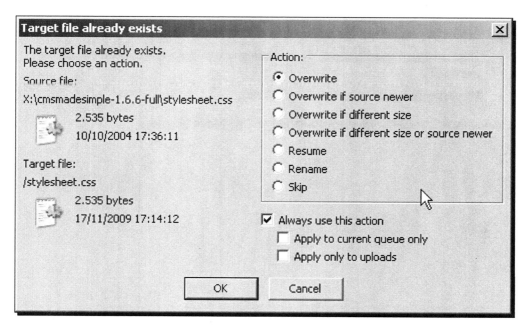

Choose **Overwrite** as the action, and check the box **Always use this action**. Wait until all the files have been transferred to the web space and until the upload is complete.

When the transfer is complete, you can start with the step-by-step installation program of CMS Made Simple. You start the installation process for CMS Made Simple in the browser by typing `http://www.yourdomain.com` in the address bar (you use your own domain name). If you do not see any installation screen, then you have uploaded the files into the wrong folder on your web space. Ask your provider where the files should be located.

Summary

In this chapter, a brief introduction to the entire book has been made.

Specifically, we covered the following:

- CMSes in general and the advantages of CMS Made Simple
- The functional specifications for the case study website that is used throughout the book
- Preparing our system for installing CMSMS.

We're now ready to start with the installation of CMS Made Simple.

2
Getting Started

Before you start creating a website with CMS Made Simple, you have to install the application on your web hosting and make some important configurations that will have an impact on everything you do with the website in future. To install CMS Made Simple, you should understand what is web hosting. You should be able to create an empty database in your web hosting account and upload CMS Made Simple's installation files through FTP.

In this chapter, we will:

- ◆ Install CMS Made Simple
- ◆ Learn about the admin console and how it is organized
- ◆ Finish the installation
- ◆ Configure the e-mail settings

CMS Made Simple is a PHP application that uses a MySQL database. This means that you need web hosting with PHP and MySQL to run CMS Made Simple. You can install a web server on a local PC for testing environments and/or on remote web hosting for live websites. The requirements for CMS Made Simple are as follows:

- ◆ Web server on Linux/Unix or Windows 2000/XP/ME/2003 or OS X
- ◆ PHP 5.2.x (not PHP 5.3)
    - ❑ safe_mode should be off
    - ❑ At least 16 MB of available memory for PHP
    - ❑ PHP tokenizer support enabled
    - ❑ At least one of ImageMagick or GDlib enabled
- ◆ MySQL 4.1+ or PostgreSQL 7+
- ◆ Enough access to your server to upload files and change some permissions

These requirements are not special and are covered by most hosting providers. To test CMS Made Simple for free without any obligation, you can even set up CMS Made Simple on free web hosting that meets the requirements stated. If in doubt, ask on the CMS Made Simple forum (`http://forum.cmsmadesimple.org`) for any hosting recommendations.

Installing CMS Made Simple step-by-step

The CMS Made Simple installer is started automatically when you enter your domain name in the address bar of the browser. The installer assists you step-by-step during the entire installation process.

Choosing a language

First you choose the installation language. In the drop-down field, you see all languages available in the installation package. In the base version of CMS Made Simple, you can choose only English. The full version has more languages included.

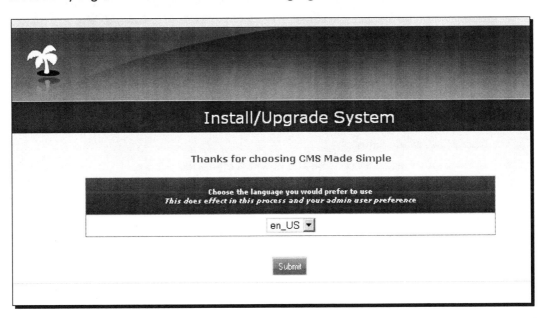

Consider that the language you choose here is used only during the installation. The language of the website and admin console can be changed later on. Click on **Submit**.

Step 1: Validating file integrity (optional)

In the first step, you can optionally validate the integrity of the installation file. This will help you identify potential problems, for example if some files have been damaged during FTP transfer or are incomplete due to network issues. If there were no issues while uploading the files to the web hosting, then ignore this step and click on **Continue**. Validation can also be done any time after the installation is complete.

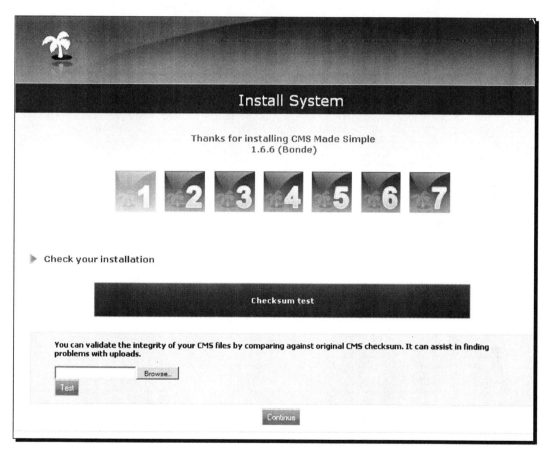

If you would like to validate, then you will need the checksum file corresponding to your version: cmsmadesimple-1.6.6-full-checksum.dat or cmsmadesimple-1.6.6-base-checksum.dat. This file is available for download from the official website. Go to http://cmsmadesimple.org, click **Downloads | CMSMS Releases**, and save the checksum file to your local disk. Choose the file in the field above, and click on **Test**.

This step is optional. Click on **Continue**.

Step 2: Checking requirements

In the second step, the installation program tests the settings of your web hosting. Check the **Result** column in the **Required settings** section. There should not be any failures or warnings.

The most common failure is:

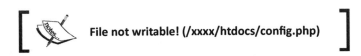

File not writable! (/xxxx/htdocs/config.php)

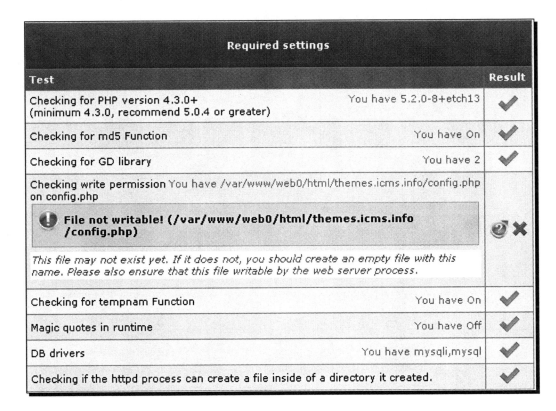

This means that the file `config.php` either does not exist in the root directory of the installation or there is no write permission for it.

If the file does not exist, create an empty file named `config.php` in a text editor (not a word processor). In Windows, open Notepad (this text editor comes with Windows), and without typing anything in the document, click on **File | Save As**. Choose a location to save the file, and use `"config.php"` (including the quotes) as the filename to ensure that the right extension (`.php`) is used. Upload that file via FTP to the folder where the CMS Made Simple installation files were uploaded. The `config.php` file should be in the same folder as the `index.php` file, as shown in the following screenshot:

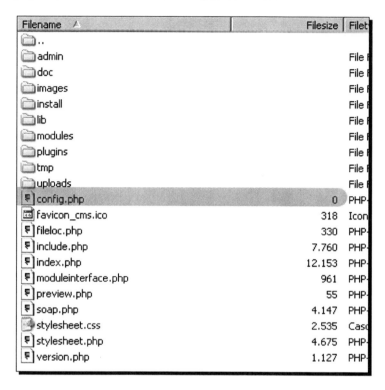

Check if the file you have created and uploaded has the file type PHP (some editors may append `.txt` extension to the end of the filename). If necessary, rename the file to `config.php`.

If the file already exists, open FileZilla or any other browser of your choice and right-click on it. Choose **File permissions** and enter *777* in the **Numeric value** field. Click on **OK**.

Go back to your browser, and click on **Try again** at the end of the settings check; the failure should disappear.

If you have other failures or warnings in the **Required settings** section and if you're unsure how to handle them, then take a screenshot of the page, and send it to your provider. He/she will help you to solve the problem.

You can ignore warnings in the **Recommended settings** section. You most probably will not encounter any problems while running your website even if you do not correct them. However, if you can follow the recommendations given to resolve the warnings, then please do it.

Recommended settings	
Test	**Result**
Checking PHP memory limit (minimum 16M, recommend 24M or greater) — You have 32M	✓
Checking PHP time limit in second (minimum 30, recommend 60 or greater) — You have 30 *Number of seconds a script is allowed to run. If this is reached, the script returns a fatal error.*	⟳ !
Checking PHP register globals — You have Off	✓
Checking output buffering — You have On	✓
Checking PHP disable functions	✓
Checking for safe mode — You have Off	✓
Check for PHP Open Basedir	✓
Test for remote URL ✓ fsockopen: Connection ok! ✓ fopen: Connection ok!	✓
Checking file uploads — You have On	✓
Checking max post size (minimum 2M, recommend 10M or greater) — You have 8M *You will probably not be able to submit (larger) data. Please be aware of this restriction.*	⟳ !
Checking max upload file size (minimum 2M, recommend 10M or greater) — You have 8M *You will probably not be able to upload (larger) files using the included file management functions. Please be aware of this restriction.*	⟳ !
Checking if /var/www/web0/html/themes.icms.info/uploads is writable — You have /var/www/web0/html/themes.icms.info/uploads	✓
Checking if /var/www/web0/html/themes.icms.info/uploads/images is writable — You have /var/www/web0/html/themes.icms.info/uploads/images	✓
Checking if /var/www/web0/html/themes.icms.info/modules is writable — You have /var/www/web0/html/themes.icms.info/modules	✓
Checking if session.save_path is writable — You have /var/lib/php5	✓
session.use_cookies — You have On	✓
Checking for basic XML (expat) support — You have On	✓
Checking for file_get_contents — You have On	✓
Checking if ini_set works — You have On	✓

On some web servers, you have to change permissions of the uploaded folders. If you're using FileZilla, then right-click on the remote folder, and select **File permissions**. In the dialog window **Change file attributes**, enter **777** in the **Numeric value** field. You should make those changes to the following folders:

- ◆ tmp/templates_c
- ◆ tmp/cache
- ◆ uploads
- ◆ uploads/images
- ◆ modules

Click on **Continue**.

Step 3: Testing file creation mask (optional)

In this step, you can optionally test if CMS Made Simple is allowed to create files on your web hosting. Click on **Test** or just ignore this step and click on **Continue**.

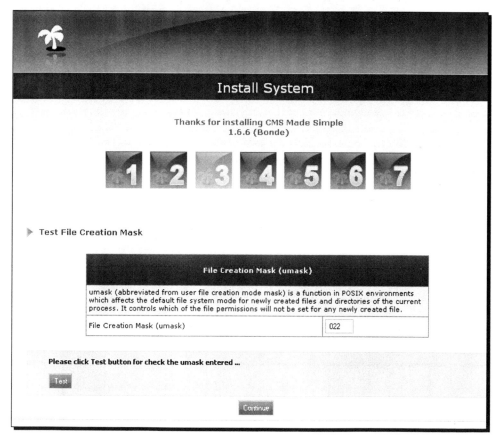

Step 4: Admin account information

Pay attention to this step. You are going to create an administrator account for your website. With this data, you gain access to the administration console of your website after it has been installed. Remember or write down the administrator's username and password that you enter in this step. Provide a valid e-mail address for your account. If you forget your password someday, then a reminder will be sent to this e-mail address.

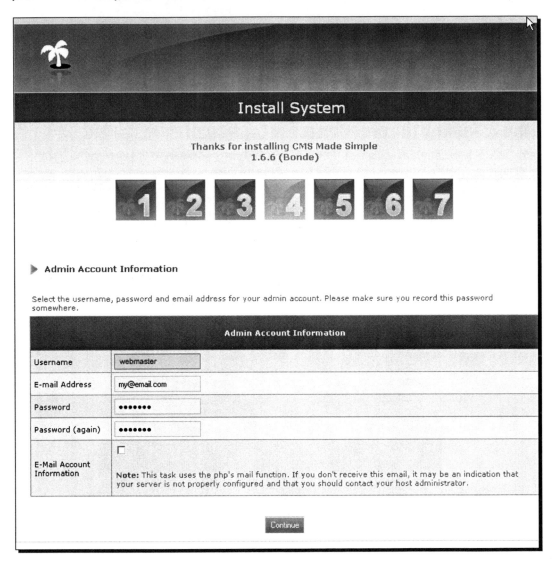

You can check the box for **E-Mail Account Information**. CMS Made Simple will try to send a confirmation mail to your e-mail account. However, do not rely on it due to the individual hosting settings. We will configure the e-mail settings of CMS Made Simple later in this chapter.

Click on **Continue**.

Step 5: Database information

In this step, change the name of the website or leave it as it is. This information can be changed any time after the installation.

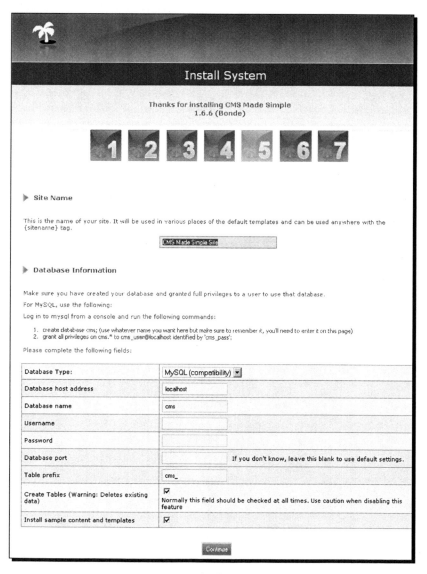

For the database information, use the access data for the database that you gained while preparing for the installation.

1. Replace **Database host address** with your individual data.
2. Replace **Database name** with the name of your database.
3. Enter the database **Username**.
4. Enter the database **Password** and optionally the **Database port** (if any).

These are the access credentials for your database. If you are not sure what to enter in these fields, then ask your hosting provider.

Sample content and templates

In the last field of this installation step, you have to decide whether you would like to install sample content and templates. Sample content is a useful resource for your first introduction to CMS Made Simple, as it includes more than twenty pages with an overview of what CMS Made Simple is and how it works. However, the default templates are difficult for beginners to understand, as they are complex and look overloaded.

For our website, we will not install any default content or templates.

Click on **Continue**.

Step 6: Creating tables

If the connection to the database was successful and the tables in the database were created, then you will see the message **Success!** at the end of this step, as shown in the next screenshot. Leave all the values in the fields below the message as they are, and click on **Continue**.

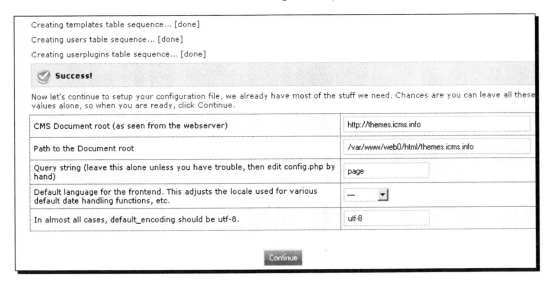

Step 7: Installation is complete

You're done! Congratulations. You can access your website by typing the domain name in the address bar of the browser, for example, `http://www.yourdomain.com`. The admin console is placed at `http://www.yourdomain.com/admin`. Click on **go to the Admin Panel**. Normally, you are already logged in to it. If not, then use the data that you entered in step 4 of the installation process.

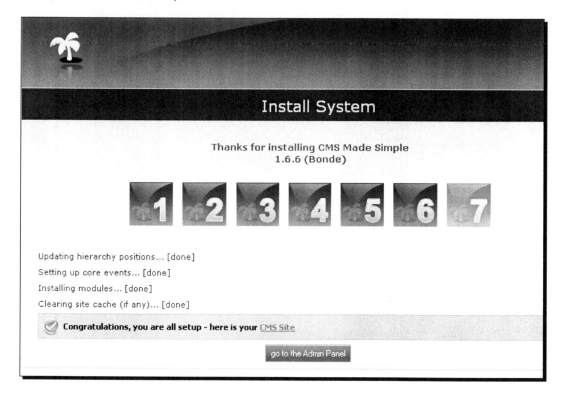

Understanding the admin console

The admin console is the heart of CMS Made Simple. This is where the website administrator (you) will work from. Here you add pages and fill them with content, choose the layout and style of your pages, install extensions for extra functionality, set permissions for users and groups, and configure the entire website.

 The admin console is the backend; as opposed to the frontend, which is what visitors to your site can see.

Log in to the admin console with the address `http://www.yourdomain.com/admin`, using the data from step 4 of the installation process. The administrator of the website can also add additional users (see Chapter 6, *Users and Permissions*).

Everything in the admin console is accessed through the main horizontal menu. When you first enter the admin area, you also see a sitemap of what can be accessed through each menu.

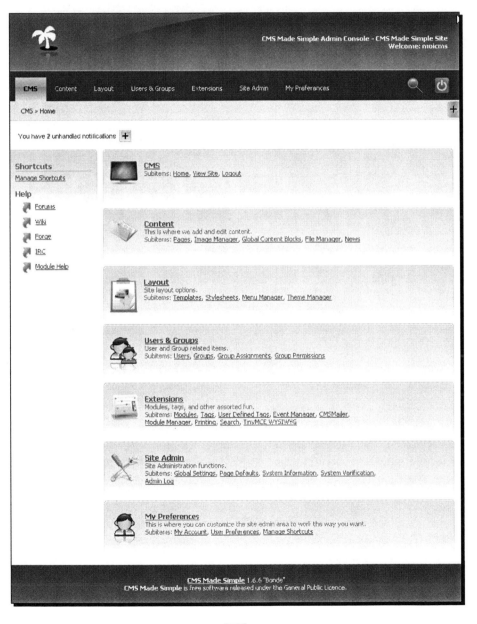

In the sitemap for any menu item, when you click on the main horizontal menu (**CMS**, **Content**, **Layout**, **Users & Groups**, and so on), all subitems of that menu item are shown.

Let's take a quick walkthrough of what's in the admin console.

- ◆ **CMS**: In the **CMS** menu, you can open the admin sitemap (see the next screenshot), the frontend page (**View Site**) in a new window, or **Logout**.

- ◆ **Content**: Here you can manage the content of your site. You can add and edit pages, upload and manage images and files, and also add, edit, and remove news. If you have installed additional content modules (such as a guestbook or FAQ), then they appear in this section as well. Lastly, in the content menu, you can create global content blocks that will be used on the entire website in different places and edited from one place.

- ◆ **Layout**: Here you can style and format the look of your page in the way you want. For the general layout, you use templates. In the layout menu, you can also access the **Stylesheets**. Using stylesheets (CSS), you can style different elements of your page.

♦ **Users & Groups**: With this menu item, you can add users that should have access to the admin console of your website and select what permissions they will have. You can put users in groups to easily select permissions for the whole group at the same time.

Users & Groups
User and Group related items.
Subitems: Users, Groups, Group Assignments, Group Permissions

♦ **Extensions**: These are add-ons that give extra functionality to CMS Made Simple. The standard installation of CMS Made Simple includes only some basic features. With extensions, you can add more or less any functionality to your site. Extensions can be either modules or tags (also called plugins).

Extensions
Modules, tags, and other assorted fun.
Subitems: Modules, Tags, User Defined Tags, Event Manager, CMSMailer, Module Manager, Printing, Search, TinyMCE WYSIWYG

♦ **Site Admin**: Here you can change the settings and preferences for the entire website, get system information, and verify the file's integrity. Any changes made to your website by you or other users are tracked in **Admin Log**.

Site Admin
Site Administration functions.
Subitems: Global Settings, Page Defaults, System Information, System Verification, Admin Log

♦ **My Preferences**: Here you can change your personal settings. You can also manage shortcuts to the pages that are most frequently used in the admin area. Click on **My Account**, if you would like to change the username of the administrator account, his/her password, or the e-mail associated with the account.

My Preferences
This is where you can customize the site admin area to work the way you want.
Subitems: My Account, User Preferences, Manage Shortcuts

Finishing the installation

Immediately after installation, you see two unhandled notifications in the dashboard area below the main menu. Click on the sign **+** beside the notifications to expand the dashboard area.

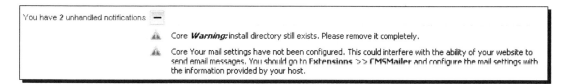

The first notification informs you that the `install` folder still exists on the web server. This folder contains the installation program you have used to set up CMS Made Simple. Once CMS Made Simple is installed and is running, you don't need this folder, and therefore, you should delete it or at least rename it. If you do not, then everybody can start the installation program again and thus replace your website with a new installation. This would be a big security issue, so delete the folder right now.

After the folder is deleted (or renamed), refresh the admin console to see the first message disappear.

The second message deals with the e-mail settings you should configure before running CMS Made Simple.

Sending e-mails with CMS

CMS Made Simple sends e-mails with the module **CMSMailer**. The configuration of the **CMSMailer** module is very important. If you do not configure it, then you will not receive the e-mail with new login information, should you ever forget your administrator password. This module is also used by many other CMS Made Simple modules that send out e-mails such as **FrontEndUsers**, **Orders**, or **FormBuilder**.

You will see this notification in the dashboard of CMS Made Simple till you have configured the module.

In the admin console, in the main horizontal navigation, select **Extensions | CMSMailer**. Set the **Character Set** to **utf-8**. Then, choose **sendmail** in the **Mailer method** field. Fill the field **From address** with an existing e-mail address. When CMS sends e-mails, the recipient will see this e-mail as the sender address. You have to enter an existing e-mail address here, as due to spam and security settings on your web hosting, CMS Made Simple will probably not be able to send out e-mails.

Fill in the **From Username** field. The name given here will be assigned to the mail address in the recipient's mail client.

Character Set:

utf-8

Mailer method:

sendmail

Mail method to use (sendmail, smtp, mail). Usually smtp is the most reliable.

SMTP host name
(or IP address):

localhost

SMTP hostname (only valid for the smtp mailer method)

Port of SMTP server:

25

SMTP port number (usually 25) (only valid for the smtp mailer method)

From address:

something@yourdomain.com

Address used as the sender in all emails.
Note, this email address must be set correctly for your host or you will have difficulty sending emails.
If you do not know the proper value for this setting, you may need to contact your host.

From Username:

Me

Friendly name used for sending all emails

Sendmail location:

/usr/sbin/sendmail

The complete path to your sendmail executable (only valid for the sendmail mailer method)

SMTP timeout:

1000

The number of seconds in an SMTP conversation before an error occurs (valid for the smtp mailer method)

SMTP Authentication:

Does your smtp host require authentication (valid only for the smtp mailer method)

Username:

SMTP authentication username (valid only for smtp mailer method, when smtp auth is selected)

Password:

SMTP authentication password (valid only for smtp mailer method, when smtp auth is selected)

Submit   Cancel

Test Email Address:

Send Test Message

Click on **Submit**, and confirm the changes.

Test your settings using the last field on the same page. In the **Test Email Address** field, enter any e-mail address (not one from the field **From Address**) where you have access to the mail box. CMS Made Simple will send a test message to the e-mail address given in this field. Click on the **Send Test Message** button, and control the incoming messages of the e-mail address given in the field **Test Email Address**. Did you receive the test message?

If not, wait for some time and then check your spam folder. Sometimes test messages are filtered out and treated as spam. If the test message has not been sent, then something is wrong with the configuration of the **CMSMailer** module.

Known issues

♦ Check the **Sendmail location** field (your hosting provider has to confirm that it is right or he/she should provide you with your individual location).

♦ Check the e-mail address entered in the **From address** field. It must be an existing e-mail address, and it has to be located on your web hosting. If you enter any other e-mail address, then your server will not be able to send out e-mails. To use e-mail addresses of the public e-mail services such as Gmail or GMX, you have to configure the module with SMTP as the **Mailer method**. This method requires that you fill in the fields considering SMTP. SMTP settings are individual for any e-mail provider.

♦ Check the spam folder and filter of the **Test Email Address**, sometimes test messages are sorted out or immediately deleted.

Summary

At the end of this chapter, you should have a clean installation of CMS Made Simple.

Specifically, we covered:

- Installation of the program: CMS Made Simple is delivered with a simple installation program that guides you step-by-step through the setup process. We have performed the steps to get CMS Made Simple running.

- Overview of the admin console: The admin console is like a cockpit in a plane. It is a place from where you can control the entire website. In the course of this book, you will learn every part in more detail.

- Sending e-mails: You have configured CMS Made Simple so that it can send mails from the admin console. If you forget your admin password, then you will receive a reminder e-mail with instructions on how to recover it. All core and most of the third-party modules of CMS Made Simple rely on this functionality. Once configured, you do not need to make it for each module separately.

In the next chapter, we will see how you create the website structure and build website navigation.

3
Creating Pages and Navigation

In this chapter, you will learn how to create new pages, edit existing pages, control the navigation of your website, and organize pages according to your website's plan. As a result, you will get a complete website structure, a kind of skeleton for your website.

Let's see how we can plan a website. Yes, we should plan before making anything material. You have to spend time on this step because you will in fact save time afterwards by avoiding the need to do some time-consuming rebuilding, recreating, or reorganizing of your website.

Take a piece of paper and write down the main parts of the website and its purpose. Write down the main idea of the website, then add the main parts (building your navigation structure) and proceed until you do not have any other ideas. Do not try to find any solution or the right tool to create your website at this time. Do not ask: "How would I realize this or that?". You have to hold everything you would like to see on the website without considering the technical details. Plan as if you have a magic wand for creating websites.

For example, a company website needs a section where the company is represented, a way to display its products or services catalog, a client center, and a contact form; refine and add each part. Refer to the example of the company website we create in this guide:

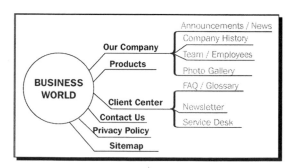

Planning your website will also help us to choose the appropriate design for it. The best design will fail if your website plan does not match the already created navigation. In the example website plan, you can easily indicate the main navigation (marked in bold), subnavigation (marked in grey), and the common structure of the website. It is important to have a rough plan and that we do not change it very often.

It is likely that you will have more and more ideas while planning the website—write them down! The advantage of planning in this way is that you are not restricted at all. You can note down all your ideas now, select the feasible tasks, and concentrate on them. Later on, you can add new parts that are not mandatory for the first implementation of your website. It is important to differentiate between nice-to-have features and something that you cannot live without.

If you create a website plan to keep all your ideas in mind, you can avoid creating pages that contain only one sentence like "Under construction". Good websites don't have any pages that are not ready. If there are any, then they should not be shown to the visitor. Imagine seeing a notice about personal style consultation in the window of a clothes shop. You go into the shop, but the clerk says: "Sorry! This service is still under construction." What was the purpose of calling attention to it? Some webmasters add such pages to the website just "to keep them in mind". You can keep them in mind in a more efficient way if you write down the main structure of your website in a separate place.

Ask your friends or family members what they plan to add to the website and keep their ideas as well. Consider different age groups and interests while planning to broaden the scope of your visitors.

If everything is perfect, then go through the main sections in your website plan and mark the parts that can be done immediately (all the sections on the previously mentioned website plan will be discussed in this guide). Other parts should not be deleted from the plan but marked as postponed. Normally, you have enough stuff at the beginning. Concentrate on these feasible points and keep the postponed points in mind.

When you are ready with the website plan, print it out, put it beside your PC, and start working on your website.

In this chapter, we will:

◆ Create and edit some pages
◆ Learn about page hierarchy
◆ Control the navigation of the website

Creating pages

We will begin by creating a rough structure for our website. A website consists of pages, which are linked to each other. The navigation of the website helps the visitor to find the pages containing the requested information. A website must have at least one page and therefore, the first page is already created in your admin console after installation. It is the start page of your website, and it is called **Home**.

Time for action – adding a new page to the website

Your website requires a page where information about the company is represented. It is the page for the section **Our Company** in the website plan. Let's create a new page as follows:

1. In the admin console of your website, click on **Content | Pages** and then on the link **Add New Content**.

2. Fill in the fields **Title** and **Content Type** as shown in the following screenshot:

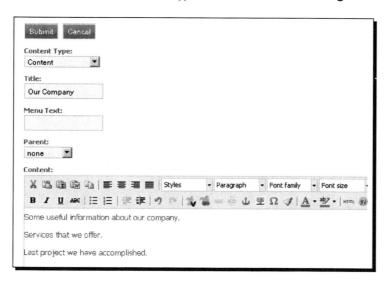

3. Click on **Submit**.

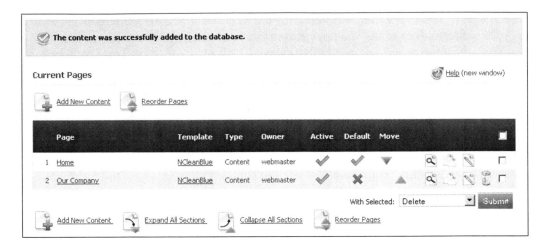

4. Click on the magnifying glass icon at the top-right of the admin console to view your website and find the new page added to the main navigation of the website.

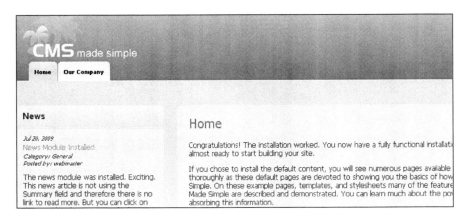

What just happened?

You have just added a new page to your website. The page has the title **Our Company** and is now listed in current pages of your website in the admin console. The page is also automatically added to the main navigation of the website. It has sample company information in the content field. This text is displayed on the **Our Company** page on the website when you navigate to the page.

You have entered only a little information to create a new page. However, other things happened.

Menu text has been created from the title of the page. A page address (URL) has been created from the title of the page. It is a part of the page link that is placed after `index.php?page=` in the address bar of the browser when you navigate to the page. In CMS Made Simple, we call this part the **page alias**. The page alias is unique within your website. You can have a lot of pages with the same title and menu text, but all these pages will have a different page alias. As the page alias is used to create a link to a specific page, you cannot have two different pages with the same link, and logically you cannot have the same page alias for two different pages.

You do not need to care about integrating the created page into the navigation of your website. All created pages will be displayed in the navigation if you do not state anything else.

Now, you can create all pages from the first level of your website, thus creating the main navigation on the top of the website. Add the following pages:

- **Products**
- **Client Center**
- **Contact Us**
- **Privacy Policy**
- **Sitemap**

Control the list of current pages in the admin console and on your website.

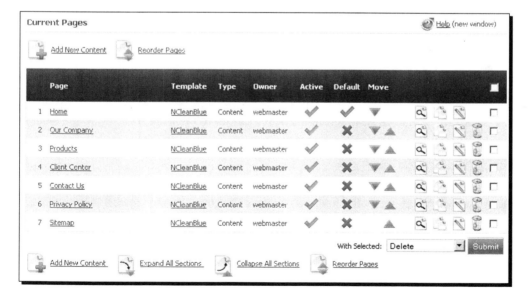

Editing pages

All pages can be edited at any time from the list of pages in the admin console.

Time for action – editing existing pages

We do not like the menu text for the page **Home** and would like to change it to **Start**. We would also like to replace the title and text on the page. In the admin console, open **Content | Pages**, and click on the **Home** page.

1. Make changes to the **Home** page, as shown in the following screenshot:

2. Click the **Apply** button to update the page.

3. Click the magnifier icon beside the **Apply** button to view the changes on the website.

What just happened?

You have changed the menu text shown in the navigation of the website. You have also replaced text on the page. At the end, you applied the changes and viewed the page in a new window.

You used the **Submit** button to save the changes and close the page in one step. The **Apply** button does not close the page. Applying changes allows you to edit the page without closing it, and thus avoid needing to reopen it for editing after each change. The **Apply** button appears only if you edit an existing page. It is not available when you are creating a new page.

Use the **Apply** button frequently, especially if you are working with large amounts of text, keep a copy of it in a separate editor window. If the connection is lost or time's out, then the page will fail to load in the browser and the modifications would be lost.

Previewing changes

If you would like to preview the changes before saving, switch to the **Preview** tab without applying the changes. You can see the changes displayed in the preview window, but they will not be visible to the visitors of your website at this moment. Once you have applied or submitted the edited page, the changes will be made visible to your site's visitors.

Changing the page alias

You can change the page alias of the page as well. Switch to the **Options** tab while editing the page, and enter the desired alias in the **Page Alias** field. Think of page alias as the link to the page. You are not allowed to enter special characters in this field, so use spaces or leave it empty. Choose the name entered here carefully as you will not be able to change it easily after your website is published online. Once your website is discovered by the search engines, the pages will be displayed in the search results with links made from the page alias. If you change the page alias, then the page will not be found and your visitors will see an error message instead of the desired information.

Deleting pages

You can delete your pages from the list of current pages in the admin console (**Content | Pages**). Find the page you do not need anymore, and click on the dust bin icon for that page. Be careful! Deleted pages cannot be restored. If you would like to keep the page for personal purposes only, then make it inactive (see the section titled *Control the navigation of the website* for more information).

Formatting page content

You have already created some pages and edited them. Notice that the text you have entered in the **Content** field appears on the website in a certain place. The text is only a fraction of the entire page. You cannot change the design of the navigation, the header, or the footer part from here.

If you were just an editor of the website (not a designer and not an administrator), then you would create or edit your articles here, but would not have the ability to change anything else on the website. This is the most important principle of a **content management system (CMS)**. We separate design from content to separate different tasks that can be accomplished by different persons. It also helps to separate the content of the layout and design so that it allows for globally changing the appearance of the website without going through all the circles of hell.

An editor needs to have the ability to format his writing by making some phrases bold and creating lists or link to other pages of the website. Normally, HTML knowledge is required for this, unless you use the **WYSIWYG editor**.

WYSIWYG means **What You See Is What You Get** and gives you the ability to format the text of a page with a common word processing feature. Additionally, the text is displayed in the editor in the same way that it will appear on the website.

> Working with the WYSIWYG editor does not require any HTML knowledge to create, edit, and format the text part of your website.

The WYSIWYG editor is the central and most important feature of every CMS. If you create a website with CMS, then you are going to consequently add content to your website. It means that apart from other modules, the WYSIWYG editor will be one of the most frequently used features of your CMS. Therefore, it is important to understand how the editor can help you and what you can do to make it suit your needs. There are some WYSIWYG editors available, for CMS Made Simple, the editor called **TinyMCE** is the most well integrated one.

In the admin console, go to **Content | Pages** and select any page for editing. The **Content** field uses a WYSIWYG editor (you can see a toolbar above the content field), which is shown in the following screenshot:

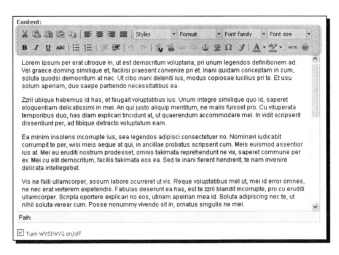

The toolbar of the editor is self-explanatory and is similar to most popular word processing programs. There are many more settings that can simplify your life if you discover them.

Often, a large amount of text is written in word processing programs like Microsoft Word. If you copy the text from Word directly into the content of the field, then it will cause a lot of problems because of the bad HTML produced by Word. In the toolbar of the editor, there is a special button (the fourth in the first line) to paste text from Word. Always use this button to copy text from Word as it will filter any messy code from your text.

Configuring TinyMCE

In the admin console, click on **Extensions | TinyMCE WYSIWYG**. You can change the width and height of the editor field here. By default, the size of the editor field is set automatically; change it according to your screen preference to gain more space to write and read.

Deselect the **Auto** field, enter the desired width and height, and click on **Save settings**. There is a test field below the settings where you can immediately see the changes. This field allows you to preview changes so that you do not need to edit pages to control the appearance of the editor.

On the **Profiles** tab, you can add even more features. For the administrator of the website, the changes have to be made in the **Advanced backend profile settings** section. Select the **Allow table operations** field to be able to create and edit tables with the WYSIWYG editor. After saving the profile, you will find the third line in the toolbar of the editor that helps to build HTML tables.

Check the **Show file management options** field if you would like to upload images directly from the editor. Click on **Save profile**, and then click on the **Insert/edit image** icon in the toolbar. A small window pops up where you can change an image URL. Click on it, and the content of your `images` folder is displayed, as shown in the next screenshot. Normally, no uploads are allowed from this window. However, as you have activated the file management option, you will find the **File operations** section above the image list where you can upload your images.

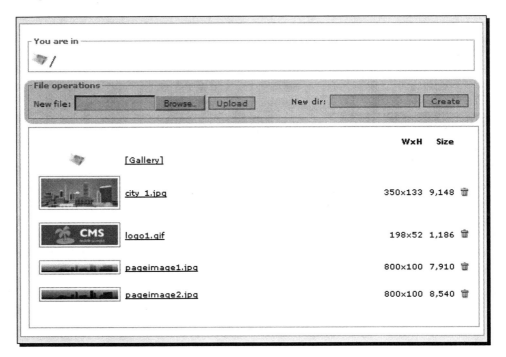

 Use folders to organize the images from the very beginning, or else you will end up with hundreds of assorted images in no time, and it will be a big problem to rearrange them, as they are already linked from various pages. Having a lot of images in one folder will slow down the loading of the file picker and finding the image you are looking for will become a challenging task.

Continue to customize the editor in the **Plugins** tab. There are some useful plugins that are not active by default, but can be activated if needed. I recommend activating the following plugins:

- **print**: Allows you to print the text from the editor
- **fullscreen**: Adds a fullscreen editing mode
- **searchreplace**: Adds search/replace dialogs for the text

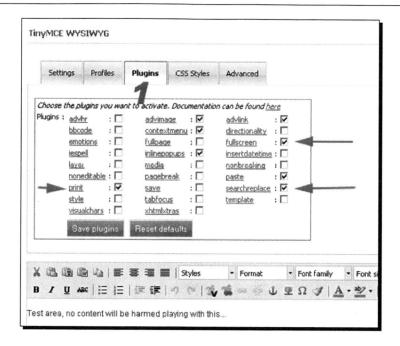

Click on **Save plugins**. Only the icon for fullscreen is added to the second toolbar before the help icon. The other two do not appear. Why? Let's take a step back and check the **Profiles** tab again. In the **Advanced backend profile settings** section, you can see three toolbar lines. These lines control the order of the icons shown in the editor in the first, second, and third (yet empty) line. The single buttons are represented with their names in the toolbar fields, as shown in the following screenshot:

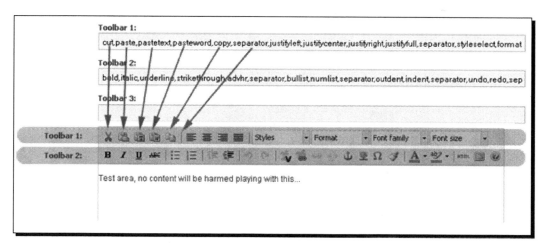

You can delete some of them, change the order, or add new ones. That is what we are going to do.

Time for action – activating search and replace function

There is a useful plugin that can search the entire contents of a page and replace all instances of a word or phrase with something different. Let's see how we can activate this plugin in TinyMCE.

1. In the admin console, click on **Extensions | TinyMCE WYSIWYG**.

2. Click the **Plugins** tab.

3. Select the checkbox beside the plugin called **searchreplace**, as shown in the following screenshot:

Choose the plugins you want to activate. Documentation can be found here

Plugins :					
advhr	: ☐	advimage	: ☑	advlink	: ☑
autoresize	: ☐	bbcode	: ☐	contextmenu	: ☑
directionality	: ☐	emotions	: ☐	fullpage	: ☐
fullscreen	: ☑	iespell	: ☐	inlinepopups	: ☑
insertdatetime	: ☐	layer	: ☐	media	: ☐
nonbreaking	: ☐	noneditable	: ☐	pagebreak	: ☐
paste	: ☑	print	: ☑	save	: ☐
searchreplace	: ☑	spellchecker	: ☑	style	: ☐
tabfocus	: ☐	template	: ☐	visualchars	: ☐
wordcount	: ☑	xhtmlxtras	: ☐		

Save plugins   Reset defaults

4. Click the **Save plugins** button.

5. Switch to the **Profiles** tab.

6. In the **Advanced backend profile settings** section, add the words **search, replace** to the **Toolbar 3** field, as shown in the following screenshot:

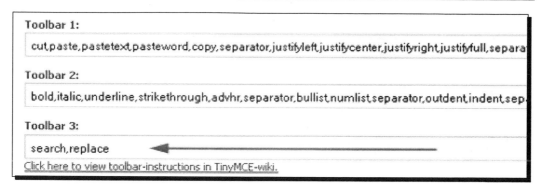

7. Click on the **Save profile** button, and see the additional functions added to the third line of the toolbar, as shown in the following screenshot:

What just happened?

Firstly, you activated the plugin in the **Plugins** tab. Activating a plugin means that the plugin is loaded with TinyMCE. But it is not enough to just activate it. In the second step, you had to customize the toolbar of TinyMCE to inform the editor where the buttons for the plugin should be shown.

You saw that a single plugin can provide two buttons. Therefore, there were two words you had to enter in the field **Toolbar 3**. The first one, **search**, was for the search button, and the second one, **replace**, was for the replace function. They must not be used together. You can omit the first or the second one if you do not need that specific functionality.

 Add the plugin `removeformat` in the **Toolbar 3** field. This is a plugin that must not be activated first as it belongs to standard. The plugin allows the removal of any formatting from the text without looking at the HTML.

There are more advanced settings in the WYSIWYG editor. To understand them, you need to know how CMS Made Simple works in general. I recommend referring to the settings of the WYSIWYG editor again and again while reading this book to make working with the editor more efficient.

Adding meta tags

Meta tags contain additional information about your website. This information is not directly displayed to the visitors of the website; as the purpose of meta tags is to supply additional information about your website to search engines and web browsers. We have to distinguish between meta tags that are the same on each page of your website and tags that are unique to a specific page of your content.

Meta elements are HTML or XHTML elements that provide additional information for search engines. They are not visible to the visitors of the website. Such elements must be placed as tags in the head section of the page. Meta elements can be used to specify the page description, keywords, and any other metadata.

Meta element specifies name and the associated content describing the page. For example:

```
<meta name="keywords" content="business company,services" />
```

In this example, the meta tag identifies the page as containing keywords relevant to the phrase business company and the word services.

Time for action – adding meta tags to pages

Let's add some specific meta tags to the start page of our website.

1. In the admin console, open **Content | Pages**.

2. Click on the start page **Start** to edit it.

3. Switch to the **Options** tab.

4. In the field **Page Specific Metadata**, add meta tags that are specific to the page.

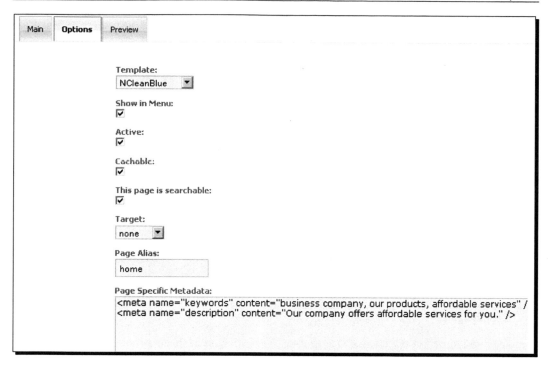

5. Click on **Apply** at the bottom of the page.

6. Click on the magnifier icon beside the **Apply** button.

7. See the head section of the website in the source code of the page.

What just happened?

You have added meta tags in plain HTML to the start page of your website. These meta tags appear only on this specific page. Generally, meta tags for the description and keywords should be different on each page.

 Any other tags (not only meta tags) for the head section of the generated page can be added here as well.

Adding global meta tags

Some global meta tags are already added to the standard installation of CMS Made Simple. You can see these meta tags in the source code of every page generated by CMS Made Simple:

```
<meta name="Generator" content="CMS Made Simple - Copyright (C) 2004-9
Ted Kulp. All rights reserved." />
<meta http-equiv="Content-Type" content="text/html; charset=utf-8" />
```

To change or delete the tags, click on **Site Admin | Global Settings** in the admin console. Find the meta tags listed above in the field **Global Metadata**. You can add your own meta tags in this field using plain HTML.

 Any other tags (not only meta tags) for the head section of all pages can be added here as well.

Understanding page hierarchy

All pages you have added in the last step are now displayed in the main navigation of your website and can be found in the current list of the pages in the admin console. But there are some more pages in our website plan that have to be added to the hierarchy.

With page hierarchy, you define the pages as being above, below, or at the same level as another page. If a page is not shown in the main navigation, then we call it a **subpage**. It also means that there is a parent page above the subpage.

Time for action – adding subpages to a website

Let's create four pages below the **Our Company** page according to the website plan.

1. In the admin console of your website, click on **Content | Pages** and then on the **Add New Content** link.

2. Fill the fields **Title** and **Content** as shown in the following screenshot and choose the page **2. -Our Company** from the drop-down field **Parent**.

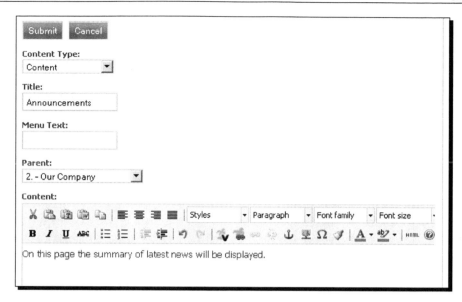

3. Click on **Submit**.

4. Click on the triangle to expand the list of pages below the page **Our Company** and to view the subpage created.

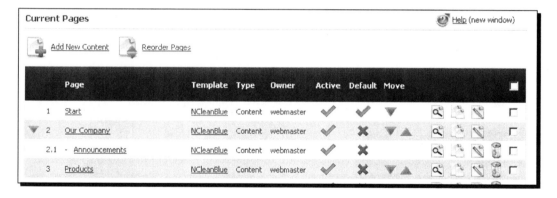

5. Click on the magnifying glass icon beside the just created page to view the page on the website.

What just happened?

You have added a new page. This time you have selected a parent page placing the new page in the hierarchy below the parent one. In the admin console, you can see that the page is now indented under the parent page. It gets the number **2.1**, saying that the page belongs to the page with number **2** and is its first child page. You will not find the page in the main navigation of the website, however, you can see the page added to the subnavigation, if you move your mouse over **Our Company** in the navigation.

We need the page hierarchy to organize our pages into main sections and to have the subnavigations built automatically.

If you would like to change the position of the page in the hierarchy, you have to edit the page by clicking on it in the page list. Select another parent page in the field **Parent** and save the changes. If you choose **none** in the drop-down list, then the page is moved to the first level and thus displayed in the main navigation.

Use the **Expand All Sections** link at the bottom of the list of current pages in order to show all hierarchy levels. With **Collapse All Sections**, you can hide all subpages and show only the first level.

You can reorder the pages that are on the same level by using icons from the **Move** column (down and up). However, if you have to move one or more pages from the very bottom to the top of the list, it can be hard to do it with move icons (especially if you have a large number of pages). Use the **Reorder pages** link in this case. This feature allows you to reorder pages by clicking on a page and dragging it to a different position within the same hierarchy level.

Reordering pages in the admin console will also change the order of appearance in the navigation of your website.

Breadcrumbs

Your hierarchy is also displayed in the so called breadcrumbs—navigation aid displayed on the website above the content. It starts with **You are here**, displays the trail of the page and provides links back to the parent page(s) of the current one.

Search engine friendly URLs

While creating your website, you probably thought about how you would promote it in search engines. Before you start to share the URLs of your website's pages, it is advisable to set up search engine friendly addresses.

Search engine friendly URLs do not contain any dynamic components in them and are more readable for visitors of your website and search engines. Compare the following two URLs:

```
http://yourdomain.com/index.php?page=products
```

```
http://yourdomain.com/products
```

Which page address is better? Search engines index your website better if your website uses the second version. Some pages with dynamic query strings in the address (as in the first example) are never indexed, and some of them will take longer to get into the search results.

If you do not care about search engines, then think about the visitors of the website. How easy is it to type or write down the address of the specific page if we do not use the second rewritten version? Imagine your visitor would like to recommend the page. He would do it without any difficulties with search engine friendly URLs and may fail with the first example.

However, after installing your website with CMS Made Simple, you will find that the URLs of your pages are built in the first way. You can easily change them to achieve better results with the website.

Time for action – creating search engine friendly URLs

To enable search engine friendly URLs on your website, perform the following steps:

1. Start FileZilla or any other FTP browser of your choice.

2. Connect to your hosting and select the file `config.php` for editing. (You can also copy the file to your local disk for editing and upload it after the following changes have been made).

3. Search `config.php` for the section "URL Settings" and replace:
   ```
   $config['url_rewriting'] = 'none';
   with
   $config['url_rewriting'] = 'mod_rewrite';
   ```

4. Close, save, and upload the file back to your web hosting.

5. Further, using FileZilla or any other FTP browser of your choice, open the `doc` directory.

6. Move the `htaccess.txt` file found in the `doc` directory to the root directory of your website (it is the same directory where the file `config.php` is present).

7. Rename the moved file to `.htaccess` (the period at the beginning belongs to the new filename!).

8. View your website in a browser, click on the top navigation area to see the new addresses for each page.

What just happened?

I am not going to bother you with technical stuff (please read about the `mod_rewrite` module if you would like to know more). You now have some pretty, clean URLs on your website.

If you have received an internal server error, then please consider the following known issues:

◆ Your hosting company does not support `mod_rewrite` (ask your hosting provider if you are not sure).

◆ You have installed CMS Made Simple into a subdirectory; for example, `http://yourdomain.com/mycms`. In this case, you will have to edit the file `.htaccess` and replace the line.

```
RewriteBase /
```

with

```
RewriteBase /mycms
```

Change the name after the slash to your subdirectory's name.

Getting more success from hierarchy

Enabling search engine friendly URLs has another useful effect. The URL of the page now contains the full path to the page including the parent page and not only the page alias.

Let's assume that you have created the page Philips TV (with page alias philips) and selected the page Plasma TV (with page alias plasma-tv) to be the parent page for it. Without rewriting the URL of the page, Philips TV gets the following address:

```
http://yourdomain.com/index.php?page=philips
```

After rewriting the URL of the page, we get:

```
http://yourdomain.com/plasma-tv/philips
```

The second version is cleaner, looks better for visitors, can easily be written down or remembered, and is better for search engines as you also have more keywords in your URL.

Remember that page aliases have to be unique. For example, you cannot have this kind of structure:

```
yourdomain.com/products/tv
```

```
yourdomain.com/news/products
```

The alias *products* can be used only once on the entire website.

If your hosting provider does not support `mod_rewrite`, then I recommend leaving them. Seriously, most web hosts have got this feature enabled by default, even free web hosting. There is no reason for not enabling it, unless the provider is not able to install it. Another reason for disabling `mod_rewrite` is that the module is quite processor-intensive, so hosts that put thousands of clients on one server would disable it to gain server performance. These are the reasons why you would not consider such a host and look for another one.

Controlling the navigation of the website

You have seen that the navigation is built automatically from the pages you have created. However, you can interfere in this process and prevent specific pages from displaying the main navigation even if they are on the top level in the page hierarchy.

Time for action – preventing pages from displaying in the navigation

In our company website, we would like to hide the pages **Privacy Policy** and **Sitemap** from the main navigation providing special links to these pages only in the footer navigation later on.

1. In the admin console, click on **Content | Pages**.

2. In the list of pages, click on the page **Privacy Policy** to open it for editing.

3. Switch to the **Options** tab on the top of the editing window and deselect **Show in Menu**, as shown in the following screenshot.

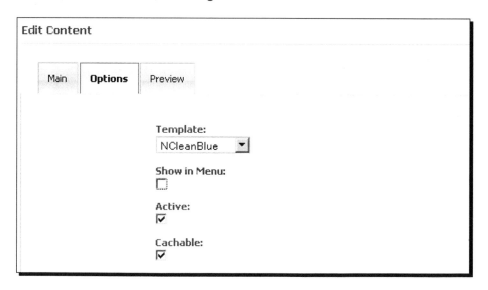

4. Scroll down to the bottom of the page, and click on the **Submit** button.

5. View your website with the magnifier icon on the top right of the admin console.

Do the same for the **Sitemap** page.

What just happened?

You have deselected **Show in Menu** to hide the page from the main navigation of your website. The link to the page disappears from the top menu.

However, the page is not deactivated. You can still view it if you enter the full address of the page in the address bar of your browser or place a direct link to it from other pages of your website. Normally you would use this feature to hide pages that are not important enough to be shown in the main navigation.

Another reason can be that specific pages have to be displayed only under certain circumstances. An example for such a page can be a *Thank you!* page that has to be displayed to the visitor when he sends us a message using the contact form on the website. We speak about service pages in this case and will learn later on how to use them on your website.

On the **Options** tab, you may have noticed another field that can be deselected: **Active**. Deactivating a page makes it unavailable to the visitors of the website. Even if a direct link is given to the page, the visitor will see an error message saying that the page could not be found.

 Think of pages that are not active as pages that do not exist as far as visitors are concerned.

You can use this feature to disable a page that you do not need any more. You can delete such pages and lose the contents of them or just deactivate them, while still being able to see their content in the admin console of your website. In this case, you are the only person who can see it. Some webmasters create inactive pages as a placeholder for future content.

What is your start page?

When your website is published online, individual pages can be reached through their links. But what page is displayed to the visitor if only the domain name of your website is given?

In CMS Made Simple, we call this the **default page**. You can define any page to be the default one. In the admin console, open **Content | Pages** and find the column **Default** in the list of current pages. Only one page has a green tick in the column and the page marked in this way is the start page of your website. You can choose another page to be the default page by clicking on the red cross in the column. Before the default page is changed, you have to confirm the question **Are you sure you want to set** (Page name) **as site default page?** See how the green tick is now moved from the previous default page to the new one. The previous page shows a red cross automatically in the column. Logically, you can have only one start page for your website.

More navigation control with content types

More control over your navigation can be achieved with different content types. You have surely noticed the **Content Type** field on the screen where the page is created or edited. The standard choice in this field is **Content** that is used to create an ordinary content page. You use this type in most cases.

With different content types (refer to the following table), you can add links to your navigation and get other behavior than ordinary pages.

Content type	Description
Internal page link	Use this content type to create a link in navigation to a specific page that is actually at another level of hierarchy. This content type generates just a link to the specific page that you select in the field **Destination page**.
Separator	Use this content type to internally separate different navigation sections from each other. This content type is mostly used to create sophisticated navigation structures or complex navigation design.
External link	As the name of the content type suggests, add an external link with this content type to your navigation. Enter complete URL starting with `http://` in the field **URL** of the content type.
Error page	This content type does not deal with navigation. It is explained in detail in Chapter 5, *Using Core Modules*.
Section header	With this content type, you create a header in the navigation. This content type is not a link itself. It just "holds" other pages placed below it in the hierarchy. You use this content type to visibly divide your menu structure into different parts.
Content	This content type is used as standard for normal content pages of your website.

Efficient work with pages

You have noticed that if you create a new page some fields are predefined; for example, the new page is active and shown in the menu. Page-specific metadata is prefilled with a comment:

```
<!-- Add code here that should appear in the metadata section of all
new pages -->
```

You can change the predefined values in the admin console. In the admin console, click on **Site Admin | Page Defaults** and set the fields the way you would like them to be set if a new page is created.

You can predefine meta tags and even the content field of the page. For example, you can create empty meta tags, which are shown as follows:

```
<meta name="keywords" content="" />
<meta name="description" content="" />
```

Now, the editor of the content has to just fill the content attribute of the meta tags (between the quotes) while creating or editing pages.

Creating a new page as a copy of existing one

You can create a new page as a copy of an existing page. In the list of current pages in the admin console (**Content | Pages**), you will find an icon for copy on the left-hand side. Click on the icon to see the next window. It is divided into two sections. The above section called **Copy From** shows the data of the page you are going to copy. You cannot change any data in it. In the section below (**Copy To**), you can enter the page alias, title, and menu text. Select another parent page for the copy if it differs from the original. Click on **Submit** and a new page is created.

New pages created as a copy do not connect to the original page in any way. You can now edit the new page the same way you would do it with other pages. You can also delete it without affecting the original page.

Changing multiple pages at once

If you have a large number of pages and would like to change more than one page at once, then you can use bulk actions in CMS Made Simple.

In the list of the current pages in the admin console (**Content | Pages**), select the checkboxes on the right-hand side of each page that has to be changed, then choose the desired action in the **With selected** field at the bottom of the page. You can activate them, show them in menu, and perform some other actions that will be explained in the next chapters.

Pop quiz – creating pages and navigation

1. How do you create new pages in CMS Made Simple?

    a. **Site Admin | Page Defaults | Add new page.**

    b. **Layout | Menu Manager | Add new page.**

    c. **Content | Pages | Add New Content.**

2. Where is the title that you fill in when creating a new page shown on the website?

    a. Title bar and menu.

    b. Title bar and heading of the site.

    c. Menu and submenu.

    d. Menu and head of the site.

3. What are the right answers considering the buttons **Apply** and **Submit**?

    a. The **Submit** button saves changes and closes the page in one step.

    b. The **Apply** button saves changes and closes the page in one step.

    c. The **Submit** button does not close the page; but saves the changes you have made.

    d. The **Submit** button does not close the page and previews the changes in the browser.

4. What will be affected if the page alias is changed?

    a. Title

    b. Keywords

    c. Menu

    d. URL

5. Where do you place the meta tags that are valid for all pages in the project?

    a. **Content | Pages | Page Title | Options.**

    b. In the section general meta tags of the stylesheet.

    c. **Site Admin | Global Settings | General Settings | Global Metadata.**

    d. **Extensions | Module Manager | GenMetaMod.**

6. Why should you use search engine friendly addresses?

    a. The RAM memory of your computer gets an overload by opening more than seven pages without search engine friendly URLs (they are too long).

    b. The URL is optimized for search engines.

    c. You should not use them at all, because you have to create a special one for every search engine, and create some duplicate content.

    d. The page is loaded much quicker.

7. If you would like to hide a page from visitors but do want to keep the content on the page for internal needs, you should:

    a. Delete the page.

    b. Deactivate the page.

    c. Assign another parent page.

    d. Copy the page and delete the original.

8. All your pages are written in English. Where would you put the meta tag for the language?

    a. In global settings.

    b. In every single page.

9. One of your pages has been linked to another website. What happens if you change the page alias?

    a. Old link will be redirected to the new page alias automatically.

    b. An error message that the page cannot be found appears after clicking on the link.

Have a go hero – create all pages for company website

Before proceeding with the next chapter, where the design and layout is explained, create all the pages you need for your website. You do not need to write the entire text for each page. The next section will simply be about preparing the structure of the website.

Use your own website plan or the sample one:

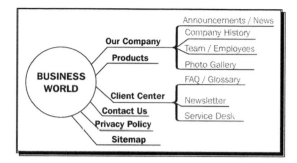

Creating pages and navigation

First add pages that are on the first level in your hierarchy (marked in bold in the preceding diagram). Then add the pages from the second level (marked in grey). You can adjust the page alias and menu text.

Add some sample text to the pages or write down what each single page will contain. If you have some ideas that are nice but should not be available on the website from the very beginning, then create some inactive pages holding these ideas.

Do not create more than two levels at the beginning. Even though it is possible to create a large number of levels, your visitors will find the navigation of the website more user friendly if they do not have to click 5 or 6 times to reach the desired information. It is better to start with two-level navigation to simplify learning layout and design in the next chapter.

The result of the website structure presented above is as follows:

Please note that the **Start** page has been renamed to **Our Company**.

Summary

In this chapter, you learned how easily pages can be created and managed. You saw that the navigation of your website is built automatically from the existing pages.

Specifically, we covered the following:

◆ **Creating pages**: You can create new pages from scratch or as a copy of an existing page.

◆ **Editing pages**: You can change everything on the page after it has been created, such as title, content, menu text, or page alias.

◆ **Adding meta tags**: Meta tags can be defined globally, if they are the same for each page. For individual meta tags on each specific page, you use the field **Page Specific Metadata** in the **Options** tab.

◆ **Page hierarchy**: Pages can be organized in a tree hierarchy. It helps to keep your pages structured and control the top and subnavigation of the website intuitively.

◆ **Search engine friendly URLs**: You modified the URLs for your pages. It gives you clean and pretty URLs that are quite noticeable for the visitors too.

◆ **Navigation control**: Pages are displayed automatically in the navigation. You can control this behavior by hiding the pages from navigation (they are still accessible by the visitors with direct links). You can also set the page to inactive so that only you, as the website administrator, are able to see the content of the links.

We also discussed how you create or change the start page of your website, gain more control by using different content types, or change multiple pages at once to save time.

Now that we've created the website structure, we're ready to start with the design and layout of our company website.

4
Design and Layout

In this chapter, we will learn what templates are. The strength of CMS Made Simple is its flexibility of design. Once you have understood how you can combine your static HTML with the dynamic parts of the website and format them with CSS, you will never lose control of your design or layout in CMS.

In this chapter, we will:

- ◆ Work with existing templates
- ◆ Create our own template from scratch
- ◆ Add and organize stylesheets
- ◆ Create and format navigation
- ◆ Port HTML templates to CMS Made Simple
- ◆ Learn the basics of Smarty
- ◆ Learn about exporting templates

CMS Made Simple uses various templates to display the content of your website. To understand templates, think of them as predefined layouts. Every time you create a new page, you choose a layout to define how this page should look.

You can easily imagine a template as a wrapper for your content. The wrapper (layout) is always the same; the content changes from page-to-page. The editor of the website just adds content to the page and chooses a template. CMS Made Simple will automatically display the page content for the visitors within a chosen layout. Thus, the design and content are entirely separated in CMS.

Working with existing templates

You will find all existing templates in your CMS in the admin console. Click on **Layout | Templates** to see all templates available in your installation. If you did not install any sample content, then only one template is available.

In the strictest sense, we have to differentiate between templates and themes. A template is just a part of a theme. A theme consists of one or more templates and one or more stylesheets. Some themes optionally include menu templates as well. So if you talk about the complete design of your website, you should think about themes. Different page layouts (1-column, 2-column, or others) within one theme are called templates in CMS Made Simple.

You can easily add ready-to-use templates to your website without any HTML or CSS knowledge by using some resources for the themes:

- `http://themes.cmsmadesimple.org`
- `http://www.icms.info/cmsms-templates`

Time for action – importing a ready-made template

Let us see how to import a ready-made template into your installation.

1. Download an XML file for your template from one of the addresses given above and save this file to your local disk.

2. In the admin console, click on **Layout | Theme Manager**.

3. Switch to the tab **Import** and choose the XML file from step 1 in the field **Upload Theme**.

4. Click on **Import**.

5. Go to **Layout | Templates** and find the new imported template in the list of templates.

6. Click on the icon with a red cross in the **Active** column (the icon should change to a green tick).

What just happened?

You have imported a new theme into your CMS Made Simple installation. A theme contains one or more templates (**Layout | Templates**), one or more stylesheets (**Layout | Stylesheets**) and sometimes menu templates as well (**Layout | Menu Manager**).

To test the template, open a page that you would like to see within the new template for editing (**Content | Pages**). Switch to the **Options** tab, and select the newly created template in the field **Template**. The screen is automatically redirected to the **Main** tab. Click on **Apply** and then on the icon with the magnifying glass icon beside the button **Apply** to see the changes on the page. Compare this page to other pages that use different templates.

This wonderful principle of CMS Made Simple allows you to give each page its own look and feel. You can use different templates to separate some parts of your website. For example, you could use one template for the company website and a completely different template for the shop if you like. Designers often use different templates to enable one, two, or three columns layouts on different pages.

To see which page uses what template, open the list of the current pages in the admin console (**Content | Pages**) and see the column **Template**.

If you would like to use one template on all pages of your website, you can assign it to all pages at once. This function is especially useful if you already have a great number of pages. In the admin console, open the list of existing templates (**Layout | Templates**) and click the **Set All Pages** link beside the name of the template. This way, the template is assigned to all pages of your website with just one click.

In the list of templates, you can also see that one template is set as default. When you create a new page, CMS Made Simple will automatically take the default template for the new page. Click on the icon with the red cross in the column **Default** beside the template name that you would like to use as the standard template.

Creating a new template

Surely, it is easier to use ready-made templates for the website. However, you often need your own style for the website. In this section, we will learn how to create a new template from scratch.

Templates in CMS Made Simple contain pure HTML. For dynamic parts of the layout, such as navigation or content, special placeholders are used. These placeholders are realized with the **Smarty** web template system. You use simple **Smarty tags** in your template to mark the places where dynamic parts in the pages are required. Smarty tags are placeholders that are substituted with simple text or even other HTML templates when the website is displayed in the browser. In contrast to HTML tags, Smarty tags are always enclosed in curly brackets.

Time for action – creating a new template

Let us see how you can easily create a new HTML template in CMS Made Simple:

1. In the admin console of your website, select **Layout | Templates**.

2. Click on **Add New Template** at the bottom of the list.

3. On the next page, type the name of the new template, **My first template**.

4. Add HTML source code to the **Content** field, as shown in the following screenshot:

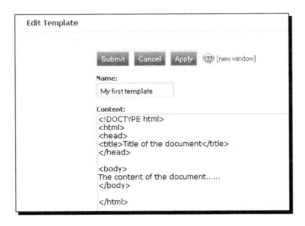

5. Click on **Submit**.

6. In the list of templates, find your new template **My first template**, click on **Set All Pages** in the same line where your template name is, and confirm the message:

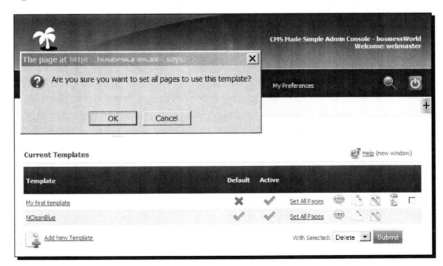

7. The message **All pages modified!** appears above the list of templates.

8. Click on the magnifying glass icon in the top-right corner of the admin console to see the result (Google Chrome was used as the web browser in this example):

What just happened?

You have created a new template with some simple HTML tags. You have then instructed CMS to use this newly created template on all pages of your website. In your browser, you see the exact output of the HTML code you have added to the **Content** field of the template.

Your template is static now. It means that no individual part of the page, such as title of the page or content, is displayed on the website. To mark the places where dynamic content should be displayed, you have to use **Smarty tags**. These tags will be substituted with an actual title or content when the page is loaded and displayed in the browser.

Adding dynamic parts to templates

Let us substitute the static page title and content with individual content of the page.

Time for action – adding Smarty tags to a template

1. In the admin console, click on **Layout | Templates**, and click on **My first template** to open it for editing.

2. Replace the static text for title and content with Smarty tags, as shown in the following screenshot:

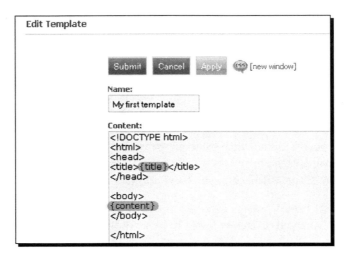

3. Click on **Apply** and then click on the magnifying glass icon in the top-right corner of the admin console to see the results of your changes. It should look as shown in the following screenshot:

What just happened?

You have replaced the static text in your template with placeholders called **Smarty tags**. These special tags are enclosed in curly brackets. When you see the page in your browser, the places where you have added Smarty tags in the HTML code are now replaced with actual content and the title of the page.

To confirm that changes were made for each page and not only for the start page, open the current list of the pages (**Content | Pages**) in the admin console, and click on the magnifying glass icon beside some of the pages to display them in the browser. You should see that every page gets an individual title. The page content is displayed in the place where the tag {content} was added in the template.

{title} and {content} are only two examples for custom CMS Smarty plugins that you can use in your template. Try out some of them from the following table to see what is displayed at the place where these Smarty tags are added.

Tag	Description
{breadcrumbs}	Prints a breadcrumb trail.
{created_date}	Prints the date and time when the page was created.
{last_modified_by}	Prints the ID of the user who has last edited the page.
{menu_text}	Prints the text entered in the field **Menu Text** for the page.
{modified_date}	Prints the date and time the page was last modified.

To try the plugins, just add the name of a plugin in the curly brackets to the template of your website in any place you like.

The preceding tags hold different information about the actual page. There are also tags that hold global information about your website, such as the website's name or the version of CMS Made Simple that is installed. They do not depend on the page where they are displayed and are the same on each page. Try them as well to see what information is displayed at the place where the tag is added.

Tag	Description
{cms_version}	Prints the current version number of your CMS.
{cms_versionname}	Prints the current version name of your CMS.
{current_date}	Prints the current date and time.
{root_url}	Prints the URL location of your website.
{sitename}	Prints the website name. The information can be changed in the admin console (**Site Admin | Global Settings | Site Name**).

With Smarty tags, you see the main principle of the separation of the code from design. As a designer, you do not need to know how the date of the last page modification is stored in the database ({modified_date}) and how exactly the location of the website is retrieved from the address line of the browser ({root_url}). You can just use the plugins declared above to retrieve the needed information.

Having control over the output

If you have already tried some of the preceding tags, then you have probably noticed that sometimes the output is not exactly what you need. You can control the output of the tags using **Smarty parameters** (also called attributes).

Parameters can be compared to HTML attributes. You can use parameters to refine the output of the Smarty tags. Parameters can be used to:

◆ Change date formats displayed by a tag

◆ Add supplementary parts to the output of the tag

◆ Remove some parts from the output

◆ Replace specific text in the output of the tag

Time for action – adding Smarty parameters to the template

Let us say you have added the tag {last_modified_by} to your template. However, you do not like the ID of the user, and you would like the username or his full name to be displayed instead of the user ID.

1. In the admin console, select your template for edit
   (**Layout | Templates | My first template**).

2. Add the {last_modified_by} tag with the format parameter, as shown in the following screenshot:

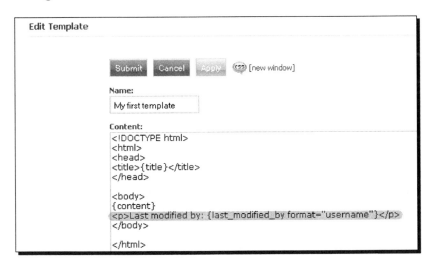

3. Click on **Apply** and then click on the magnifying glass icon in the top-right corner of the admin console to see the result of your template changes.

What just happened?

You have added a tag {last_modified_by} to the template in order to display the name of the user who made the last modification to the page. Normally, if you do not say anything else, the ID of the user is displayed at the place where the tag is added. By adding a format parameter to the tag, you can now control what exactly should be shown.

As templates in CMS Made Simple consist of a mixture of HTML and Smarty, you need to understand the definition of tag, plugin, parameter, and parameter values. The tags we used in the example are **Smarty plugins**. Smarty plugins are custom functions defined for your convenience. Almost every plugin can take parameters (sometimes also called attributes). You add parameters to the plugin name separated with a space. The parameter name is followed by an equals sign and parameter value enclosed in double or single quotes. See the following image to understand the anatomy of the Smarty tag:

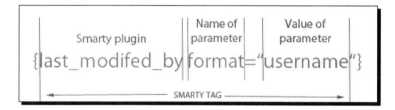

Now, how do you know what parameters you can use with what plugin and what parameter values are allowed? You will find a complete list of custom CMS plugins in the admin console of your website. These plugins are called **tags** in CMS Made Simple. Click on **Extensions | Tags** to see the complete list of plugins that you can use in the template right now.

If you click on the name of the tag, you will get help on it. You will find a short description what this tag does in general, and then see an example of how you can use it in your template. You will also see a list of available parameters (if any) and the values you can use for them.

Similar to HTML attributes, you can use more than one parameter in a tag. The order of the parameters is not important.

For the tag {last_modified_by}, only one parameter is listed in the **Help** section. There are three values that are accepted by this parameter—id, username, and fullname, so that you can use another parameter value to display the full name of the person who has edited the page last:

```
{last_modified_by format="fullname"}
```

The full name of the user is shown if it is given in the user's account. In the admin console, open **Users & Groups | Users** and click on the username that you would like to modify. Enter the **First Name** and the **Last Name** of the user.

Using plugins in content

In the last section, you added Smarty plugins to the template. However, it is also possible to add them directly into the content of the page. You use the tags in the content in the same way that you used them in the template. Write the name of the plugin enclosed in curly brackets in the field **Content** of a specific page. Try it out now. Open any page for editing (**Content | Pages**) and add one or more tags in the field **Content**. You can mix tags and static text in the same way you did in the template.

A small example for the start page of your website can be:

```
Welcome! Today is {current_date}.
```

The preceding code will automatically display the current date on the start page of your website.

You should add plugins that need to be displayed on every page of your website to the template. If you need a special plugin on only one page (for example, the start page), then you should add the plugin into the field **Content** of this page.

Adding stylesheets to the template

Nowadays, designing websites requires not only pure HTML, but also CSS. The most professional websites use HTML to structure the website and CSS to style them. CSS gives you full control over your layout. With CSS you can easily change the complete look and feel of your website without changing any HTML. You can see some good examples of CSS layouts based on the same HTML at http://www.csszengarden.com.

CMS Made Simple takes pure CSS code for your page layout and saves it in the database. In this section, you will learn how you can create a new stylesheet, add your styles to it, and attach it to the template.

Creating a new stylesheet

To create a new stylesheet, you have to accomplish three simple steps:

1. Create and save the new stylesheet containing your CSS code.

2. Attach the stylesheet to the template.

3. Add a special tag in the template that will be replaced by an HTML tag `<link>` pointing to the stylesheet.

Time for action – creating the stylesheet

Normally, in static HTML pages, you create a CSS file and attach it to your template using an HTML `<link>` tag. In CMS Made Simple, stylesheets are saved in the database, and therefore cannot be linked directly. Let us see how stylesheets can be created and attached to the templates.

1. In the admin console, click on **Layout | Stylesheets**.

2. Click the **Add a Stylesheet** link at the bottom of the list.

3. Type in the name of the new stylesheet and enter the CSS code in the **Content** field, as shown in the following screenshot:

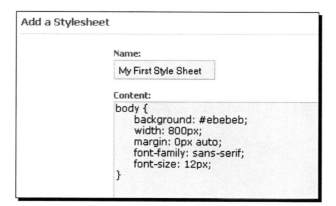

4. Click on **Submit**. The new stylesheet is added to the list of stylesheets.

5. To attach the new stylesheet to your template, in the admin console, click on **Layout | Templates**.

6. In the list of templates, click on the blue CSS icon, as shown in the following screenshot:

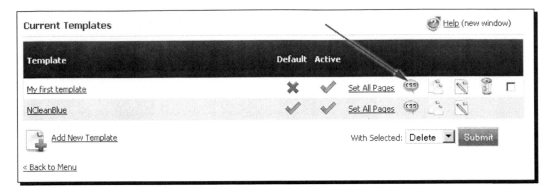

7. Select **My First Style Sheet** from the drop-down field, and click on **Add a Stylesheet**.

8. The last step is to add a Smarty plugin that will call the attached stylesheet in the template. In the admin console, click on **Layout | Templates**, and select your template for editing.

9. Add the {stylesheet} tag to the template, as shown in the following screenshot:

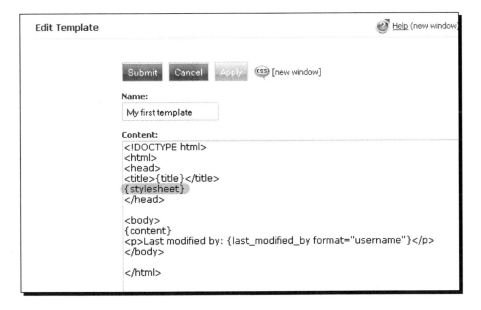

10. Click on **Apply** and then click on the magnifying glass icon in the top-right corner of the admin console to see the result of your template changes. It should look as shown in the following screenshot:

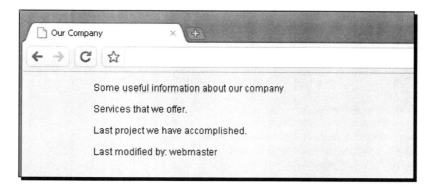

What just happened?

You have created a new stylesheet that contains pure CSS code. Then, you have attached this stylesheet to your template. By attaching the stylesheet, you have stated which stylesheet is relevant for your template. The {stylesheet} tag that you added to your template, is substituted by the HTML <link> tag when the page is displayed in the browser.

Open the page source in the browser to see what is set at the place where the {stylesheet} tag has been added to the template. In my example, it looks like:

```
<link rel="stylesheet" type="text/css" href="http://www.yourdomain.
com/stylesheet.php?cssid=51" />
```

In your special installation, the name of the domain will be different, and the last number in the URL of the stylesheet is also likely to be different. The tag is formed automatically, and you do not need to care how it is made technically.

You can define and attach more than one stylesheet to the template. For example, you can define a stylesheet with general styles and then add another one containing print styles. We will create and add more stylesheets in the course of the book so that you can see how it works later on. For each stylesheet, a separate HTML link tag is added at the place where the {stylesheet} tag is added. There is no need to add the tag twice or more if you have attached more stylesheets, as this plugin will create as many links as there are stylesheets attached to the template.

Media types for stylesheets

While creating a stylesheet, you have probably seen the area **Media Type** with some checkboxes at the bottom of the page where stylesheet code is added. You can see the area if you open your stylesheet for editing in the admin console (**Layout | Stylesheets**) and scroll down. It appears as shown in the following screenshot:

```
Media Type:

  Media type

  □  all : Suitable for all devices.
  □  aural : Intended for speech synthesizers.
  □  braille : Intended for braille tactile feedback devices.
  □  embossed : Intended for paged braille printers.
  □  handheld : Intended for handheld devices.
  □  print : Intended for paged, opaque material and for documents viewed on screen in print preview mode.
  □  projection : Intended for projected presentations, for example projectors or print to transparencies.
  □  screen : Intended primarily for color computer screens.
  □  tty : Intended for media using a fixed-pitch character grid, such as teletypes and terminals.
  □  tv : Intended for television-type devices.
```

The media type corresponds to the HTML attribute `media` and is automatically added to the HTML `<link>` tag (if you select any type here):

```
<link rel="stylesheet" type="text/css" media="screen" href="http://
www.yourdomain.com/stylesheet.php?cssid=51" />
<link rel="stylesheet" type="text/css" media="print" href="http://www.
yourdomain.com/stylesheet.php?cssid=52" />
```

The styles from the first stylesheet are used to display your website in the browser. However, the browser will use the print stylesheet if your page is printed:

If you use any CSS framework with more than one CSS file, then you can copy the content of each CSS file into a separate stylesheet in CMS Made Simple and then attach them all to your templates. You can also change the order of the stylesheets while assigning them to the template.

Creating navigation for the website

The heart of each website is surely the navigation. The navigation consists of links to the pages and is often divided into main navigation and sidebar navigation. In CMS Made Simple, the navigation is automatically built from the list of active pages. You can create navigation of any complexity grade in CMS Made Simple due to the very powerful concept explained in the following sections.

Time for action – adding navigation to the template

Let us add navigation links to the website.

1. In the admin console, click on **Layout | Templates**, and select **My first template** for edit.

2. Add a special tag for navigation before the {content} tag, as shown in the following screenshot:

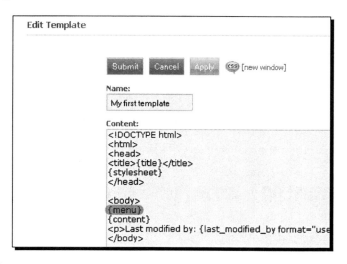

3. Click on **Apply** and then click on the magnifying glass icon in the top-right corner of the admin console to see the result of your template changes. It should look as shown in the following screenshot:

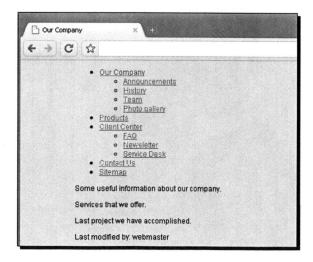

What just happened?

With the custom CMS tag {menu}, a complete structure of the website is displayed at the place where it is added in the template. Each active page is displayed according to its position in the hierarchy and order in the list of pages.

The {menu} tag is very powerful. You can use numerous parameters that help you to create navigation of any complexity grade. For example, you can limit the navigation to only one level, so that only pages from the first hierarchy level are shown:

```
{menu number_of_levels="1"}
```

Try the preceding code to create some navigation limited to the main pages. This is a common way to create the main navigation for the website; normally placed at the top of each page. The subpages are not shown with this parameter but we can display them in the sidebar navigation later on.

We will learn more parameters for the {menu} tag and see more examples on how it can be customized later on. In this chapter, our main subject is design and layout. That is why we will now learn to customize the look and feel of top navigation.

Designing navigation—the pure CSS way

With the simple plugin {menu} the navigation of the website is displayed on every page. CMS Made Simple creates a simple unordered HTML list for the navigation as you can see in the source code of the page. Let us see how you can easily style a top navigation bar with pure CSS.

Time for action – design navigation with pure CSS

We are now going to style the top navigation so that it looks like buttons displayed beside each other instead of below each other.

1. In the admin console, click on **Layout | Templates**, and open **My first template** for edit.

2. Add the HTML `<div>` tag around the {menu number_of_levels="1 "} tag, as shown in the following screenshot:

```
Name:

My first template

Content:
<!DOCTYPE html>
<html>
<head>
<title>{title}</title>
{stylesheet}
</head>

<body>

<div id="top-navi">
{menu number_of_levels="1"}
</div>

{content}
<p>Last modified by: {last_modified_by format="username"}</p>
</body>

</html>
```

3. Click on **Submit**.

4. Open **My First Style Sheet** from the list of stylesheets (**Layout | Stylesheets**) for editing.

5. Add style formats for the container `top-navi` at the end of stylesheet, as shown in the following code snippet:

```css
#top-navi ul
{
        height: 22px;
        padding: 0px;
        margin: 10px 0;
        border-top: 1px solid #e5e4e2;
        border-bottom: 1px solid #e5e4e2;
}
#top-navi li
{
        list-style: none;
        float:left;
}

#top-navi li a
{
        color: #a2a2a2;
        text-decoration: none;
        display: block;
        padding: 5px 15px;
}
```

```
#top-navi li a:hover
{
        color: #ffffff;
        background: #3d648a;

}
```

6. Click on **Apply** and then click on the magnifying glass icon in the top-right corner of the admin console to see the result of your changes. It should now look as shown in the following screenshot:

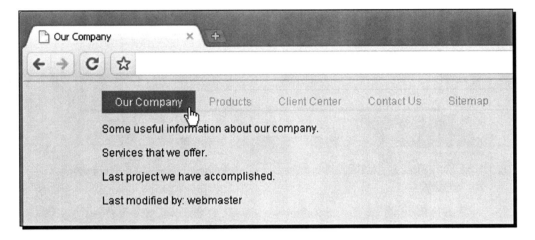

What just happened?

You have limited the output of the navigation to the first level by adding the parameter number_of_levels to the {menu} tag. Then you have placed an HTML <div> tag around the Smarty plugin {menu}. With the last step, you have added some CSS styles to give the top navigation the desired look and feel. Notice that you do not need any special "CMS design" knowledge to add styles to your navigation. You have used pure and common CSS to format the navigation.

If you click on each page in the browser and see how the navigation is displayed on other pages, you will notice that there is some additional formatting which CMS uses to display active pages. For example, <h3> is used to display the name of the active page within navigation. Open the page source in your browser to see the formatting of active pages. You can add more styles to change the formatting of <h3> tag. On the other hand, to save your time you can reduce all these special formats to pure ordered lists by using the built-in template minimal_menu.tpl. This template is automatically provided with a standard installation of CMS Made Simple. To use it, add another parameter to the tag {menu}, as shown in the following line of code:

```
{menu number_of_levels="1" template="minimal_menu.tpl"}
```

In this way, all additional tags are deleted from the navigation and a clear unordered list is displayed on each page.

If you look into the page source of the website, you will notice that there were also some special class attributes added to the menu. CMS knows what page is actually shown and adds a special class to the HTML tag <a> of the active page:

```
<li><a href="http://www.yourdomain.com/" class="currentpage"> Our
Company </a>
```

You can use this information to give another style to the navigation item of the page that is currently displayed. The easiest method is to combine the a:hover and a.currentpage classes to give them the same style.

```
#top-navi li a:hover, #top-navi li a.currentpage
{
  color: #ffffff;
  background: #3d648a;
}
```

If you can design websites with CSS, you are now able to design simple navigation of the website without any special coding knowledge.

Adding sidebar navigation

However, this is only half of the story. The pages displayed in the top navigation are limited to the first level. We need some sidebar navigation to display the list of subpages belonging to the parent page.

We have to discuss another important parameter of the plugin {menu}. With the parameter number_of_levels, you set how many levels from your page hierarchy are to be shown. For the sidebar navigation, you do not need to limit the number of levels, but to define a start level for your navigation. As the first level is added to the top navigation already, for the sidebar, you start with the second level:

```
{menu start_level="2" template="minimal_menu.tpl" }
```

With parameter start_level, you say from what level the pages are shown in the menu. Second level means that pages with a minimum of two numbers in the hierarchy are shown, for example, 1.2, 2.3, or 4.2. CMS Made Simple also knows what page is selected in the top navigation and displays in the sidebar only pages that are children of the page selected above. This means that if the page with number 3 is selected in the top navigation, the sidebar will only contain the children of this page: 3.1, 3.2, 3.3, and so on.

With the parameter template, you again reduce the output of the navigation to the pure HTML unordered list to make formatting easier at this point.

An interesting and popular parameter is collapse, for example, {menu collapse="1"}. This parameter allows the collapsing of sub items in the menu, so that only the sub items of the current menu item are shown. It should have at least three levels in the page hierarchy to see how automatic collapse hides menu items that do not belong to the currently displayed page.

We have learned the most important parts of a template: title, content, and menu. This is enough information to be able to port ready-made HTML template to CMS Made Simple.

Porting a HTML template

Normally, you do not design a complete template from scratch in CMS Made Simple. You can use any HTML/CSS editor to create a design outside of CMS Made Simple. It is also possible that you have downloaded or purchased a ready-made HTML template or you work with a designer who has created the design for your website. In all the cases listed above, you get an HTML file, CSS file, and one or more images. In this section, we learn to port an HTML template to CMS Made Simple.

Imagine, you get an HTML template that looks like the following screenshot.

This template consists of three files: HTML, CSS, and a logo image in the upper-right corner. Notice that there is nothing but pure HTML and CSS at this point. Let us create a new CMS Made Simple template from the preceding template.

Time for action – porting a HTML template to CMS Made Simple

1. In the admin console, click on **Layout | Templates**, and click on **Add New Template**.

2. Enter **Business World** as **Name** of the template, and replace the whole suggested **Content** with the HTML code of the example template given in the preceding screenshot. The HTML code for the template is:

```
<!DOCTYPE html>
<html>
  <head>
    <title>Our Company</title>
    <link rel="stylesheet" type="text/css" media="screen"
      href="style.css" />
    <meta name="description" content="" />
  </head>
  <body>
    <div id="container">
      <div id="header">
        businessWorld
      </div>
      <div id="top-navi">
        <ul class="clearfix">
          <li><a href="#"> Our Company </a></li>
          <li><a href="#"> Products </a></li>
          <li><a href="#"> Client Center </a></li>
          <li><a href="#"> Contact Us </a></li>
          <li><a href="#"> Sitemap </a></li>
        </ul>
      </div>
      <div id="content">
        <h1>Our Company</h1>
        <p>
        Lorem ipsum quo ea eruditi epicuri dolores, mea no
        delicata reprehendunt. Mea possit aperiri iracundia in, ad
        veri ocurreret scribentur his, justo qualisque adipiscing
        pro an. Has congue dissentiunt an, ea summo simul
        repudiandae sit. Omnium aliquam disputationi est no, etiam
        deleniti eos in, te pro reque torquatos. Adhuc cetero
        alienum te mei, nec id solum partem populo.
        </p>
        <p>
        Sit putent fabulas complectitur ne, pro te velit viris
        ocurreret. Eam dico habeo aeterno ei, ut deserunt
        eloquentiam pri. Vim ad alii populo expetendis, et pro
        dolorum scaevola partiendo. Mea te timeam delicata
```

```
           deterruisset, ius no molestie lobortis definiebas, etiam
           inciderint eos ea. Ea sit fugit audiam, nec clita alterum
           intellegebat cu, nonummy fuisset id mel. Eam ut amet
           sensibus consequat, erant legimus vim id.
         </p>
       </div>
       <div id="sidebar">
         <ul class="clearfix">
           <li><a href="#"> Announcements </a></li>
           <li><a href="#"> History </a></li>
           <li><a href="#"> Team </a></li>
           <li><a href="#"> Photo gallery </a></li>
         </ul>
       </div>
       <div id="footer">
         2009 businessWorld
       </div>
     </div>
   </body>
 </html>
```

3. Click on **Submit**.

4. In the list of templates (**Layout | Templates**), click on **Set All Pages** and confirm the message: **Are you sure you want to set all pages to use this template?**

5. Click on the icon with the red cross in the column **Default** to set the template as the standard template for all new pages.

6. Now, create a new stylesheet. In the admin console, open **Layout | Stylesheets**, and click on **Add a Stylesheet**.

7. Enter **Business World Style Sheet** as **Name**, and paste the CSS code from the example template above into the **Content** field. The CSS code for the template is:

```
body
{
  background:#ebebeb;
  font-family:sans-serif;
  font-size:12px;
}
#container
{
  width:800px;
  margin:15px auto;
}
```

```css
#top-navi ul
{
  height:22px;
  padding:0px;
  margin:10px 0;
  border-top:1px solid #e5e4e2;
  border-bottom:1px solid #e5e4e2;
}
#top-navi li
{
  list-style:none;
  float:left;
}
#top-navi li a
{
  color:#a2a2a2;
  text-decoration:none;
  display:block;
  padding:5px 15px;
}
#top-navi li a:hover
{
    color:#ffffff;
    background:#3d648a;
}
#header
{
  height:105px;
  background:#a83b06 url(logo.jpg) top right no-repeat;
  color:#fde5d9;
  font-size:90px;
  padding-top:20px;
  font-family:serif;
  padding-left:15px;
  letter-spacing:-3px;
  border:1px solid #c48769;
}
#content
{
  width:540px;
  float:left;
  background:#ffffff;
  padding:10px;
  margin-bottom:20px;
```

```
}
#sidebar
{
   width:200px;
   float:right;
   background:#ffffff;
   padding:10px;
   margin-bottom:20px;
}
#footer
{
   clear:both;
   width:780px;
   background:#a83b06;
   padding:10px;
   font-size:11px;
   color:#ffffff;
   font-weight:bold;
}
#footer a
{
   color:#eeeeee;
   text-decoration:none;
   font-weight:normal;
}
h1
{
   color:#062d53;
   font-size:20px;

}
```

8. Click on **Submit**.

9. In the list of stylesheets (**Layout | Stylesheets**), click on the blue CSS icon 🔵 in the same line where a new stylesheet is.

10. Select template **Business World** from the drop-down field, and click on **Attach to this Template**.

11. Click **Business World** to open the template for editing and replace the static link to the stylesheet with the Smarty placeholder shown as follows:

```
<!DOCTYPE html>
  <html>
    <head>
```

```
<title>Our Company</title>
{stylesheet}
<meta name="description" content="" />
</head>
<body>
 <div id="container">
<div id="header">
businessWorld
</div>
```

12. Click on **Apply** and see the new template on the website.

What just happened?

You have created a new HTML template and a new stylesheet. You attached the stylesheet to the template, so that CMS Made Simple knows what stylesheet has to be loaded with the template. Normally, you would use an HTML `<link>` tag to point to `style.css`. In our case, we do not really have a file, as the stylesheet is saved in database. Therefore, we have replaced the HTML `<link>` tag in the head section of the HTML template with the Smarty plugin `{stylesheet}`.

The image used as the background in the CSS stylesheet is not found.

```
background:#a83b06 url(logo.jpg) top right no-repeat;
```

With any graphics editing program, create an image of 215 x 125 pixels and name it `logo.jpg`. Create a new folder under the folder `uploads` in your installation, name the folder `design`, and upload the image `logo.jpg` to this folder. You can upload it with FileZilla or any other FTP client of your choice. Then replace the path to the image in your stylesheet (**Layout | Stylesheets**), as follows:

```
background:#a83b06 url(uploads/design/logo.jpg) top right no-repeat;
```

The path to the images is relative to the currently displayed page. Writing `uploads/design/logo.jpg` tells CMS to look for the image in `http://www.youdomain.com/uploads/design/logo.jpg`. However, you do not need to add a domain name to the path. If you export your template later on and use it on another domain, it is better to use relative paths without a domain name in front of them.

Now, you can start replacing the static text in your template with Smarty tags. Find and replace title, content, and menu in HTML. Open your template in the admin console and make the following changes:

```
<!DOCTYPE html>
  <html>
    <head>
      <title>{title} - {sitename}</title>
      {stylesheet}
      {metadata}
      <meta name="description" content="" />
    </head>
    <body>
      <div id="container">
      <div id="header">
      businessWorld
      </div>
      <div id="top-navi">
      {menu number_of_levels="1" template="minimal_menu.tpl"}
      </div>
      <div id="content">
        <h1>{title}</h1>
        {content}
      </div>
      <div id="sidebar">
      {menu start_level="2" template="minimal_menu.tpl"}
      </div>
      <div id="footer">
      2009 businessWorld
      </div>
      </div>
    </body>
  </html>
```

Below the Smarty {stylesheet} plugin, you can add the {metadata} plugin. This plugin will add global metadata (**Site Admin | Global Settings**) and the **Page Specific Metadata** from the tab **Options** of the page. It will also set the HTML <base> tag with the attribute href to the root of your installation. In this way, all images can be defined in relation to the root folder.

Congratulations! Your template is now ported to CMS Made Simple.

Learning Smarty basics

You have learned how to use Smarty tags and refine them with a parameter so far. You have also ported an entire HTML template to CMS Made Simple. However, if you would like to create professional sophisticated designs, you will need more knowledge about Smarty. With the powerful combination of Smarty and HTML, there are no limits to the flexibility of the sites you design.

Working with Smarty variables

Smarty variables are much simpler than complex Smarty plugins. They are placeholders that contain plain information about the actual page ID, page alias, or position of the page in the hierarchy. Some Smarty variables that you are not aware of, are already defined in your template. You do not need to know or remember all of them if you know how you can figure out their names and values.

Time for action – getting Smarty variables

We are going to get the number of the page in the page hierarchy to integrate this information into the design of the page title. How do we figure out the name of the Smarty variable that contains this information? We can get it from the template as follows:

1. In the admin console, click on **Layout | Templates**.

2. Open the **Business World** template for edit and add the plugin
   `{get_template_vars}` just before the last `</div>` tag, as shown
   in the following code snippet:

```
<!DOCTYPE html>
  <html>
    <head>
      <title>{title} - {sitename}</title>
      {stylesheet}
      {metadata}
      <meta name="description" content="" />
    </head>
    <body>
      ..........
      {get_template_vars}
    </div>
    </body>
  </html>
```

3. Click on **Apply** and then click on the magnifying glass icon on the top-right corner of the admin console to see the result. It should now look like the following screenshot:

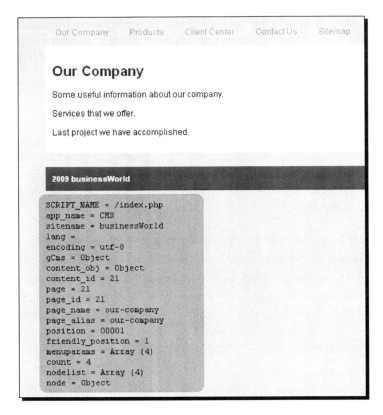

What just happened?

With the Smarty {get_template_vars} plugin, you displayed all **Smarty variables** available in your template. In the list of variables on each line, one variable is displayed with its name and its value separated by an equals sign. These values change from page to page. For example, the variable with the name friendly_position contains the position of the page in the page hierarchy. If you navigate to other pages, you will see that the value of this variable is different on every page.

How do you add a variable in your template? Smarty variables are enclosed in curly brackets as well, but unlike the Smarty plugins, they have a dollar sign at the beginning. To use the variable friendly_position, you just need to add the following Smarty tag to your template:

```
{$friendly_position}
```

You can delete the {get_template_vars} plugin now. It is helpful for you to see which Smarty variables exist and what values are stored there. You can add this plugin again, when you need to look for another variable.

Let us use the information we have learned about Smarty plugins and Smarty variables by combining them both to create a title of the page. Open the template **Business World** (**Layout | Templates**) for editing and change the title of the page between the body tags and before the tag {content} shown as follows:

```
<h1><span>{$friendly_position}</span> {title}</h1>
```

Then open **Business World Style Sheet** for editing (**Layout | Stylesheets**), and add a CSS style to format the title of the page:

```
h1 span
{
    color: #ffffff;
    background: #cccccc;
    padding: 0 5px;
}
```

The result of the above formatting should look as shown in the following screenshot:

You can use any Smarty variable from the template, except for variables with the value Array(). We will look at these special variables in the following section.

Controlling output with the IF function

You can create numerous templates for your website and assign different templates to different pages. This is useful if you use layouts with a different number of columns. However, sometimes there is only a tiny difference between the templates, and it is not efficient to create a new template each time you need only slight changes.

For example, imagine you would like to display the last editor of the page, as we did with the {last_modified_by} tag. It is a useful piece of information on most pages but we would like to hide it on the contact page. You do not need to create a new template where this tag is not added. For such slight changes, it is better to know how to control the output in the same template with an IF structure.

Time for action – displaying tags in dependence of the page

We are going to hide the {last_modified_by} tag on the page **Contact Us**. However, it has to be still displayed on all other pages.

1. Open the template **Business World** for editing (**Layout | Templates**).

2. Add the Smarty IF code around the {last_modified_by...} tag, as shown in the following code snippet:

```
<!DOCTYPE html>
  <html>
    <head>
      <title>{title} - {sitename}</title>
      {stylesheet}
      {metadata}
      <meta name="description" content="" />
    </head>
    <body>
    <div id="container">
    <div id="header">
    businessWorld
    </div>
    <div id="top-navi">
    {menu number_of_levels="1" template="minimal_menu.tpl"}
    </div>
    <div id="content">
      <h1>{title}</h1>
      {content}
      {if $page_alias neq "contact-us"}
        <p>Last modified by {last_modified_by format=
                              "fullname"}</p>
```

```
    {/if}
  </div>
  <div id="sidebar">
  {menu start_level="2" template="minimal_menu.tpl"}
  </div>
  <div id="footer">
    2009 businessWorld
  </div>
  </div>
  </body>
</html>
```

 In this book, you may occasionally come across a single line of code appearing on two different lines. Please note that this has been done only for the purpose of indentation due to space constraints. When using such code make sure it's on one line in your script file.

3. Click on **Apply** and then click on the magnifying glass icon in the top-right corner of the admin console to see the result.

What just happened?

The IF code that you have added around the paragraph containing the last modification causes CMS to check the page alias of the displayed page. If the page alias is equal to "*contact-us*", then everything between the IF structure is not shown, otherwise the information about the last modification is displayed.

You have seen from the previous section that CMS knows what page of our website is currently being displayed. This information is stored in the Smarty variable {$page_alias}. With the built-in IF function, you can compare the page alias of the actual page with the page alias of the page **Contact Us**. If the value of the variable {$page_alias} is NOT equal to contact-us, then everything between the IF tags is displayed. If the page alias is equal to contact-us, then nothing is displayed. In this way, you can control the output of the template depending on the page alias.

The abbreviation neq (meaning **not equal**) between the variable {$page_alias} and the value contact-us is called a **Qualifier**. Qualifiers are used to build a logical condition in the IF code. The result of the logical condition can be true or false. If the result of the IF condition is true (and it is true if the page alias IS NOT EQUAL to contact-us), then everything placed in between the IF tags is displayed. If the result of the IF condition is false (and it is only false if the page alias IS EQUAL to contact-us), then everything between the IF tags is suppressed.

There are more qualifiers that can be used to build logical conditions in Smarty. Some of them are listed in the following table:

Qualifier	Meaning	Example
eq	equals	`$page_alias eq "contact-us"`
neq	not equal to	`$page_alias neq "contact-us"`
gt	greater than	`$friendly_position gt 2`
lt	less than	`$friendly_position lt 3`
gte	greater than or equal	`$friendly_position gte $count`
lte	less than or equal	`$friendly_position lte 5`
not	negation	`not $lang`
		(Negation can be used to check if a variable contains any value or if it is empty. If no value is given, then the result of the condition is `true`, or else the result of the condition is `false`).
mod	modulo	`$count mod 2`
		The modulo operation finds the remainder of division of one number by another. You can use the above example to figure out if the number of pages in the first hierarchy level is even or odd.

The IF structure is a useful tool for handling slight changes in one template depending on the page name or the position in the hierarchy. In the preceding example, you saw that you can use every variable from the template to build a logical condition.

Creating navigation template with Smarty loop

You can also change the HTML markup of the navigation. In this chapter, the great principle of a "template in template" giving you full control of your design is explained. Before you can learn this principle, you have to understand some Smarty basics.

When we added the top navigation to the website, we used a standard template for the navigation. It displays the navigation as an unordered HTML list. Imagine that you need a kind of footer navigation where all the links from the top navigation are shown. You do not need an unordered HTML list in this case. You just would like to show all links in one line separated by a pipe (|) shown as follows:

Our Company | Announcements | History | Team | Photo gallery ......

This means that you need a completely different HTML markup for this kind of navigation. The great advantage of CMS Made Simple is the ability to display a template in template. While you can use the main template to define the whole layout for the page, the HTML markup of the navigation is saved in its own template. This navigation template is just a piece of the HTML code that is added to the main template at the place where the tag {menu} is placed.

The menu template contains some HTML markup for the navigation. Let us see how you can create a fully new template for the menu and add your individual HTML markup.

Time for action – creating a menu template

We need a simple footer navigation where all pages of the website are listed, separated by a pipe (|) sign, as shown earlier.

1. In the admin console of the page, click on **Layout | Menu Manager**.

2. Click on **Add Template**.

3. Fill in the fields for **New Template Name** and **Template Content**, as shown in the following screenshot :

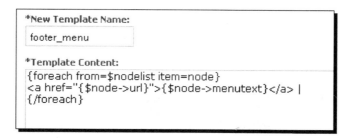

4. Click on **Submit** to save the new menu template.

5. Open the **Business World** template for editing (**Layout | Templates**).

6. Add footer navigation with the {menu} tag, and provide the name of the menu template, as shown in the following code snippet:

```
<!DOCTYPE html>
  <html>
    <head>
      <title>{title} - {sitename}</title>
      {stylesheet}
      {metadata}
      <meta name="description" content="" />
    </head>
    <body>
```

```
<div id="container">
<div id="header">
businessWorld
</div>
<div id="top-navi">
{menu number_of_levels="1" template="minimal_menu.tpl"}
</div>
<div id="content">
  <h1>{title}</h1>
  {content}
  {if $page_alias neq "contact-us"}
    <p>Last modified by {last_modified_by
                           format="fullname"}</p>
  {/if}
</div>
<div id="sidebar">
{menu start_level="2" template="minimal_menu.tpl"}
</div>
<div id="footer">
  <p>{menu template="footer_menu"}</p>
  2009 businessWorld
</div>
</div>
</body>
</html>
```

7. Click on **Apply** and see the footer navigation on your website. It should look as shown in the following screenshot:

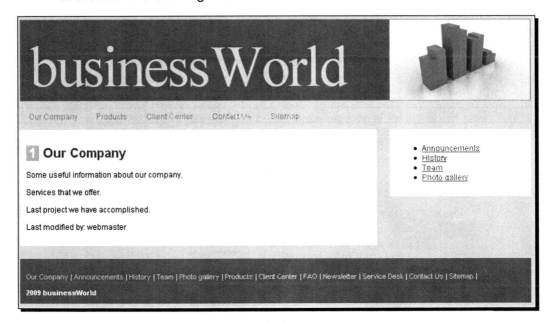

What just happened?

You have just created a new menu template. In the menu template, you have used some Smarty code that needs to be explained. The most important part in the code is the Smarty variable $nodelist. It is not an ordinary Smarty variable like the ones we have already learned. This variable is an **array**. It means that more than one value is saved in it. This variable contains all the information, such as menu texts or URLs of all active pages of our website. With the built-in Smarty function `foreach`, we can run through all the values of this variable and display the same piece of HTML code for each page. Let us see exactly how a loop works.

`foreach` goes through every single page saved in the variable {$nodelist} and prints the HTML code placed between the `foreach` tags as many times as there are pages found in the variable. For each run, the values for the single page are saved in the variable $node. We name and create this variable with parameter item=node in the `foreach` tag. The loop starts its run with the first menu item—the page **Our Company**. At this point, the menu text and URL are saved in the variable $node. We can reach the required information with {$node->menutext} and {$node->url} and use the tags in the HTML code. With the next (second) run, the next page is saved in the variable $node. So beginning with the second run, another menu text and URL is pasted into the same HTML code. The `foreach` loop runs through every page and stops automatically when no more pages are found.

Footer navigation displays all pages independent of their position in the hierarchy. You can limit the footer navigation only to the first level as well. Do it the same way you did it with the top navigation. Use parameter number_of_levels in the tag {menu} shown as follows:

```
{menu number_of_levels="1" template="footer_menu"}
```

`foreach` loops are a powerful way to construct any form of navigation you can imagine. This way, you can use images instead of text in your navigation.

One more example, how a graphical navigation can be created, is as shown:

```
{foreach from=$nodelist item=node}
<a href="{$node->url}">
    <img src="uploads/design/{$node->alias}.jpg"
         alt="{$node->menutext}" border="0" />
</a>
{/foreach}
```

To understand what HTML is produced by the preceding Smarty code, in your mind, replace the bold Smarty tags with the actual values of a page, for example, Contact Us:

```
<a href="contact-us">
    <img src="uploads/design/contact-us.jpg" alt="Contact Us" />
</a>
```

As the previous code is placed in the `foreach` loop, the markup will be repeated for every page. You can see that for the graphical example to work, you will need to create a JPG file for every page. The name of the files has to correspond to the page alias. In our example, for the top navigation, you will need five images:

- `our-company.jpg`
- `products.jpg`
- `client-center.jpg`
- `contact-us.jpg`
- `sitemap.jpg`

Create the images (buttons) in the graphics editing program of your choice and upload them to the `uploads/design` directory on your web server. Create a new menu template with the name `graphical_menu`, and add the Smarty `foreach` code into it, as shown earlier. Then replace the top navigation in the main template (**Layout | Templates**) with the following line:

```
{menu number_of_levels="1" template="graphical_menu"}
```

Now, the navigation is made of graphics instead of text.

There is even more information about each page available in menu template which is given in the following table:

Variable	Explanation
`$node->pagetitle`	Title of the page
`$node->depth`	Number of levels in the page hierarchy
`$node->prevdepth`	Number of levels of the previous page in the page hierarchy
`$node->haschildren`	Prints 1 if the page has child pages
`$node->target`	The target of the page can be set by the editor from the drop-down menu. In your template, you use it in the following way, as shown in the following example: `<a href="{$node->url}" target="{$node->target}">`
`$node->alias`	Prints the alias of the page
`$node->current`	Prints 1 if the page is currently displayed
`$node->type`	The type of the page. Possible values are: `sectionheader` (Section header) `separator` (Separator) `content` (Content) `pagelink` (Internal page link) `link` (External link)

With the information given, you can now enhance your navigation. For example, you can add the HTML attribute `target` to consider if the link should open in the same window or in the new one.

If you would like to add a special CSS class to the current page, then you will use an IF code within the `foreach` tags. See how you can combine both structures:

```
{foreach from=$nodelist item=node}
<a href="{$node->url}" {if $node->current}class="current"{/if}
>{$node->menutext}</a> |
{/foreach}
```

This IF code will add `class="current"` to the HTML tag `<a>` only to the link of the page that is currently displayed.

If you would like to know more about Smarty, use the documentation and support forum at `http://www.smarty.net`.

Exporting templates

Once your theme is finished, you can export it from CMS Made Simple. Exporting a theme means making an XML file containing template(s), attached stylesheets, and optionally menu templates. It also includes all images used in HTML or CSS. This XML file can be saved as a backup of your design, `http://themes.cmsmadesimple.org`, or to hand it over to your customer.

Time for action – displaying tags in dependence of the page

1. In the admin console, click on **Layout | Theme Manager**.

2. Select the checkbox on the line where the **Business World** template is, and enter a name in the field **Export Theme As**:

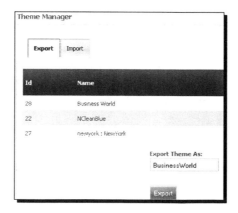

3. Click on **Export**.

4. In the download window of the browser, choose where on your hard drive this XML file should be saved.

You can either open the XML file or save it as backup for your design.

Pop quiz – testing what you have learned

1. Where in the admin console can you find all the templates, which you have at your disposal in your project?

   a. **Layout | Templates**

   b. **Layout | Stylesheets | Templates**

   c. **Content | Pages | Main | Templates**

   d. **Extensions |Templates**

2. How can you replace static text with dynamical components?

   a. Integrate Smarty tags like {content} in the template.

   b. Integrate Smarty tags like <content> in the template.

   c. Integrate modules like 'DynTxt' in the CSS stylesheet.

   d. Integrate a Smarty tag like <breadcrumbs> in the content field of the page.

3. If you have a closer look at the Smarty tag {last_modified_by format="username"}, which part of it is the "name" of the parameter?

   a. last_modified_by

   b. format

   c. username

   d. by format

4. What do you do if you want to have special and dynamic information on every page?

   a. Add Smarty plugins directly into the content of the page by using the content field.

   b. Add Smarty plugins directly into the content of the page by using the stylesheet.

   c. Add Smarty plugins directly into an inactive template, because you can fit the output easier in the layout of the site.

   d. Add Smarty plugins directly into the active template, because this is the only way to display it.

5. Where do you place the {stylesheet} tag in the template?

    a. Head

    b. Keywords or description

    c. Title

    d. Body

    e. Footer

6. How many stylesheets can be defined for one template?

    a. Just one stylesheet for each template.

    b. It depends on the number of themes in the template, you can define as many stylesheets as you have themes for it.

    c. Maximum seven, because of program restrictions.

    d. As many as you want.

7. How can you generate the navigation?

    a. The main menu and the sidebar navigation have to be connected in the admin console **Content | Pages** and the drop-down menu **parent**.

    b. The sites have to be connected to the whole navigation at once with a Smarty tag.

    c. The navigation is generated automatically.

    d. The main menu is generated automatically, the sidebar menu has to be integrated by using the module 'SideNav3.1'.

8. What is the meaning of the plugin menu in combination with the parameter start_level set to 2 ({menu start_level="2"})?

    a. The menu is only shown when you click twice on the button.

    b. The value 2 depends on the number of the line of the code in the template where it is integrated.

    c. When you set the value 2, there will only be 2 navigation links shown, when you set all instead of 2, the whole navigation structure is displayed.

    d. The value 2 is responsible for the first level not being shown in the navigation.

9. What is the special feature of an array like $nodelist, which is a Smarty variable?

    a. There is more than one value saved in it.

    b. There is exactly one value saved in it.

    c. Arrays only contain numeric values.

    d. Arrays only contain text values.

10. What is the right definition for a custom CMS plugin (function)?

    a.   It is a built-in function, which is the inner working of Smarty.

    b.   Custom plugins are additional functions.

    c.   It is everything that is placed between the curly brackets.

    d.   It starts with a $ sign and contains simple values or a number of values called array.

Have a go hero – creating custom templates

Now, it is your turn to create a design for your website of any complexity. If the design can be sliced into HTML and CSS templates, then it can be converted to CMS Made Simple. There are no restrictions in using technologies such as JQuery, Flash, or even frames.

Summary

We learned a lot in this chapter about templates and design with CMS Made Simple.

Specifically, we covered:

♦ Working with existing templates: You learned how to import templates into your installation and assign them to one or more pages.

♦ Creating a new template and stylesheet from scratch: You started to create a simple template with CMS Made Simple to see how static HTML interacts with dynamic Smarty tags. You also learned how to attach stylesheets to a template.

♦ Creating navigation: It was very important to see how easily the navigation of the website can be created. You created a top navigation and a sidebar with only one Smarty plugin {menu}. You also saw how you can control the output of your navigation with some simple parameters. Later on, you created your own template to see how the principle of "template in template" is covered in CMS Made Simple.

♦ Porting templates: You created your HTML and CSS template in any editor of your choice. Once the template was finished, you could port it to CMS Made Simple.

♦ Learning Smarty Basics: You learned a lot about Smarty tags. You saw how this easy and powerful language can help you to customize your template. Understanding Smarty means that you can get complete flexibility with your design. You also learned some Smarty terms that are important for understanding how Smarty can be used. See the following table to reflect on what you have learned so far:

Definition	Explanation
Smarty tag	Everything that is placed between the curly brackets
Smarty built-in functions	Built-in functions are the inner workings of Smarty, such as {if} and {foreach}. A reference of them can be found on http://smarty.net
Custom CMS plugins (functions)	Custom plugins are additional functions. {content} and {menu} are examples of custom functions. The list of them can be found in the admin console **Extensions | Tags**.
Parameters/Attributes	Most of the plugins above take parameters that specify or modify their behavior.
Smarty variables	Template variables start with the dollar sign, like {$page_alias} or {$friendly_position}. They contain simple values or a number of values (**array**).

5

Using Core Modules

We have learned how to set up a website, plan and create a complete website structure, and design the website. These were the first steps we had to take before writing content and implementing additional features such as news articles or search functionality.

What are core modules?

Core modules are a few basic modules that offer important features and are shipped with CMS Made Simple. They are installed by default and are supported by the official development team of CMS Made Simple. These modules are not essential, and your CMS website will work well without them. You can use them if you need functionality such as news management, search function, or custom navigation.

In this chapter, we will:

- ◆ Create global content blocks
- ◆ Implement news article and categorize them
- ◆ Add a search function
- ◆ Use a built-in **Image Manager** and **File Manager**
- ◆ Create a sitemap with **Menu Manager**
- ◆ Create a print version of the content pages or news articles
- ◆ Learn how to install additional modules that are not included in the standard installation of CMS Made Simple

In the following examples, I assume that you have a template like the one which was created in the last chapter and that your website structure is built according to the one shown at the end of Chapter 3, *Creating Pages and Navigation*. However, you can still proceed with this chapter if your structure or design is different.

Understanding global content blocks

You can use global content blocks to add some repeated parts containing text and/or images in your website. These blocks contain the same information and can be used at any place in your template or in the content of any page. For example, you can create a contact box with the address and phone number of your company as a global content block and then add it at multiple places in your website.

Sure, you can design the contact box every time you need it and add the contact information individually for each page. You can even copy the box from one page and paste it into another. It works until the phone number of your company changes. Now, you have to open each page where the contact box is added and change the phone number. Depending on the number of the pages, you could spend hours changing every page. Using the global content block, you can edit all the information in one place and just call the same content from any place on your website. If the phone number of the company has changed, then you adjust it in the global content block, and it is automatically changed on each page that uses this global content block.

Let's see how to use global content blocks on your website.

Time for action – adding a global content block to the website

Let's say that we need a contact box as described earlier on some of the pages placed somewhere in the content.

1. In the admin console, click on **Content | Global Content Blocks**.

2. Click on **Add Global Content Block**.

3. Enter the **Name** of the block and then the contact information in the field **Content**, as shown in the following screenshot:

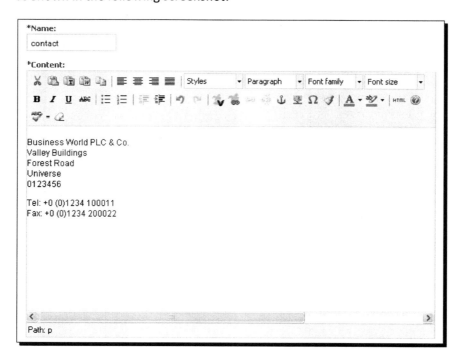

 Use *Shift + Enter* on your keyboard to add line breaks.

4. Click on **Submit**.

5. In the list of the global content blocks, copy the Smarty tag from the column **Tag to Use this Block** to the clipboard.

6. In the admin console, open a page of your choice (**Content | Pages**) for editing and paste the tag at the place where the contact box should be shown.

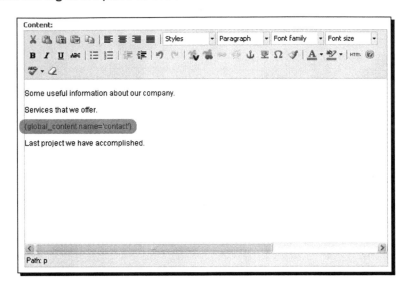

7. Click on **Apply**, and see the result on your website.

What just happened?

For the contact information, you have created a new global content block. Every time you need to display contact information on your website (whether in the page or in a template), you add the Smarty tag instead of the complete information. From now on, you make your changes only in the global content block, and each page and template using it will display the same information.

Try it out. Add a new global content block to another page and see the result on both pages. Then in the admin console, open **Content | Global Content Blocks**, choose the content block with your contact information, and change something in it. Save it, and see the changes on both pages using it.

Managing news articles with module News

Until now, we have added content pages which are under the control of the hierarchy manager of CMS Made Simple. For announcements or events in your company, you use the core module **News**. This module allows you to create quick, short statements, and then place them at any place on your website, templates, or pages. Your news should be really new. Nothing is as disappointing as websites containing news dated a year ago. "Aged" news gives a website an abandoned look.

For your company website, you can announce the last project the company accomplished or any customer events. With the news section, you can also advertise the new products or services that your company offers. You can present your new customers or partners and wish your customers on holidays. When the visitors of the website find news articles dated just some days ago, they know that your website (and your company) is alive.

If you cannot imagine what could be announced on the website, then skip this module. Do not place it only because it is standard and easy to use and other websites have news on them.

Displaying news on the website

The **News** module is very flexible and can be displayed in many different ways. Let's see how you can add news to the page **Announcements**. I assume that you have created this page already. If not, then you can put the news on the start page of your website as well. The next step will work on every page.

Time for action – displaying news on the page

1. Open the page **Announcements** for editing (**Content | Pages**).

2. Add the Smarty tag {news} at the place where news articles should be displayed, as shown in the following screenshot:

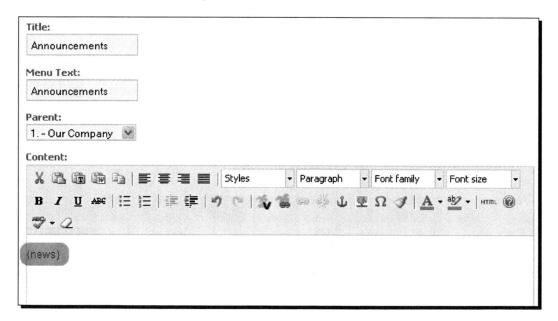

3. Click on **Apply**, and see the result of this Smarty tag on your website. It should look as follows:

What just happened?

With only one short Smarty tag, you can display the first news article on your website. This article is already added with the standard installation of CMS Made Simple. But where can this article be edited and how can new articles be created?

Adding news

All news that has ever been created can be found in the admin console. Open **Content | News**. You see the admin area of this module with many settings. On the first tab, **Articles**, you can search through the news if you have got lots of them. But at this point, you have just one news article that is displayed below the list and called **News Module Installed**. This news article is created automatically during installation of CMS Made Simple and is also shown on the page where the tag {news} has been added.

Let's add a new article to the list of news and see what can be changed to suit your requirements.

Time for action – adding news items

1. In the admin console, click on **Content | News**.

2. Click **Add Article**.

3. Enter the **Title** of the news article, **Summary** text, and **Content** of the article.

4. Click on **Submit**.

5. Open the page **Announcements** to see the new article published. It should look as shown in the following screenshot:

What just happened?

You have published a new announcement in the admin console of your website. For the summary and content fields, the WYISWYG editor was automatically displayed. The difference between the first article added during installation and the article published by you is the link **More** at the end of the article. This link is only shown if the **Summary** field of the news article is filled. In this case, only the summary text of the article is shown on the page. If you click the **More** link, you can read the complete text of the news article. However, if you do not use the **Summary** field, then the whole **Content** of the news item is displayed in the summary view, and there is no link **More** at the end of the article. Normally, you would not use the field **Summary** for short articles, so that the entire text can be read in the summary view.

Let's see what fields can be changed while editing and adding news articles.

Open the last edited article by clicking on it in the list of articles (**Content | News**). The author name is added automatically. It is your username. The field **Category** shows all categories available. In the standard installation, there is only one category **General**. We will see how to add new categories later on. Below the field **Content**, you see the field **Extra**. This field can be used for any additional information. However, the field is not shown in the template automatically. The field **Post Date** shows the publishing date of the article and can be changed to whatever you like. While adding new articles, the field is automatically filled with the actual date.

Status is a very important field. You can choose between **Published** and **Draft**. Drafts are never displayed on the website. In this way, you can work on your article as long as you need it. Save it as draft and change the status to **Published**, once the article text is ready.

News articles can also have a start and expiration date. Normally, if no expiration date is set, the article is published on your website forever. But what if you just would like to wish your visitors Merry Christmas? It would look strange if the article is still published some weeks or even months after December 25th. In this case, you select the field **Use Expiration Date**, and choose the date when the article expires. Expired articles are automatically removed from your website, but they can still be found in the list of articles in the admin console. If you add a date in the future in the field **Start Date**, the article will be published on the website at the given date. In this way, you can set the exact date and time for your announcements to appear on the website.

Keep in mind that dates are saved according to the local time zone defined on your server. If you develop the website on a different server and then transfer the finished version to another one, you have to double check that both the servers are configured with the same time zone.

News categories

You can categorize your news by adding new articles and assigning news to the different categories. This feature will not only allow you to sort and display news articles in the admin console, but also gives you power to display news from different categories on different pages or even in the same page on different locations. Categories can be created as a tree, so that there are parent and child categories. The tree structure of news categories is very similar to the page hierarchy of the content pages.

Open the **Categories** tab in the admin area of **News** module (**Content | News**) and create a new category. Once created, the category can be used for new articles. The old articles can be assigned to this category as well.

By using categories, you can publish any sort of information with this module, not only announcements. For example, you can publish job opportunities at your company as well.

Time for action – creating news categories

We are going to create a new category that will contain job offers and then show the list of jobs on the start page.

1. In the admin console, click on **Content | News**.

2. Under the **Categories** tab, click on **Add Category** and create a new category with the name **Vacancies**, as shown in the following screenshot:

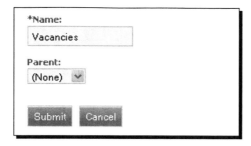

3. Click on **Submit**.

4. Under the **Articles** tab, click **Add Article** and create a new article with the following information:

    a.   **Category: Vacancies**

    b.   **Title: Marketing Manager**

    c.   **Content: We are looking for an excellent person who will be able to develop the European market for our company. Please contact our human resources department.**

5. Click on **Submit**

6. Open the start page of the website for editing and add the Smarty tag somewhere in the **Content** field, as shown in the following screenshot:

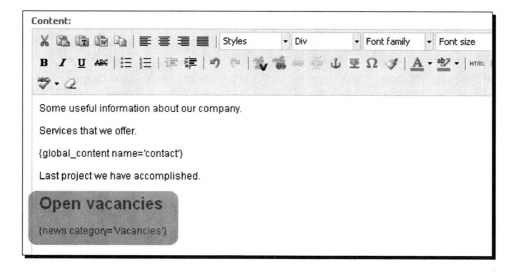

7. Save the page, and see the changes on the website.

Open vacancies

Sep 1, 2009
Marketing Manager
Category: Vacancies
Posted by: Sofia Hauschildt

We are looking for an excellent person who will be able to develop European market for our company. Please contact human resources.

What just happened?

You have used the **News** module to display job opportunities on the start page. You have used the parameter `category` to limit the shown items to only one category. Therefore, only the items assigned to this category are shown at this place. On the page **Announcements**, all news are still displayed (including job opportunities), as there was no limitation to one category. If you would like to limit announcements on this page to the items assigned to the category **General**, then you would modify the Smarty tag, which is shown as follows:

```
{news category="General"}
```

You see that you can display news articles at different locations of your website and limit them to one category. You can use the **News** module for anything that you would like to categorize. Another example is the list of last accomplished projects. Even a company blog can be realized with this module.

Customizing news templates

Remember how you have customized the menu template in the previous chapter. The principle of "template in template" is valid for each module in CMS Made Simple. It means that all module templates can be edited separately from the main layout to fit in the entire website. At the place where the Smarty tag for the module is placed (in the content page or in the template), the template of the module is shown. It is just like using one template inside another template, so is using module templates in the main templates.

There are different templates for the news article of your website:

◆ **Summary Templates**: The list of news with the summary fields and links for further reading

◆ **Detail Templates**: The complete text of the news article

◆ **Browse Category Templates**: The list of all news categories

◆ **Form Templates**: Used when **User Management** is installed, and will be discussed later

Each template can be created or modified by using a combination of Smarty variables and HTML. If you call the module with the Smarty tag {news}, then the sample template for news summary is called. If you add the attribute action to the Smarty tag {news}, then another template according to the following list is called:

Action	Template
{news action="default"}	**Summary Templates**
{news action="detail"}	**Detail Templates**
{new action="browsecat"}	**Browse Category Templates**
{news action="fesubmit"}	**Form Templates**

You will find templates in the admin console (**Content | News**) on the tabs next to **Articles** and **Categories**. For each action, more than one template can be created, but only one template can be set as the default one.

Now, let's see how you can create and use a new summary template in your website.

Time for action – creating a new summary template

Assume that you need just a list of the news articles without their summary text and date. The titles of the news items should be linked to the full news article (detail view).

1. In the admin console, open **Content | News**, and select the tab **Summary Templates**.

2. Click on **Create A New Template**.

3. Enter **NewsList** as the **Template Name** and replace the **Template Source** with the following code snippet:

```
<ul>
  {foreach from=$items item=entry}
    <li><a href="{$entry->moreurl}"
          title="{$entry>title|cms_escape:htmlall}">
                {$entry->title|cms_escape}</a>
    </li>
  {/foreach}
</ul>
```

4. Click on **Submit**. The template appears in the list of the summary templates.

5. Open the page template **Business World (Layout | Templates)** and add the list of news articles below the sidebar navigation, as shown in the following code snippet:

```
<!DOCTYPE html>
  <html>
    <head>
```

```
      <title>{title} - {sitename}</title>
      {stylesheet}
      {metadata}
      <meta name="description" content="" />
   </head>
   <body>
      <div id="container">
      <div id="header">
      businessWorld
      </div>
      <div id="top-navi">
      {menu number_of_levels="1" template="minimal_menu.tpl"}
      </div>
      <div id="content">
        <h1>{title}</h1>
          {content}
          {if $page_alias neq "contact-us"}
            <p>Last modified by {last_modified_by
            format="fullname"}</p>
          {/if}
      </div>
      <div id="sidebar">
      {menu start_level="2" template="minimal_menu.tpl"}
      <hr />
      {news summarytemplate="NewsList"}
       </div>
       <div id="footer">
          <p>{menu template="footer_menu"}</p>
          2009 businessWorld
       </div>
       </div>
   </body>
</html>
```

6. Click on **Submit**, and view the result on the page. Your sidebar should look similar to the following screenshot:

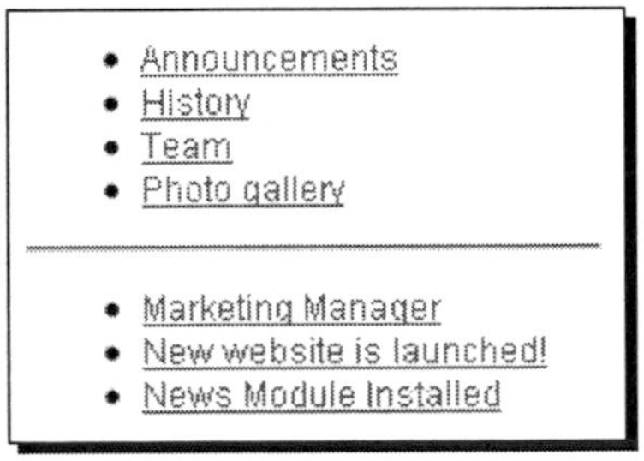

What just happened?

You have created a new summary template for the news articles. The summary template includes an ordered list of the news articles, and each article is linked to the detail view. Then, you have added a Smarty tag in the template below the sidebar menu. You have used the parameter `summarytemplate` to specify exactly what template should be used to display the summary view of the news articles in this place. If you do not use the parameter, then the default template is used. In the standard installation of CMS Made Simple, the **Sample** template is taken by default. You can change the default template by clicking on the icon with the red cross in the column **Default** in the list of templates (**Content | News | Summary Templates**).

You can edit existing templates or create new custom templates. If you use the module for different tasks such as job opportunities, announcements, and company blog, you can create as many templates as you need. You can also specify which template should be used to display the output of the module at the place where the tag is called. An example call for displaying job opportunities on the website can be:

```
{news summarytemplate="Jobs" detailtemplate="Job"
  category="Vacancies"}
```

For the preceding example, you should create a summary template with the name **Jobs** and a detail template with the name **Job**. You also need a **Vacancies** category where you add at least one job opportunity.

Adding custom fields to the module News

Sometimes, you need custom information to be displayed in the announcements. For example, you would like to add a department or a special location, or you would like to associate files with the news announcing new products. In this case, you would have to define custom fields in the **News** module.

Let's see how the location of the news can be added in the special field.

Time for action – adding custom fields

1. In the admin field, open **Content | News** and select the tab **Field Definitions**.

2. Click **Add Field Definition** and enter the fields, as shown in the following screenshot:

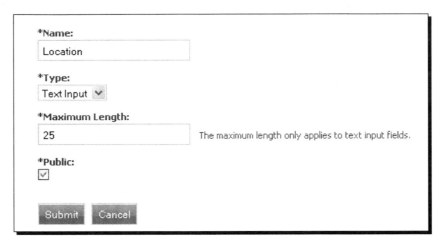

3. Click on **Submit**.

4. Open the last article item you have added, for example, **Marketing Manager** (**Content | News**), and you will find the new field **Location** at the bottom of the page.

5. Enter **Washington** in the field **Location**, and click **Submit**.

6. Open your page and you can find the location added below the news article. (Attention: This works only with *Sample* templates or templates based on default templates!). It should look similar to the following screenshot:

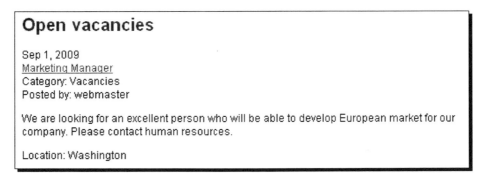

What just happened?

You have added a new custom field to the news articles. As the field is marked as **Public**, it will be displayed on the website. The field is automatically added to the news editing window. If you like to change the position of the field, you should edit the template. In the default template **Sample**, all additional fields are added at the bottom of the news article. In your own template, you can get any custom field value with the following line of code:

```
Location: {$entry->fieldsbyname.location->value}
```

The previous line will display the value saved in the field **Location**. You can use this line in the summary and detail template.

There are even more parameters that you can use to refine the output of the Smarty plugin {news}. For each module, the list of parameters can be found in the **Help** section of the module. In the admin console, open **Content | News**, and click on the **Module Help** link to the right of the module name.

There are some useful parameters for the **News** module, as listed in the following table:

News parameter	Description
browsecat="1"	Shows a browseable category list.
showall="1"	Shows all articles, irrespective of the end date.
showarchive="0"	Shows only expired news articles.
sortasc="true"	Sort news items in an ascending date order rather than descending.
sortby="news_title"	Field to sort by. Options are: news_date, summary, news_data, news_category, news_title, news_extra, end_time, start_time, and random. Default is news_date.
moretext="more..."	Text to display at the end of a news item if the field **Summary** is not empty. By default, it is set to "more..."
start="0"	Starts the list of articles with the item number given.

 If you would like to display a detailed view of the news article in another page template other than your main template, then create a new page template (**Layout | Templates**), create a new page, and assign the new template to the page. Call the **News** module with {news page="alias"} where the alias is the name of the page where a detailed view of every news item should be displayed.

You can even allow your site visitors to add news articles to your module if you install the module **FrontEndUsers** which will be described in Chapter 7, *Using Third-party Modules*. The news articles submitted by the website's visitors will be saved as drafts, and you can publish them after approving them in the admin content page.

Using the news title as the page title

Pay attention to the title bar of the browser on the page where the full article is displayed. You discover that the title tag will be the same for each item, as there is only one real page to display each news article. However, search engine optimization requires a unique title for every page. You can customize the title of the generated pages with a small trick. Open **Content | News** in the admin console, and choose the **Detail Templates** tab. At the very top of the template, add the following line:

```
{assign var="pagetitle" value=$entry->title|escape}
```

This line will generate the Smarty variable `{$pagetitle}` containing the title of the news article. To add the variable to the main template, open it, and add the tag `{process_pagedata}` at the very top of your template and replace the title tag with an IF structure, as shown in the following code snippet:

```
{process_pagedata}
  <!DOCTYPE html>
    <html>
      <head>
        {if isset($pagetitle) && !empty($pagetitle)}
          <title>{title} - {sitename}</title>
        {else}
          <title>{sitename} - {title}</title>
        {/if}
  . . .
```

This piece of code checks if the variable `{$pagetitle}` is defined and is not empty. If the variable exists, then the news title is used for the title tag and is displayed in the title bar of the browser. If not, then the ordinary page title is taken.

Using the search function with the module Search

The next standard feature that should be explained is a **Search** module. It is installed by default and allows the visitors of the website to search the content pages and the news articles on your website. Normally, you add the search field to your template rather than to every single page.

Let's add the search feature to the template at the top of the website.

Time for action – adding a search form

1. Open the template **Business World (Layout | Templates)**

2. Add the Smarty tag {search} to the sidebar, as shown:

```
<!DOCTYPE html>
  <html>
    <head>
      <title>{title} - {sitename}</title>
      {stylesheet}
      {metadata}
      <meta name="description" content="" />
    </head>
    <body>
      <div id="container">
      <div id="header">
        businessWorld
      </div>
      <div id="top-navi">
        {menu number_of_levels="1" template="minimal_menu.tpl"}
      </div>
      <div id="content">
        <h1>{title}</h1>
        {content}

        {if $page_alias neq "contact-us"}
          <p>Last modified by {last_modified_by
          format="fullname"}</p>
        {/if}

      </div>
      <div id="sidebar">
        {search}
        {menu start_level="2" template="minimal_menu.tpl"}
      <hr />
        {news summarytemplate="NewsList"}
      </div>
      <div id="footer">
        <p>{menu template="footer_menu"}</p>
          2009 businessWorld
      </div>
      </div>
    </body>
  </html>
```

3. Click on **Submit** and view your page in the browser, it should look as shown in the following screenshot:

What just happened?

You have added the search feature to your website. It works out of the box if you try to search in the content of your pages or news articles.

You can define the list of **Stop Words** in the admin console (**Extensions | Search | Options**). These words are excluded from the search index, and there is also a predefined list of common stop words for your convenience. Normally, you would add your company name or any word that can be found on every page or in templates. To avoid that, search functions show all pages in the found results. You can add your custom words separated by a comma at the end of the list or define your own list. Do not forget to click on the button **Reindex All Content** after saving the list of stop words. It would create a new search index for your website.

If your website is in English, you can use a word stemming search. This means that the words in the search index are reduced to their stem, base, or root form. For example, you have a content page where the word *steps* is found and indexed. However, the visitor of your website searches for *step*. Without activating the stemming feature, nothing is found as literally *step* is not the same as *steps*. With stemming search, all forms of the search word are considered, such as "step", "steps", and even "stepped".

Excluding pages from search

If you would like some pages, like **Policy** or **Disclaimer** to be excluded from search, then open the page that you would like to exclude in the admin console (**Content | Pages**) and select the **Options** tab. Deselect the field **This page is searchable**, and save the page. Now the page is not found even if the searched word appears on this page.

You can customize the template of the search template (search field itself) and search result template in the admin console (**Extensions | Search**). As usual, you use a mix of HTML and Smarty tags to change the order of the elements. Use stylesheet to change to suit the form into your layout.

If you would like to output search results in the template different from the main one, you have to create the desired template yourself (you have learned how to create templates in the previous chapter) and assign the template to the page where the search results should be shown. The alias of this page should be passed to the parameter `resultpage` as shown In the example. Modify the Smarty tag `{search}` by adding the parameter `resultpage` as follows:

```
{search resultpage="search-result"}
```

You have to assign the alias of the page created previously to the parameter `resultpage`, so that the search results are always shown on this page now.

The search feature also tracks the search activity on your website and allows you to figure out what the visitors of your website need or miss. You can track single search words or phrases to see how often they have been used by the visitors. In the **Options** tab of the **Search** module (**Extensions | Search**), you can select **Track Search Phrases, not Individual Words** to enable statistic for phrases.

The **Search** module of CMS Made Simple is not as sophisticated as large search engines. You can use customized Google search for your website if you would like to show the searched words in the text and have stemming features for languages other than English. But if your website is not indexed in Google, then you do not have any other option but to use the standard search feature of CMS Made Simple.

Browsing files with File Manager

You can upload any files in CMS Made Simple with **File Manager**. **File Manager** is like a built-in FTP browser where you can upload, move, delete, and copy files or directories. In the admin console, open **Content | File Manager**, and find the list of all the files that are saved in the folder `uploads` on your web hosting.

On the **Upload files** tab, you can upload more than one file or even an archive file that will be unpacked after uploading in this folder.

On the **Settings** tab, you can enable the advanced mode that will let you gain access to the whole file structure of your CMS Made Simple website so that **File Manager** is no longer restricted to the folder `uploads`. Be careful with this setting, as you can easily move and delete core files of CMS Made Simple, and as a result, damage your entire website.

If you would like to upload and edit images, then you should use **Image Manager**.

Using Image Manager

Surely, you would like to add images to your website. Whether they are placed in the content of your pages or used in templates or photo galleries, they have to be uploaded to your web host first. You should optimize your images before displaying them on your website. Do not upload images that are larger than 200KB. This restriction is not from CMS Made Simple. You can upload and display even larger images with **Image Manager**. The restriction is suggested in consideration of your visitors who want your website to load quickly. If you use large images, your website will load very slowly, and a certain percentage of your visitors will close the browser before they have seen what you offer on the website.

The rule of thumb
One image should not be larger than 20KB and all images on one page together should not account for more than 200KB.

Resize your images with graphics program before using them on the website. Or, use the built-in image editor in CMS Made Simple to resize, crop, rotate, and flip your images.

Let us upload some images to CMS Made Simple, edit, and display them on the page or in the template. There are three formats that can be displayed by any browser—JPG (or JPEG), GIF, and PNG. No other graphics should be used on the websites, because some browsers on some operating systems will not display BMP, TIFF, PSD, or other files. Prepare one image that you will use for the next step on your local disk with any graphics application.

Time for action – using the image editor

Assume we have an image that is too large for the page. Ideally, you have to create images with a graphics application before uploading them to your web hosting. But if you have no graphics application or would just like to make few quick changes, you can use the built-in **Image Manager** for the task.

1. In the admin console, open **Content | Image Manager**.

2. Choose the image you would like to upload in the field **Upload File** at the bottom of the page, and click on **Send**.

3. When the image is uploaded, click on the edit icon below the image to start the image editor.

4. Resize the physical size of the picture to the required width and height in pixels by clicking on **Resize** in the left control panel and giving the desired dimensions in the fields above the image.

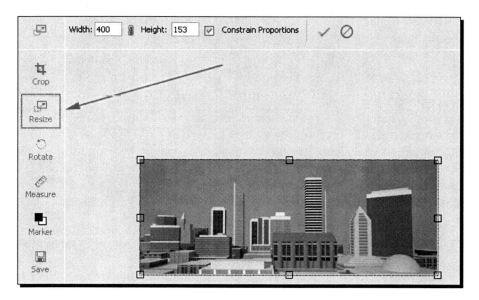

5. Click on the icon with a green tick mark above the image to apply the changes.

6. Click on the **Save** icon in the left control panel, and choose the image format for the resized image, as shown in the following screenshot:

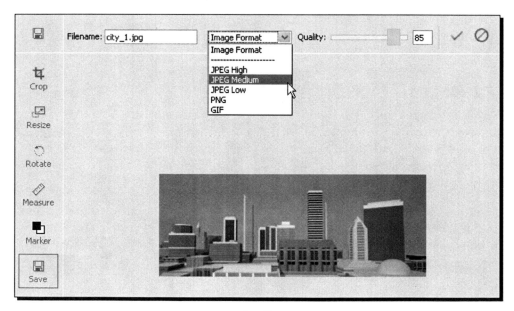

7. Click on the green tick mark again to apply the changes. When the image has been saved, you can close the window.

8. Refresh the page with the image thumbnails or open **Image Manager** again (**Content | Images**). The new version of the image with the changes applied is now shown in the list of available images.

What just happened?

You have uploaded a new image to CMS Made Simple. After uploading, a 96x96 pixels thumbnail (small version of the picture used for previewing) is automatically created by CMS. You have changed the size of the image and then saved it at a lower quality to reduce the weight in kilobytes as well. Choosing a quality of 60 percent to 85 percent for JPEG images will not cause any visible quality loss. Try it out. Your original image will not be changed after saving, but a new version of the image will be created. You can delete the new version at any time and start with the original picture once again if you have made a mistake.

For more advanced graphical work, you can use special graphics applications such as the free GIMP or the commercial Adobe Photoshop.

With an FTP browser, you can find your image files and automatically created thumbnails in the directory /uploads/images. If you have a lot of images, you can upload them to this directory using an FTP browser in this directory as well. However if you do this, the thumbnails are not created automatically. After uploading through FTP, you have to open **Content | Image Manager**. The **Image Manager** will discover the newly uploaded files and then create the missing thumbnails.

Thumbnails' filenames are prefixed with thumb_. For example, the image file city.jpg will get an automatically generated thumbnail with the name thumb_city.jpg in the same folder where the original image was uploaded.

Using images in template and content

The uploaded images can be used in the content of the pages with the WYSIWYG editor (refer Chapter 3, *Creating Pages and Navigation*). Normally, the editor of the content does not have the ability to change the template of the website. But there is also a functionality that can help him/her to assign an image to the page and display it anywhere in the template.

Consider that the design (template) and the text can be strictly separated from each other in CMS Made Simple. In order to give a little more responsibility for the appearance of the site to the editor, you can allow him to change the pictures of the template in a defined way.

Let's create a new image that can be chosen by the editor of the page to be displayed above the navigation. First of all, create two images having a width of 800 pixels and height of about 100 pixels. Name them `pageimage1.jpg` and `pageimage2.jpg`. Upload the images with **Image Manager** to CMS Made Simple. Do not upload them to subfolders, but directly to the start folder of **Image Manager** (`uploads/images`).

In the admin console, open any page (**Content | Pages**). Choose the **Options** tab, and in the **Image** field, select the picture you would like to associate with this page, as shown in the following screenshot:

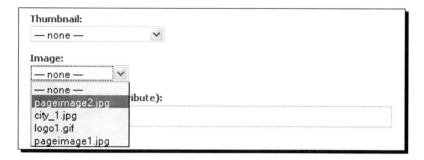

Do the same with other pages and assign other images to them.

 If you cannot see the image in the drop-down field, then it is not uploaded into the right folder. Page images have to be found in **Content | Image Manager** or `/uploads/images` (not subfolder) on the web server.

Then add the image to the template. Open the **Business World** template (**Layout | Templates**), and add the page image to display it:

```
<!DOCTYPE html>
  <html>
    <head>
      <title>{title} - {sitename}</title>
      {stylesheet}
      {metadata}
      <meta name="description" content="" />
    </head>
    <body>
      <div id="container">
      <div id="header">
      businessWorld
      </div>
```

```
<img src="uploads/images/{page_image}" width="800" height="100"
alt="{title}" />
<div id="top-navi">
{menu number_of_levels="1" template="minimal_menu.tpl"}
</div>
<div id="content">
  <h1>{title}</h1>
  {content}
```

. . .

Now the editor of the page can select from the predefined images to display them in the template without having to modify the template itself.

Using Menu Manager in content

You have already worked with the **Menu Manager** to create top, sidebar, and footer navigation for the website. Top navigation displays pages that are placed on the first level of the page hierarchy. Sidebar navigation automatically displays only the children of the page selected in the top navigation. Navigation in the footer includes all pages independent of their position in the hierarchy.

Additionally, you can display the complete website structure (or some parts of it) in the **Content** field as well. In this way, you can easily output a sitemap that helps your visitors to find the required information on your website.

Time for action – creating a sitemap

Let's create a sitemap in the page **Sitemap** that we had created in Chapter 3, *Creating Pages and Navigation*. If you do not have the page, then please create it now.

1. In the admin console, open the page **Sitemap** (**Content | Pages**).

2. Add the Smarty tag {menu template="minimal_menu.tpl"} to the content of the page.

3. Click on **Apply**, and use the magnifying glass icon beside the button **Apply** to see the result on the website. It should look as shown in the following screenshot:

What just happened?

Using the already known Smarty tag {menu}, you have added a sitemap to the website. It displays the complete structure of the website with all pages that are marked as **Shown in Menu** (tab **Options**). You can refine the output of the {menu} tag with further parameters:

♦ show_all="1": This option will show all pages even if they are set to not be shown in the menu. However, it still will not display inactive pages.

♦ number_of_levels="1": This setting will help to limit the output to a certain number of levels.

You can combine as many parameters as you like. For example, to display all active pages and to limit the hierarchy by two levels, you would add the following line:

```
{menu show_all="1" number_of_levels="2"}
```

Another example of the use of an additional navigation option in the content is the list of pages (not news articles) on the start page independent of their actual position in the hierarchy. Assume that you would like to create some kind of quick navigation on your start page giving the visitor the possibility to access some pages directly from the start page. To create a list of subpages, use one of the following parameters in the content of the start page:

- `start_element="1.2"`: Displays the list of pages starting at the given `start_element` (position in the hierarchy) and shows that element and its children only

- `start_page="home"`: Displays the list of pages at the given `start_page` (alias of the page) and shows that element and its children only

It's up to you, which of the two parameters you prefer to use. Surely you can simply create the list of links to the pages manually. But in this case, the list is not dynamic. If new pages are added, then you have to add them manually to the link list as well. If you use the Smarty tag `{menu}` instead, it automatically displays all new pages as well.

Another useful parameter is:

- `show_root_siblings="1"`: This option only becomes useful if the `start_element` or `start_page` parameters (as shown previously) are used. It will display pages in the same level as the selected start page or element.

See the following example for page structure and how it can be outputted on every page with different parameters:

▼	1	Our Company
▼	1.1	- Announcements
	1.1.1	- - All announcements
	1.2	- History
	1.3	- Team
	1.4	- Photo gallery
	2	Products
▼	3	Client Center
	3.1	- FAQ
	3.2	- Newsletter
	3.3	- Service Desk

If your website structure looks like the preceding screenshot, then you will get the output shown in the second column by using the tag from the first column.

Smarty tag	Output
{menu start_element="3"}	
{menu start_element="1.1" show_root_siblings="1" }	
{menu start_element="1.1" show_root_siblings="1" number_of_levels="1"}	

You can see how flexible the navigation layout can be on CMS Made Simple. On every page, you can precisely define your navigation structure and even create a kind of articles' catalog by adding article category first and then assigning articles to the categories and displaying them with **Menu Manager** on the website in any page or in the template.

Printing pages

With CMS Made Simple, every page and news article can be automatically prepared for print preview with the built-in **Printing** module.

Time for action – adding a print link

Let's see how you can add a link to the print version of every page or news article.

1. In the admin console, open the template **Business World** for edit (**Layout | Templates**).

2. Add the Smarty plugin {print} above the {content} tag in the template, shown as follows:

```
...
<div id="content">
    <h1><span>{$friendly_position}</span> {title}</h1>
    {print}
    {content}
...
```

3. Click **Apply**, and see the changes in your website.

What just happened?

With the custom Smarty tag {print}, you use the core module **Printing**. At the place where you have added the tag, a link **Print this page** is displayed. When you click on the link, a new page is opened with a print friendly version of the page. It does not have any special styles in it, and it does not display a main template but only the content of the page.

There are some useful parameters that help you to customize the link **Print this page** and its behavior.

- `text="Print this page"`: Overrides the default text for the print link.
- `popup="false"`: Set this to `true` and the page for printing will be opened in a new window. Be careful, some browsers block popup windows!
- `script="false"`: Set this to `true` and the print version will automatically open the print dialog of the browser.
- `includetemplate="false"`: If this is set to `true`, not only the content of the page, but the whole page template including the content of the page, header, navigation, and footer area will be displayed.
- `showbutton="false"`: Set this to `true` to show a graphical button instead of the text **Print this page**.

If the preceding parameters do not offer enough ways for you to customize the look and feel of the print link and print view, you are free to customize the module in the admin console (**Extensions | Printing**). There are four tabs:

- **Link template**: The template that is used to display the link to the print (or PDF) version of your website.
- **Print template**: The template that is used to display the print version. You can add your own HTML markup here, like URL of the website, website company, or contact details, so that this information is automatically displayed in the print version of the website.
- **Override print stylesheet**: Gives you the possibility to insert your own, custom CSS to the print version. Normally, you would use it to define the font size and set it in points as often used in print works.
- **PDF settings**: We will discuss this tab later in the section *Generating a PDF version of the page*.

Adding media type to stylesheets

Sometimes a visitor of the page does not use the special print button but the default print dialog of the browser. In this case, the whole page is printed out, as shown on the screen. You can use media type for the stylesheets to customize the printed version in this case as well. In pure CSS, you can define different media types as HTML attributes in the link tags as follows:

```
<link rel="stylesheet" type="text/css" media="screen" href="sheet.
css">
<link rel="stylesheet" type="text/css" media="print" href="print.css">
```

In CMS Made Simple, you add the Smarty tag {stylesheet} to the template that generates the HTML link tags automatically, so that you cannot add HTML attribute media to it. Nevertheless, you can attach two different stylesheets to your template and mark them as **screen**, **print**, or any other allowed type.

In the admin console, open your stylesheet (**Layout | Stylesheets**) for editing and scroll down to the **Media Type** section:

Media Type:
┌─ Media type ───
│ ☐ all : Suitable for all devices.
│ ☐ aural : Intended for speech synthesizers.
│ ☐ braille : Intended for braille tactile feedback devices.
│ ☐ embossed : Intended for paged braille printers.
│ ☐ handheld : Intended for handheld devices
│ ☐ print : Intended for paged, opaque material and for documents viewed on screen in print preview mode.
│ ☐ projection : Intended for projected presentations, for example projectors or print to transparencies.
│ ☐ screen : Intended primarily for color computer screens.
│ ☐ tty : Intended for media using a fixed-pitch character grid, such as teletypes and terminals.
│ ☐ tv : Intended for television-type devices.

Select the media types that you would like to serve with this stylesheet, for example, **screen**. To add a special stylesheet containing formatting for the print view of your page, create a new stylesheet with print formats. Select **print** as the media type in the **Media Type** section (see the preceding screenshot), then attach this stylesheet to the template. CMS Made Simple will automatically add the HTML attribute media to the link tags generated at the place where {stylesheet} was added to the template.

Generating a PDF version of the page

You can produce a PDF output of the page with the **Printing** module. Activate PDF settings to allow PDF generation for the website. On the **PDF Settings** tab (found at **Extensions | Printing**), select the option **Enable PDF-generation**. Then add a PDF print link or button to the template or page as follows:

```
{print pdf="true"}
```

The **Generate PDF** link is displayed wherever the preceding tag is added. Customize the PDF settings (**Extensions | Printing**) such as the header, font size, font type, or page orientation. If PDF generation is enabled, you can also see an additional tab for the PDF template so that you can enhance it to meet your needs.

Adding more modules to your website

Additional features, such as **News**, **Search**, **File Manager**, **Menu Manager**, and **Printing** are found in the core modules of CMS Made Simple. These modules are installed with CMS Made Simple by default. These modules are developed by the CMS Made Simple development team.

In the admin console, click on **Extensions | Modules** and find a list of all the modules that are available on your installation, their versions, and additional information. You will also find a **Help** link beside each module that helps you to understand how the module can be used and what parameters are available. Installed modules have a green tick in the **Active** column and their **Status** is **Installed**.

You can enrich your website with more features by installing additional modules that are developed and supported by third-party developers. There are over 300 modules available for CMS Made Simple. Just to name some of the optional features that you can add to your website: login functionality for your visitors, creation, and automatic update of the Google sitemap according to the website page structure, photo gallery, e-commerce functions, discussion board, products catalog, feedback form, and more.

Most of the modules can be easily installed and used without any special knowledge by using the **Module Manager**.

Using the Module Manager

To choose and install new modules, click on **Extensions | Module Manager** in the admin console. Notice that the modules listed here are not standard modules of CMS Made Simple, and therefore not all of them have got the same good quality as the core modules. Therefore, you see the **Use at Your Own Risk** message above the list of modules. Nevertheless, there are a lot of modules that are very useful and sophisticated, and are thoroughly supported by their developers.

The **Available Modules** tab is your research centre for available modules. The modules are sorted alphabetically by their names and have mostly good explanations which can be found by clicking on the **Help** link beside the module name.

There is no possibility to search for a module functionality by keywords in **Module Manager**. However, you can use the search feature in **CMSMS Forge**. CMSMS Forge is a hub for all features such as modules, plugins, or translations. It can be found at http://dev. cmsmadesimple.org. Enter the search word or phrase in the top-right corner in CMSMS Forge and find the list of modules, plugins (also called tags), or translations that match your search criteria. If you are interested in any module found in the list; note its name, return to the admin console in **Extensions | Module Manager**, and search in the alphabetical list for the module name in question. Read the **Help** section to see if the module suits your requirements.

Installing additional modules

Before installing a module, you should check the **Dependencies** link beside it in the list of modules in the **Module Manager**. Some modules depend on other modules in order to function, so you have to install the other modules first.

Time for action – module installation

Let's install an additional module that allows us to manage FAQ on the website.

1. In the admin console, click on **Extensions | Module Manager**, and choose the tab **Available Modules** tab.

2. In the list of modules, select the letter **Q**, and find the module **Questions**.

3. Click on the **Dependencies** link to see what modules have to be installed first.

> **Module Name:** Questions
>
> **Version:** 1.0.3
>
> **XML File:** Questions-1.0.3.xml
>
>   CGExtensions => 1.13

4. Return to the list of available modules (**Extensions | Module Manager**) and select the letter **C**. Find the module **CGExtensions**, and click on the **Download & Install** link. The module **CGExtensions** will be installed.

5. Return to the list of available modules (**Extensions | Module Manager**), and select the letter **Q** again. Find the **Questions** module.

6. Click on **Download & Install**. The module **Questions** will be installed.

7. Open the page **FAQ** for edit (**Content | Pages**).

8. Add the Smarty tag in the page, as shown in the following screenshot:

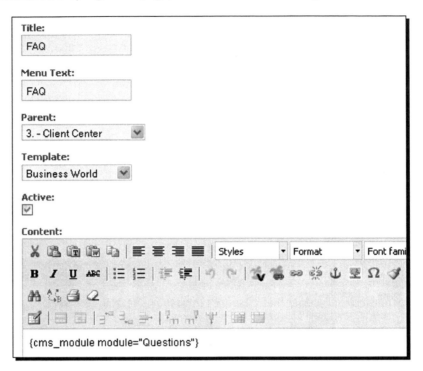

9. Click on **Apply,** and then click the magnifying glass icon beside the **Apply** button to see the changes on the page. It should look as shown in the following screenshot:

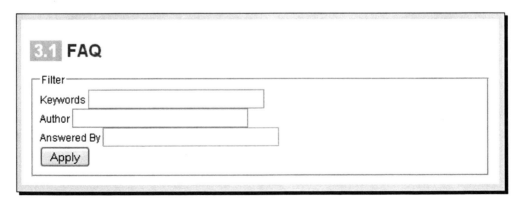

What just happened?

You have installed a new module. The **Questions** module is now available on every page or template of your CMS Made Simple website. You will find the **Questions** module in the list of installed modules in the admin console (**Extensions | Modules**) as well.

Each module that you have installed can be used in the content of a page or template by using the Smarty tag {cms_module ...}. This tag has a required parameter module that is set to the name of the module, as shown in the module list (**Extensions | Modules**). Generally, all modules can be used with this tag:

```
{cms_module module="MODULE_NAME"}
```

Just replace MODULE_NAME with the name of the installed module to see how the module acts by default. The **Questions** module displays the FAQs which can be created, edited, deleted, and categorized in the admin console (**Content | Questions and Answers**). It is self-explaining how the FAQ can be built (use the link **Add New Question** to add a new pair of questions and answers). Please use the **Help** link in the list of installed modules (**Extensions | Modules**) to find some usage examples and an additional parameter for the module **Questions**.

For example, if you do not like the filter form in the list of questions and answers, remove it with the parameter nofilter shown as follows:

```
{cms_module module="Questions" nofilter="yes"}
```

Some modules have a short version and can be called only by their names.

Short notation	Long notation
{news}	{cms_module module="News"}
{search}	{cms_module module="Search"}
{menu}	{cms_module module="MenuManager"}
Not available	{cms_module module="Questions"}

There is no difference in functionality. Every module can be used with long notation and only some of them have short notation implemented. Please see the **Help** module to determine whether or not short notation is available.

Installing modules with XML file

On some web hosting, there is no possibility to connect to external resources (such as CMSMS Forge). In this case, you will not see any module in the list of available modules. Nevertheless, you can install modules manually as well, if you download the XML installation file for them.

To find the module installation file, open CMSMS Forge (`http://dev.cmsmadesimple.org`) and search for a desired module. Click on the module name, and select the **Files** tab to the right of the module name. Find the newest XML file in the list of files shown, and save it to your local disk. In the admin console, click on **Extensions | Modules**, and select the saved XML file in the field **Upload**, below the list of the modules. Click on **Submit**, and the module will be shown in the list of modules. However, it is not installed yet. Click the **Install** link beside the module to complete its installation. You can now use it the same way as if it had been installed automatically with the **Module Manager**.

Available upgrades

From time to time, new versions with new features or bug fixes are released. In the **Available Upgrades** tab, you can see which of your installed modules have newer versions compared to the version installed on your system.

To upgrade modules, search for their names in the list on the **Available Modules** tab and click the **Upgrade** link that is shown at the place of **Download & Install** link. Before upgrading, make a backup of your website so that you have the ability to roll back if something goes wrong.

How to find the best CMS Made Simple module for your purpose

There are a lot of modules for CMS Made Simple, but not all of them are of the same quality. The version of the module normally indicates how mature it is. Module versions that start with 0, like 0.3 or 0.5, are alpha versions. This means that these modules are in the first phases of testing and could exhibit some errors or unexpected behavior. Use these modules with caution if you are not a technical person.

The **About** link beside the module name in the list of **Available Modules** (**Extensions | Module Manager**) will inform you when the latest version of the module was released. A last release date of 2006 or 2007 could indicate that there is no scope for development for the module anymore, and it has been abandoned by its developer. In this case, it is better to look for another module or use this one at your own risk.

The **Help** link gives you extended information about the module functionality. See the **parameter** section to figure out if your requirements can be solved with the module in question.

Uninstalling and removing modules

All modules that you do not need can be uninstalled from the list of modules (**Extensions | Modules**). If you do not need the module and uninstall it, then all data that is saved in it will be lost. The module itself will be inactive but still shown in the list of modules. By removing modules from the list, you also physically remove the associated module files from your website.

You cannot remove core modules as they are a part of the standard installation of CMS Made Simple.

Pop quiz – using core modules

1. What is the main feature of a global content block?
    a. It can add repeated texts and pictures to your website.
    b. It can place different company addresses (HQ and subsidiaries) on different pages.
    c. The Smarty tag has to be added to the template.
    d. The global content block has to be installed with the **Module Manager**.

2. What happens if the summary text in the news is not written?
    a. You can only place it in the category **General**.
    b. The whole text is shown on the website in the news section.
    c. The news will not be displayed on the website in the news section.
    d. You cannot save the news without the summary.

3. Which is the standard folder that the **File Manager** uses to store the files?
    a. `uploads`
    b. `downloads`
    c. `images`
    d. There is no standard folder.

4. Which image format should not be used in websites?
    a. JPEG
    b. GIF
    c. TIFF
    d. PNG

5. In order to print out PDF Documents, you have ...
    a. to use the Smarty tag `{pdf_onpage pdf="true"}`.
    b. to first download Adobe Reader.
    c. to be sure that your visitors have got Acrobat.
    d. to use the Smarty tag `{print pdf="true"}`.

6. How can you find the best CMSMS module?

   a. Be sure that it is an alpha version, because alpha is a synonym for high quality every time.

   b. Be sure that the last release is not too long ago because you can be sure that the developer keeps the module alive.

   c. Be sure that the last release is at least 18 months ago because you can be sure that the developer made a stable module.

   d. Be sure that the module's version starts at least with a 0.5, because 0.3 or further versions are not stable.

Have a go hero – applying customization to the core modules

You can integrate news, search, and printing features on your website according to your individual requirements. Use the **Help** section for each module to figure out how you can customize it. Use module templates to suit the layout of each module according to your design. When finished, the result will be a rudimentary website build with CMS Made Simple. If you do not have any additional requirements, you can stop at this point. Congratulations! You are almost ready with the website that can now be filled with content and published.

Summary

In this chapter, you have learned how to use and customize standard modules (core modules) installed with CMS Made Simple.

Specifically, we covered:

- How to use global content blocks in the pages. A global content block is not really a module, but an additional feature that can be used to display the same content in different locations on your website.

- Using news feature for adding news articles to the website, placing them in different categories and displaying them, depending on the category at different locations on your website.

- Using and customizing a search feature for the content of the pages or news articles on the website.

- Using the **Image Manager** to upload images to your website, edit them online, and using them in the content or in the template of the website.

- Using the **Menu Manager** to display any part of your website structure in the content. You learned how a sitemap or any dynamic list of pages can be created.

◆ Using the **Printing** module to create a print version of the website pages or even to create a PDF version of the website without any special knowledge.

◆ Using the **Module Manager** to install third-party modules, and thus add new features to the website like the FAQ feature. We will learn additional modules in Chapter 7, *Using Third-party Modules.*

For each module, you saw how the powerful concept of "template in template" allows you to fully customize the look and feel of each module template. By combining Smarty tags, HTML, and CSS, you do not have any design restrictions and can use a design of any complexity on your website.

Now that we've learned about modules, we're ready to learn about roles and permissions that users with access to the admin console of your website can have—which is the topic of the next chapter.

6
Users and Permissions

This chapter is important to read if you are going to grant access to the admin console of your website to other users. Users with access to the admin console of CMS Made Simple are different from standard visitors to the website. In this chapter, we are talking about users involved in the development of the website. We speak about editors, who write content, create and edit pages; designers, who edit templates and stylesheets; and administrators, who manage website modules, other users, and their permissions in the admin console.

You do not need to read this chapter if you are the only person who develops the website and thus has an unrestricted administrator account. However, if you (or your customer) have a team where different tasks are shared between the team members, then you have to understand how you can grant different permissions to different users. It will safeguard your website and makes it simpler for a CMS Made Simple novice to concentrate on the features that they are allowed to access.

In this chapter, we shall look into:

- Roles, users, and groups
- Permissions on content
- Special designer permissions
- Archiving and restoring different versions
- Overview of all default permissions
- User notifications

Understanding users and their roles

A **role** is a collection of permissions grouped by general tasks that the user has to be able to perform on the website. An **editor** may be responsible for creating, reorganizing, and editing pages. A **designer** does not need to have any permission for page operations, but for creating and editing templates (including module templates). An **administrator** is a person who has all permissions in the admin console and has unrestricted access to the entire admin console.

In CMS Made Simple, three roles are suggested by default—editor, designer, and administrator. The first user created during installation of CMS Made Simple gets the administrator role by default. This user cannot be deleted, deactivated, or removed from the administrator group, as it would mean that there is no administrator for the website at all. You should choose the name of this user and pay attention to the password strength. Members of the administrator group automatically get all the permissions.

Let's see how you can create a new user and learn about the minimum features that every user has, independent of his/her role.

Time for action – creating a new user

1. In the admin console, click on **Users & Groups | Users**.

2. Click on **Add New User**, and fill in the fields, as shown in the following screenshot:

3. Click on **Submit**.

4. Log out (**CMS | Logout**) and log in as **Peter**. The admin console should now look as shown in the following screenshot:

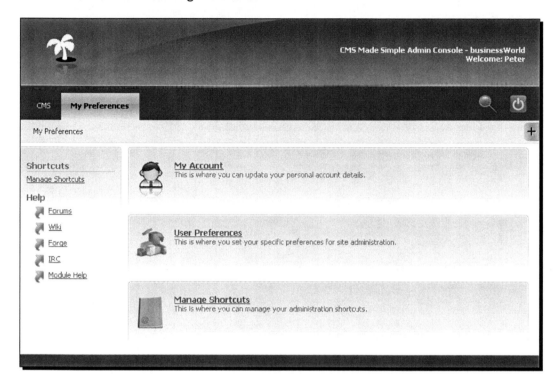

What just happened?

You have created a new user without assigning him to any group. This user can log in to the admin console. There are only two main menu items that the user can access—**CMS** and **My Preferences**. The user can change his name, password, and e-mail address in the **My Account** section. He can define his personal preferences such as language, admin template, set default start page for the admin console, and more. He is also able to manage his personal shortcuts.

It is important to define an e-mail address for every user, as this e-mail is used to recover the password, in case the user forgets it. On the login screen of the admin console of CMS Made Simple (when you are not logged in), you will find the link **Forgot your password**. Click it, enter **Peter** in the **Username** field, and click on **Submit**. An e-mail will be sent to the e-mail address associated with this user. If no e-mail address has been set for this user, then automatic password recovery is not possible. In this case, only the administrator of the website can reset the user's password.

The administrator of the website can set any user as inactive by clicking the icon with a green tick in the column **Active (Users & Groups | Users)**. The user account is not deleted, but the user is not able to log in to the admin console until his account has been activated again. If you delete the user, all permissions and personal user preferences will be irrevocably removed.

If the user is not assigned to any group, then he is not allowed to do anything other than changing his personal settings. Let's assign the user **Peter** to the editor group to see what tasks he will be allowed to perform as an editor.

Time for action – assigning a user to a group

1. In the admin console, click on **Users & Groups | Users**.

2. Select the user **Peter** for edit by clicking on his username.

3. Select the **Editor** checkbox at the bottom of the screen, as shown in the following screenshot:

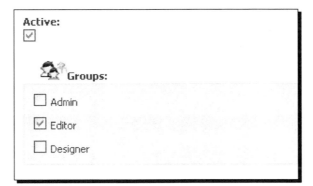

4. Click on **Submit**.

5. Log out (**CMS | Logout**) and log in as **Peter**. The admin console should look as shown in the following screenshot:

What just happened?

You have given the user additional permissions. Now, he can access a new menu item called **Content**. There are no content pages, but only **News** that Peter can submit. Let's see what permissions Peter has now. In the admin console, click on **Users & Groups | Group Permissions**. In the first column, all available permissions are listed. To the right of the permission, there are three columns, one for each group—**Admin**, **Editor**, and **Designer**. You can limit the view to only one group by selecting the group at the top of the table from the drop-down list.

Find all selected checkboxes in the **Editor** column to see what permissions the user assigned to this group gets. You can see that only the **Modify News** permission is checked for the group. This means that the user can create news articles and edit existing news. When the user creates a new item, the news is automatically saved as a draft, so that only the administrator of the page or a user who has the **Approve News For Frontend Display** permission can publish the article on the website.

Peter is not allowed to delete news articles (permission **Delete News Articles**) and has no access to the content pages (permission **Modify Any Page** or **Manage All Content**).

Content permissions

As the target goal of CMS Made Simple is content management, the permissions on editing content are the most flexible. You can create and manage as many editors for the website as you like. Moreover, you can create editors with different access levels thus thoroughly separating who is allowed to do what on your website.

For example, the permission **Manage All Content** will give the group full access to all the features that are available with the administrator account in **Content | Pages**. A user assigned to this group can:

- Create new pages
- Reorder and move them through the hierarchy
- Make pages inactive or prevent them from showing in the navigation
- Change the default page of the website
- Delete pages
- Edit pages including all the information placed in the **Options** tab

To restrict the features mentioned above, you can grant the permission **Modify Any Page**. This permission allows us to edit the content only. The **Options** tab is not shown for the users with this permission, so that any information placed in the **Options** tab cannot be changed.

In addition to the last permission, you can allow some fields from the **Options** tab, so that the editor is able to change the template or mark the page as inactive.

Time for action – creating an editor account

The company page will be edited by the office assistant Mary. The office assistant must be able to edit existing pages, edit meta tags, assign templates, and set the page as inactive.

1. In the admin console, create a new user (**Users & Groups | Users**), and assign the user to the group **Editor**, as shown in the following screenshot:

2. Click on **Submit**.

3. Modify the permissions of the group **Editor** (**Users & Groups | Group Permissions**), and check the box for **Modify Any Page**.

4. Click on **Submit**.

5. In the admin console, click on **Site Admin | Global Settings**, and choose the **Advanced Setup** tab.

6. In the **Basic Properties** field, choose options **Template**, **Active**, and **Page Specific Metadata** , as shown in the following screenshot (hold the *Ctrl* key to mark three options at the same time):

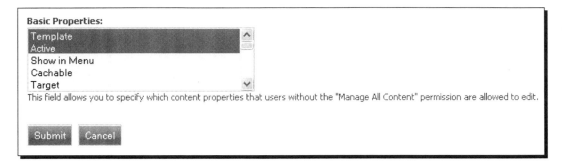

7. Click on **Submit**.

8. Log out (**CMS** | **Logout**) and log in as **Mary**. Check that all of the required features are available when the page is opened for editing.

What just happened?

You have created a new user and assigned the user to the group **Editor**. The group is allowed to edit any page of the website. Additionally, the fields **Template**, **Active**, and **Page Specific Metadata** are available to Mary when she edits the content.

 Your template should have a Smarty plugin {metadata} in the head section, so that **Page Specific Metadata** can be placed in the source code of the page.

Note that the permission **Modify Any Page** does not give you the possibility to restrict access to certain pages. If Mary is not allowed to edit every page on the website, but only some of them, then you should switch to the concept of additional editors, which will be described in the next section.

Additional editors

For every content page, **additional editors** can be defined. You can add additional editors to a certain page in the **Options** tab in the field **Additional Editors** (you must be logged in as the administrator to do it). The additional editor of the page will be able to see and edit only the pages that he is assigned.

To explain it in our example and make it more practical, assume that Mary is not allowed to edit all the pages but only pages **History**, **Team**, and **Contact Us**. Remove Mary from the group **Editor (Users & Groups | Group Assignments)** by deselecting the group in line with Mary's account. Then open the three pages listed earlier, and assign Mary in the field **Additional Editors**, in the **Options** tab for every page. Now, log in as Mary, and open the list of content pages (**Content | Pages**).

Additional editors automatically get the permission **Modify Any Page**, but are restricted to the pages where they have been set as additional editors. You do not need any special group or permissions for such users. Mary, as with every additional editor, is not allowed to create new pages.

Creating new pages

The **Add Pages** permission depends upon other permissions that the user has. It is not enough to add the permission **Add Pages** for the editor. This is because creating new pages will automatically impact the whole website structure. Remember that the navigation is built entirely of the existing pages.

Only those groups having the **Manage All Content** permission are allowed to create pages at every level of the website structure. Beware that these users will not only be able to create new pages, but also modify the whole website structure by reordering or even deleting pages.

Time for action – adding page permissions

Assume that Mary was not only allowed to edit some pages, but also to create pages at certain places in the hierarchy. However, Mary is still not allowed to create pages at the top level of the website. In the last example, we added Mary as an additional editor to some pages. Let's give her the right to create new pages.

1. In the admin console, click on **Users & Groups | Groups**, and create a new group named **Additional Editors**.

2. Click on **Users & Groups | Group Permissions**, and assign the permission **Add Pages** to the group **Additional Editors**, as shown in the following screenshot:

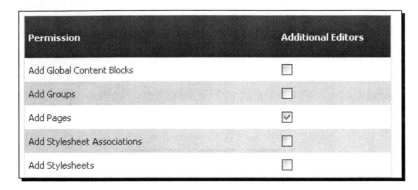

3. Click on **Submit**.

4. Assign **Mary** to the group **Additional Editors** (**Users & Groups | Group Assignments**).

5. Log out (**CMS | Logout**) and log in as **Mary**.

6. Click on the link **Add New Content** (**Content | Pages**), and see the options in the **Parent** field, as shown in the following screenshot:

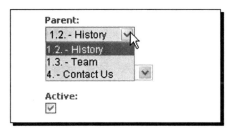

What just happened?

Mary is an additional editor of the pages **History**, **Team**, and **Contact Us**. Assigned to the group with the permission **Add Pages**, Mary can now create new pages under the pages in which she has permission to. However, she is not able to create pages in other sections of the website. For all pages that she creates, Mary will be set as the owner of the page.

If you would like to approve pages created by editors before showing them in the menu of the website, click on **Site Admin | Page Defaults** and deselect the field **Show in Menu**. This way, all newly created pages are not shown in the navigation. By default, the editor cannot change these settings. He/she has to wait for the administrator of the website or for the user with the permission **Manage All Content** for the page to be shown in menu.

In the same manner, you can grant the permission **Remove Pages**. Assign the permission to the group **Additional Editors**, so that they can delete only those pages where they have been assigned as editors.

Designer permissions

If you have a user with strong HTML and CSS knowledge who is able to make reasonable changes to the entire layout of the website or just to the module templates, then you can assign that user to the group **Designer**.

A designer must have the following set of permissions:

- **Add Stylesheet Associations**
- **Add Stylesheets**
- **Add Templates**
- **Manage Menu**
- **Manage Themes**
- **Modify Files**
- **Modify Stylesheet Associations**
- **Modify Stylesheets**
- **Modify Templates**
- **Remove Stylesheet Associations**
- **Remove Stylesheets**
- **Remove Templates**
- **View Tag Help**

This set of permissions allows the designer of the website to perform any task related to the design of the template. However, the designer will not be able to edit the content, submit news, or set any site preferences.

The designer still needs a content page that he can use for design or layout tests. In order to prevent the test page being shown in the menu or in the sitemap, you should do the following trick.

Time for action – creating a test area for the designer

1. In the admin console, click on **Content | Pages**.

2. Click on **Add New Content** and create an inactive **Section Header** named **Design Test** as shown:

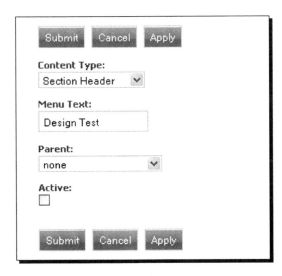

3. Click on **Submit**.

4. Click on **Add New Content** again, choose the section header **Design Test** (created in step 2) in the field **Parent**. Select the **Options** tab, scroll down, and select the user or the whole group **Designer** in the field **Additional Editors**.

5. Click on **Submit**.

6. Log out and log in again as **Designer**. Click on **Content | Pages** to see the test page.

What just happened?

You have created a new page and placed it below an inactive **Section Header**. The pages placed below inactive pages cannot be displayed in the website structure. Even if you use the parameter show_all with the Smarty plugin menu (for example, in the sitemap) the page will not be displayed. However, it is active, and it can be accessed directly through the magnifying glass icon, and can be used by the designer as a test area.

In the admin console (**Site Admin | Global Settings**), under the **Advanced Setup** tab, you can define **Basic Properties** for the additional editors such as **Image**. We used this field in the last chapter. Here, the editor can choose an image from a drop-down list and thus assign an image to a certain location in the template defined by the designer.

> There is a useful third-party module called **Template Externalizer**. It allows you to use any external editor to edit your templates and stylesheets. After installing and turning on **Development Mode**, the module automatically extracts all stylesheets and templates into the specified directory.
>
> If you modify templates in this external directory, changes are automatically detected, imported to the database, and take effect immediately. When the module is installed, there is the permission **Template Externalizer** that can be granted to the group **Designer**.

Viewing the admin log

The admin log records the details of the changes made to the site by all users. This log can be found in the admin console (**Site Admin | Admin Log**) and includes records about the creating, deleting, and changing of:

- Pages and global content blocks
- Templates and stylesheets
- Users, groups, and permissions
- Site preferences
- Modules

At the top of the log, you will find a navigation section providing links to the first, next, previous, and last pages of the log. There is also a link to download the complete log as a tab separated text file. At the bottom is the **Clear Admin Log** link. This will clear the entire log.

> Important! You won't be asked to confirm the **Clear Admin Log**, and this action cannot be undone once completed.

Once the admin log is cleared, there is no evidence of who has changed anything on the website and what the changes were. Therefore, there is even a separate permission called **Clear Admin Log** that is granted separately from the permission **Modify Site Preferences**.

There are five columns in each log entry, which are as follows:

- ♦ **User:** This shows the username of the user who performed the action. Even if the user is deleted later, the username is still saved in the log.
- ♦ **Item ID:** This shows the database ID of the affected item. Note that item IDs are only unique to the **Item Name** shown in the next column and not across the whole database, so the same item ID may appear repeatedly.
- ♦ **Item Name:** This shows the name of the item affected.
- ♦ **Action:** This describes the type of change made to the item.
- ♦ **Date:** This saves the date and time the change was made.

If you have novice users with access to the admin console, then you probably would like to keep all versions of the content to be able to restore them if something goes wrong. There is no such feature in the standard installation of CMS Made Simple, but there is a nice third-party module that you can install additionally.

Archiving changes and restoring them

Once the **Archiver** module is installed, it keeps a copy of every content page, global content block, stylesheet, or template that is edited or deleted. It also provides the possibility to restore anything in the archive to the current state. This means that your users can edit various aspects of the site, and you can reverse their changes later.

To install the **Archiver** module, open the admin console, and click on **Extensions | Module Manager**. Click on the **Available Modules** tab, and then click the **Download & Install** link which can be found in the same line as the module name. The module is installed.

After installation, the module will automatically start saving changes into the archives. For example, if you would like to track the changes of the start page, open the page, and save it without any changes, so that the first version of the page is created. This version will be used as a base for future restorations.

Time for action – restoring changes made by an editor

Assuming that you have installed the **Archiver** module, as just described, you can restore the changes made by the editor as follows:

1. Log in as the editor and edit any page that you are allowed to.

2. Log out and then log in again with the administrator account.

3. Click on **Content | Archive Manager Module**.

4. Search for the name of the page that has been edited in step 1, and click on it.

5. In the **Expanded Archive View**, find the second last version (revision) of the page and click on the last icon in the column **Operation**.

6. View the page.

What just happened?

You have restored the older version of the content and made it to the current one. The editor's version is not deleted but just replaced, so that you can restore it any time.

You can automatically purge archives either by the number of stored versions for each item (that is, keep only the last five versions of each page, global content block, stylesheet, or template) or by date (that is, keep the versions of the last seven days only). For automatic purge setup, click the **Archive Preferences** link in the admin area of the module (**Content | Archive Manager Module**).

You do not have to purge archives, though you can keep accumulating all changes. However, if you have a lot of changes made daily, you must purge your archive to prevent an overflow of the database.

 This module is not a substitute for the regular offsite database backups. The data is still stored in the same database, which might render the archives useless upon a database crash. Read the appropriate section in Chapter 11, *Administration and Troubleshooting* to learn how to create database backups.

Overview of all default permissions

Permissions are always given to the group and are shared by all users assigned to this group. In the following table, the first column is the name of the permission, the second column is a suggestion as to what role the permission can be granted to, and the third column advises you if there are some preconditions for the permission to take effect.

Permission	Suggestion for the role	Description
Add Global Content Blocks	Editor	The group is allowed to create new global content blocks (**Content | Global Content Blocks**). Depends upon the permission **Modify Global Content Blocks**.
Add Groups	Admin	The group is allowed to create user groups (**Users & Groups | Groups**). Depends upon the permission **Modify Groups**.
Add Pages	Editor	The group allows the creation of children content pages below the pages where the user is an owner or an additional editor. The user must be set as **Owner** of the page or an **Additional Editor**.
Add Stylesheet Associations	Designer	The group is allowed to associate stylesheets with templates.
Add Stylesheets	Designer	The group is allowed to create new stylesheets.
Add Templates	Designer	The group is allowed to create new templates.
Add Users	Admin	The group is allowed to create new users with access to the admin console.
Allow usage of advanced profile in TinyMCE	Editor	Users in this group will automatically get advanced profile settings made for the **TinyMCE** module. However, they are not able to change the profile itself.
Approve News For Frontend Display	Editor	Allows changing the **Status** field of the news item from **Draft** to **Published**. The user in this group is also able to edit news articles.
Clear Admin Log	Admin	Clear the history in **Site Admin	Admin Log**. Depends upon the permission **Modify Site Preferences**.
Delete News Articles	Editor	The group is allowed to delete news articles. Depends upon the permission **Modify News**.
Manage All Content	Editor	The group is allowed to create, move, and delete pages. The group is allowed to access the **Options** tab while editing the pages and change anything that can be found on the tab in contrast to the permission **Modify Any Page**.
Manage Menu	Designer	The group can modify menu templates and create new menu templates.

Permission	Suggestion for the role	Description
Manage Themes	Designer	The group is allowed to export themes. If dependant permissions are available, the user is also able to import themes.Depends upon the permissions **Add Stylesheet Associations**, **Add Stylesheets**, and **Add Templates**.
Modify Any Page	Editor	The group is allowed to edit content pages. There is no **Options** tab while editing the content for this group. However, some fields from the **Options** tab can be added from **Site Admin | Global Settings** (tab **Advanced Setup**, field **Basic Properties**).
Modify Events	Admin	The group is allowed to add and reorder events (refer to Chapter 8).
Modify Files	Editor	Allows using **File and Image Manager**, thus giving full access to the /uploads folder of your installation.
Modify Global Content Blocks	Editor	Allows editing and deleting of global content blocks.
Modify Group Assignments	Admin	Allows assigning users to different groups.
Modify Groups	Admin	Allows changing group names.
Modify Modules	Admin	Allows managing of **Extensions | Modules** and **Extensions | Module Manager**, thus installing, upgrading, uninstalling, and removing modules.
Modify News	Editor	Allows editing news and creating new articles with status **Draft**.
Modify Permissions for Groups	Admin	Allows modifying permissions for the group.
Modify Site Preferences	Admin	This is a set of multiple permissions including the tabs **Preferences**, **Settings**, or **Options** in different modules. For example, the user is able to access the **Options** tab on the **News** module, the **Settings** tab in **File Manager**, **CMSMailer**, the **Options** tab in the **Search** module, and so on.
Modify Stylesheet Associations	Designer	Allows attaching stylesheets to the templates and resolving the attachment as well.
Modify Stylesheets	Designer	Allows editing existing stylesheets.
Modify Templates	Designer	Allows editing existing templates including templates in modules **News**, **Search**, and **Printing**.
Modify User-defined Tags	Admin	Allows adding user defined tags to the website (refer to Chapter 10).

Permission	Suggestion for the role	Description
Modify Users	Admin	Allows editing the user with the exception of the administrator user account.
Remove Global Content Blocks	Admin	Allows editing the global content blocks. Depends upon the permission **Modify Global Content Blocks**.
Remove Groups	Admin	Allows deleting user groups.
Remove Pages	Editor	Allows deleting content pages where the user is an **Owner** or **Additional editor**.
Remove Stylesheet Associations	Designer	Allows removing stylesheet associations.
Remove Stylesheets	Designer	Allows removing stylesheets.
Remove Templates	Designer	Allows removing layout templates, but not the module templates.
Remove Users	Admin	Allows removing users with exception of the own account and the administrator account.
Advanced usage of the File Manager module	Admin	Allows viewing the complete structure of the website and not only the /uploads directory. For this permission to work, the advanced mode setting should be enabled in **File**.
View Tag Help	Editor	Allows reading help for the custom smarty plugins.

Module permissions

Not only can the core functions and core modules of CMS Made Simple have permissions, but every third-party module you have installed on your page can add the module's specific permissions to the list. If you still have the **Questions & Answers** module installed, as described in the last chapter, you will find the permissions **Manage Questions** , **Can Answer Questions**, and **Can Approve Questions** in your list of permissions (**Users & Groups | Group Permissions**).

The **Archiver** module has the permission **Manage Archives** that can be granted to advanced users with access to the admin console or to the main editor with the permission **Manage All Content**.

User notifications

There is a notification area in the admin console of CMS Made Simple located below the main menu.

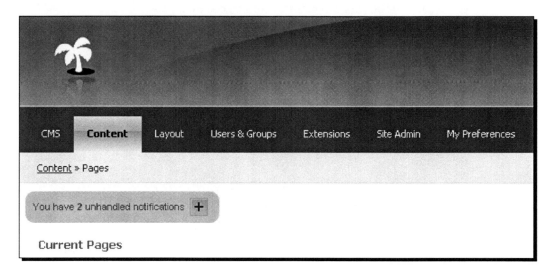

You saw the message just after the installation of CMS Made Simple advising you about the next steps to secure and configure the system. Later on, this area is used to notify us when a new version of CMS Made Simple is released. The **News** module uses the area to notify when there are some unpublished news articles that must be approved and published.

Normally, each user logged into the admin console is able to read these notifications even if it is something that is not devoted to him.

You can disable notifications in the admin console. Click on **Site Admin | Global Settings**, and select the tab **Advanced Setup**. Deselect the field **Allow users to view notifications** and the messages will disappears.

Pop quiz – users and permissions

1. What is a role?

    a. A bunch of permissions.

    b. Another term only for editors.

    c. A term for a special visitor group.

    d. A term for visitors, whose permissions to read special contents can be defined.

2. Who has the right to change or delete the administrator account?

   a. Absolutely nobody—an administrator cannot be deleted.

   b. Each user, who is an administrator, can delete all other administrators.

   c. Additional editors can edit the admin accounts.

   d. Only the user who owns the first created administrator account can delete and edit all other admin accounts.

3. Which user group is not created by default?

   a. Administrator

   b. Designer

   c. Additional editor

   d. Editor

4. Why is it important to create an e-mail address for each user?

   a. Because the CMS does not work properly without an e-mail address.

   b. Because the administrator can contact the other users easily.

   c. Because the e-mail is needed to recover a forgotten password by the user himself.

   d. Because the e-mail address is a check for the existence of the user.

5. What can an editor who has the permission **Modify Any Page** do?

   a. Edit all pages.

   b. Delete all pages.

   c. Change the alias of all pages.

   d. Change the owner of all pages.

6. What can an editor who has the permission **Manage All Content** not do?

   a. Set pages as inactive or prevent showing them in the navigation.

   b. Delete pages.

   c. Edit pages including all information placed on the **Options** tab.

   d. Change the owner of the pages.

7. What is the most important fact concerning an additional editor?

   a. He can create only one page per section.

   b. He can only administrate his own pages.

   c. He gets more rights than an editor with default permissions.

   d. There can be an unlimited number of additional editors in contrast to standard editors.

Have a go hero – users and permissions

Analyze how many persons will get access to your website. Separate them in different groups according to their tasks. Create the groups and assign permissions to the group. It is better if you give minimum set of permissions to each group then ask the person assigned to the group to log in and see whether he/she is able to accomplish his/her tasks in the admin console. If there are some undesired restrictions, add more permissions. Consider that giving more access would make your system more vulnerable. Be careful and apply permissions sparingly.

Summary

In this chapter, we learned how teamwork can be effectively managed with access to the admin console.

Specifically, we covered:

- ◆ Standard user roles in CMS Made Simple
- ◆ Permissions for the editors
- ◆ Permissions for the designers
- ◆ Viewing the admin log and working with the **Archiver** module to be able to restore older versions of the content

Now that we've learned about permissions, we're ready to enrich the website with additional features typically found on business websites, which will be discussed in the next chapter.

7
Using Third-party Modules

CMS Made Simple has only some basic features that belong to the standard installation. Any additional functionality can be installed with other modules. Think of CMS Made Simple modules as Lego bricks. Modules can be installed in any combination you choose. Some modules are combinable with or even dependant on other modules. Modules are additional features that anyone can put on their website.

To choose and install new modules, click on **Extensions | Module Manager** in the admin console. Notice that the modules listed here are not standard modules of CMS Made Simple and therefore not all of them are of the same high quality as the core modules. That is why you see the message "*Use at Your Own Risk*" above the list of modules. Nevertheless, there are many modules which are very useful, sophisticated, and were thoroughly tested by their developers.

The **Available Modules** tab facilitates the installation of packages you already know about. The modules are sorted alphabetically by their names and a good explanation about them can be found by clicking on the **Help** link beside the module name.

In this chapter, we shall install and use the following:

- Gallery
- Form Builder
- Newsletter
- YouTube videos

So, let's get started with it...

Creating a photo gallery

The most popular feature for websites is a photo gallery. Photo galleries are popular parts of private portfolios, music bands', or company websites. On a business website, photo galleries are often used to display office buildings or photos of the team members. Products, samples, or results of the projects are often implemented as photo galleries as well.

If you are not using any special module for gallery, you could upload all images in one folder on your web hosting and manually add each image to the content page. This kind of static gallery is difficult to maintain and design. It is not flexible enough and requires deep HTML knowledge from the page editor.

A better solution is to use a special module that will read a folder on the web host and display all images from this folder using some impressive blending effects. The module will offer a special admin area where each image's caption can be entered.

To install the **Gallery** module, log in to admin console and click on **Extensions | Module Manager**. On the **Available Modules** tab, click the letter **G** in the alphabetical navigation, and find the module called **Gallery**. Click the **Download & Install** link in line with the module name. The module will be installed.

After installation of the **Gallery** module, a new folder called `uploads/images/Gallery` will be automatically created on your web hosting. This folder is empty by default, so you have to upload some images into it. You can upload images with **Image Manager** or **File Manager** or even with an FTP browser if you have a lot of images to upload.

Time for action – creating the first gallery

Let's see how images from the folder `uploads/images/Gallery` can be displayed on the **Photo Gallery** page. Perform the following steps:

1. In the admin console, open the **Photo Gallery** page for editing (**Content | Pages**).

2. Enter the Smarty plugin in the **Content** field, as shown in the following screenshot:

3. Click on **Apply** and then on the magnifying glass icon beside the **Apply** button to see the first gallery on the website.

What just happened?

You have uploaded some images into the folder /uploads/images/Gallery. This folder was automatically created after the module installation. Your first gallery is displayed on the **Photo Gallery** page.

You will find the admin area of the **Gallery** module in the admin console (**Content | Gallery**). Open the admin area, and click on the folder named Gallery to see what you can change in the module output. Change **Gallery Title** and **Comment** to suit your needs. Choose another **Template** for different blending effects in the gallery. If no template is specified for the gallery, then the default template (**Content | Gallery**, tab **Templates**) is used.

The size of thumbnails (small preview versions of the images) is set to 96x96 pixels (standard thumbnail size in CMS Made Simple). In the photo gallery, you can enter your own thumbnail size and then choose any of the following resize methods:

- ◆ **crop**: Crops the original image to the thumbnail size taking smaller detail of the image. Proportions of the original image are ignored.

- ◆ **scale**: This will resize the original image to the custom thumbnail size. The proportions of the original image are held, so that only the width or height can be taken into account while resizing.

- ◆ **zoom & crop**: This is the same as 'crop', but the details of the image are slightly zoomed. Crops the original image to the thumbnail size while taking zoomed details of the image. The proportions of the original image are ignored.

- ◆ **zoom & scale**: The same as 'scale crop', but the thumbnail is slightly zoomed. Resizes the original image to the custom thumbnail size. The proportions of the original image are held, so that only the width or height can be taken into account while resizing.

When the thumbnail size is changed, you have to click on the link **(Re)Create Thumbs** for the new thumbnails to be created.

At the bottom of the screen, a list of the images that are uploaded into the folder uploads/images/Gallery are displayed. For each image, you can enter a **Title** (image caption) and a **Comment** (is not shown in any template by default). You can deactivate images rather than delete them. In this case, the image is not shown in the gallery, but the caption and comment will be kept.

The images in the gallery are sorted alphabetically by their filenames.

Adding albums to a gallery

New albums are created from new folders. Create a new folder below the folder uploads/images/Gallery with **File Manager** or **Image Manager**. Upload your images into the new folder. In the admin area of the **Gallery (Content | Gallery)**, find the new folder, and edit it the same way as your main album.

To display images from one or more directories, use the parameter dir. This parameter specifies the directory (or directories) where the images are uploaded. For example, if you have created two folders below the /uploads/images/Gallery and named them buildings and projects, then to display images from the folder buildings only, use the Smarty tag as shown:

```
{Gallery dir="buildings"}
```

You can override the template for the gallery directly in the Smarty tag by adding the parameter template to it. If this parameter is not specified, then the template assigned to the directory will be used, or else the default template will be used.

Using the gallery on other pages

Use images from the gallery on other pages and not only in the page **Photo Gallery**. For example, display recently added images from your gallery on the start page and link them to the page where the entire gallery can be found.

Time for action – adding random images to the template

Let's add two recently added images from the gallery to the start page of the website.

1. In the admin console, click on **Content | Gallery**, and choose the **Templates** tab.

2. Click the **Create a new template** link. Enter **Latest** as the template name and in the **Template Source** field add the following Smarty code:

```
{foreach from=$images item=image}
  <a href="{cms_selflink href="photo-gallery"}" title="{$image-
    >title}"><img src="{$image->thumb}" alt="{$image->title}" />
  </a>
{/foreach}
```

You should replace photo-gallery in the example with the alias of the page where the whole image gallery can be found.

3. Delete everything from the fields **Template CSS-stylesheet** and **Template JavaScript**.

4. Click on **Save**.

5. In the admin console, open the start page for editing (**Content | Pages**).

6. Add the Smarty tag to display the latest images from the gallery, as shown in the following screenshot:

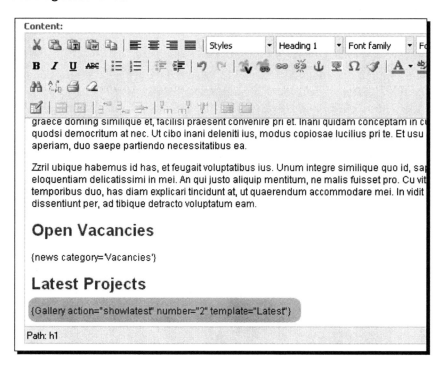

7. Click **Apply** and see the result on the start page.

What just happened?

You have created a new template for the **Gallery** module. This template displays two recently added images from the gallery. Each image is linked to the **Photo Gallery** page (`{cms_ selflink href="photo-gallery"}`). Then, you have added the Smarty tag `{Gallery action-"showlatest" number="2" template-"Latest"}` to the start page. There are three parameters, which are as follows:

◆ `action="showlatest"`: Displays the most recently added images (by default, it displays a total of six images). Subdirectories are automatically included.

◆ `number="2"`: The maximum number of images to display. All images will be displayed if the value for this parameter is not specified.

◆ `template="Latest"`: Uses a separate database template for displaying the photo gallery. This template must exist. However, it does not need to be set as default. If this parameter is not specified, then the default template will be used.

If you do not want to display recently added images, but some random images from the gallery, then set the parameter action to showrandom.

Additional parameters for each module can be found in the **Help** module (see the link **Module Help** to the right of the module name in the admin area of the module).

Creating your own gallery template

It is possible to implement any template in your gallery. I would like to show you how it works with the **AD Gallery** plugin (http://coffeescripter.com/code/ad-gallery/). **AD Gallery** is a jQuery plugin and consists of HTML, CSS, JavaScript, and images. We have to put all these components in the right order to use the plugin as a gallery template.

Open the link http://coffeescripter.com/code/ad-gallery, and scroll down to the **Downloads** section. Save the file placed under **The whole kit and kaboodle** to your local disk and unzip it.

On your web hosting, create a new folder adgallery in modules/Gallery/templates. Upload the file jquery.ad-gallery.js into this folder. Then upload all images (PNG and GIF files) from the same folder to modules/Gallery/images.

In the admin console, create a new template for gallery (**Content | Gallery**, tab **Templates**). Enter **Ad Gallery** as the **Template Name**, and replace the **Template Source** with the following code snippet:

```
<div id="gallery" class="ad-gallery">
  <div class="ad-image-wrapper"></div>
  <div class="ad-controls"></div>
  <div class="ad-nav">
    <div class="ad-thumbs">
      <ul class="ad-thumb-list">
        {foreach from=$images item=image} {if !$image->isdir}
        <li>
          <a href="{$image->file}">
            <img src="{$image->thumb}" title="{$image->title}"
              longdesc="{$image->comment}" class="image0">
          </a>
        </li>
        {/if} {/foreach}
      </ul>
    </div>
  </div>
</div>
```

This code was taken from the file `example.html` and was modified to use the Smarty tag `foreach` to take all images from the gallery.

Proceed with the stylesheet. On your local disk, open the file `jquery.ad-gallery.css`. This file has to be slightly modified for the images to be found on the server. Find any occurrences of:

```
background: url(
```

and replace them with:

```
background: url(../../images/
```

Then, in the first line, adjust the width of the entire gallery:

```
ad-gallery {
  width: 500px;
}
```

Copy the entire contents of the modified stylesheet, and replace the content of the field **Template CSS-stylesheet** with it.

In the last step, copy the following code, and replace the entire content in the field **Template JavaScript**:

```html
<script type="text/javascript"
  src="modules/Gallery/templates/jquery/jquery.js"></script>
<script type="text/javascript"
  src="modules/Gallery/templates/adgallery/jquery.ad-gallery.js">
</script>
<script type="text/javascript">
  $(function() {
    var galleries = $('.ad-gallery').adGallery();
    $('#switch-effect').change(
      function() {
        galleries[0].settings.effect = $(this).val();
        return false;
      }
    );
    $('#toggle-slideshow').click(
      function() {
        galleries[0].slideshow.toggle();
        return false;
      }
    );
  });
</script>
```

Click on **Save**, and find the new template in the list of templates. Set the template as **Default** and see your photo gallery on the website. Your gallery is now using the AD Gallery plugin. In the same way, you can use any plugin for your gallery. Separate HTML, images, CSS, and JavaScript from each other and place them in the appropriate fields so that all required parts are composed on the website in the right order as before.

Adding forms with the module Form Builder

Almost every business page has a contact, feedback, or inquiry form. The **Form Builder** module helps you to create forms with any level of complexity without writing any HTML. You can add different input fields to it, set validation rules, and define how the data from the form must be stored and/or sent by e-mail.

Install the **Form Builder** module in the same way as you installed other third-party modules on the website (for example, **Questions** or **Gallery**). After installation, the admin area of the module can be found in **Extensions | Form Builder**.

Before you start configuring the module, ensure that the module **CMSMailer** is properly configured (refer Chapter 2, *Getting Started*) and you are able to send e-mails from your CMS Made Simple website.

Time for action – adding a contact form to the website

Let's add a simple contact form to the **Contact Us** page and send the submitted content of the form to our e-mail address.

1. In the admin console, click on **Extensions | Form Builder**.

2. Click the **Contact Form** link.

3. Scroll down to **Form Fields**, and click the **Send To** link.

4. Replace the e-mail address in the fields **"From address" for email** and **Destination Email Address** with your real e-mail address, as shown in the following screenshot:

"From address" for email:

my.real.mail@businesswo

Do not just pick a random address here -- many ISPs will
not deliver the mail if you are using a different domain name than your actual
host name (i.e., use something like name@business.icms.info)

Destination Email Address:

Destination Email Address   **Delete?**

my.real.mail@businessworld.c

5. Click on **Update** to save the changes.

6. Click on **Save** below the form fields.

7. Copy the Smarty tag from the column **Form Alias** in the line **Contact Form**, as shown in the following screenshot:

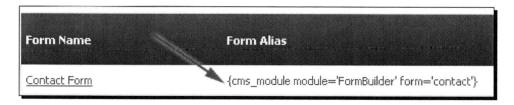

8. Open the page **Contact Us** for editing (**Content | Pages**) and add the copied Smarty tag into it.

9. Click **Apply** and view the page. It should look as follows:

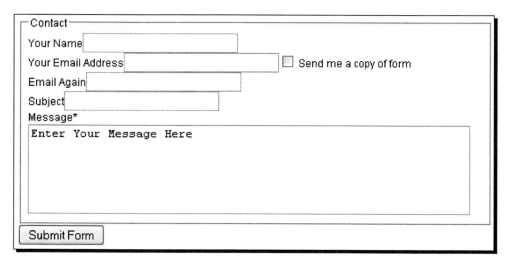

10. Fill out the form, and click **Submit Form**, you should get an e-mail sent from this contact form to the e-mail address given in step 4.

What just happened?

You have added a simple contact form to the page. This contact form consists of the field set (a border around all fields), five visible fields, and the **Submit Form** button. You have changed the e-mail address to be sure that the results from the form are sent through e-mail to the right address. This contact form can be fully customized to suit your needs.

Customizing the contact form

Let's see exactly what the contact form is made up of and how you can customize its appearance, the text of the e-mail message sent, and the confirmation message shown to the visitor after submitting the form on the website. In the admin console, click on **Extensions | Form Builder** and choose **Contact Form**. Scroll down to the section **Form Fields** where all fields for the contact form can be customized.

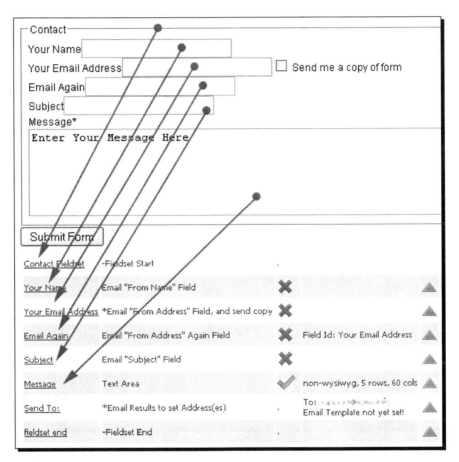

You can reorder, delete, and add new fields in this section. **Contact Fieldset** is an optical border around the fields. You can delete it (using the dustbin icon at the end of the line), if you do not like it. In this case, do not forget to remove **fieldset end** (the last line) as well.

To edit labels in front of the fields on the page, edit the field (click on it in the list) and change the **Field Name**. Check the box for **Required**, if the field must be filled, so that if it is empty, the form is not sent, and an error message is shown to the visitor.

Edit the field **Your Email Address**. Set it to **Required**, and select **Email Address** in the **Field Validation** option. This will ensure that visitors must provide a valid e-mail address, otherwise an error message will be displayed. Set the value in the field **Send User a Copy of Submission** to **Never**. If you send a copy of the message to the visitor, you reveal the destination e-mail address, and probably get undesired communication bypassing the feedback form. Update the field and return to the list of fields in the form.

The **Email Again** field is optional. You can remove it if you like.

The **Message** field is defined as a **Text Area**. This means that more than one line can be entered in the field by the website visitor. The height and width of this field can be changed by setting the number of **Rows** (number of lines shown without scroll bar) and **Columns** (number of characters shown in one line before line break). The size of the field can also be customized using CSS.

For each form, different types of template can be defined and configured. You can use a combination of HTML and Smarty tags as you learned in Chapter 4, *Design and Layout*.

Template	Description
Form Template	This template defines how the form should look. Open the **Contact Form** (Extensions | Form Builder), and click on the **Form Template** tab. Some default templates can be chosen from the **Load Template** drop-down list. You can also create your own template by using instructions and variables shown in the section **Form Template Variables**. The default **Form Template** is very complicated. The reason for it is that it includes everything that you can customize for the single fields.
Submission Template	This template defines how the response message should look like after the form is submitted. Open the **Contact Form** (Extensions | Form Builder), and click on the **Submission Template** tab. Customize the message in the field **Response to display**. You don't need to use any variables in this field. I also recommend removing the part **Other information** as it is too technical for website visitors.
Email Template	This template defines how the e-mail message should look. Open the **Contact Form** (Extensions | Form Builder), and click on the field **Send To** in the list of fields. Choose the **Advanced Settings** tab, scroll down, and click on the button **Create Sample HTML Template**. Now, you can edit the e-mail message in field **Email Template**.

Form Builder not only offers default templates, but offers default stylesheets as well. The stylesheet is automatically added after installation to **Layout | Stylesheets**. Attach the **FormBuilder Default Style** to the **Business World** template by clicking on the blue CSS icon in the list of stylesheets if you would like to use it. You can customize the attached stylesheet to suit the form to your individual page layout.

Adding new fields to the forms

The contact form can be enriched with more fields. Let's see how you can add a radio button group, drop-down group, and checkbox group to the form. New fields are created in the admin area of the **Form Builder** (**Extensions | Form Builder**). Open the **Contact Form** for editing, and click the **Add New Field** link below the list of fields. Then you have to select the **Field Type** you would like to add.

Every time you add a new field to the form, you must adjust the **Email Template** and **Submission Template**. New fields are added automatically to the form but not to other templates.

To update the **Email Template**, open the **Send To** field for editing, and select the **Advanced Settings** tab, scroll down the page, and click the **Create Sample HTML Template** button. In the field **Email Template** above you will see the sample template that will be used for sending out messages. Edit the template if needed and click **Update** to save it. This would automatically add new fields to the e-mail message. On the **Submission Template** tab, you can edit the message that the visitor sees after the form is sent. You can create a sample HTML template here as well, and then alter it according to your needs.

In the following three sections, we will add three new fields to the contact form, so that it looks like the following screenshot:

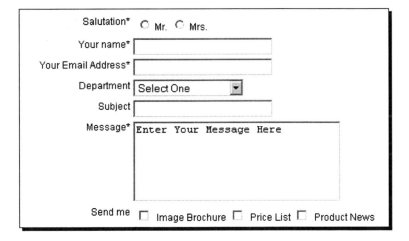

Adding salutation as a radio button group

For salutation fields, you create a new field with radio buttons that are grouped so that only one radio button in the group can be selected at any time. Select **Radio Button Group** in the **Field Type** and enter the fields as shown:

Field Name:

Salutation

Field Type:
Radio Button Group

Required:
☑ Require a response for this Field

Field Validation:
Automatic

Radio Button Group Details:

Radio Button label	Value when checked	Checked by Default?	Delete?
Mr.	Mr.	No ▾	☐
Mrs.	Mrs.	No ▾	☐

Add More Options   Delete Marked Options

The **Radio Button label** is what visitors of the website see while filling in the form. The **Value when checked** is what will be sent to you when they submit the form. Here you can enter different values if you like. Initially, you see only one option that you can fill, so click the **Add More Options** button to add more radio buttons to the group.

Click **Add** when you are ready, and the field will be added to the list of fields. Below the list of fields, you will find the **Reorder Fields** link where you can easily drag-and-drop the fields to adjust their appearance order on the page. Place **Salutation** at the very top of your form so that it appears before the **Your Name** field.

 Do not forget to update the **Email** and **Submission** templates after adding the field to the form.

Adding department as a pulldown field

Another type of field that you can easily add to the form is a drop-down field, which is called **pulldown** in CMS Made Simple. Click on the **Add New Field** link, and select **Pulldown** as the **Field Type**. Enter the fields as shown in the following screenshot:

Just as in radio buttons, here you can differentiate between what the visitor sees while filling in the form (**Option Name**) and the value of the field sent to you (**Value Submitted**).

 Do not forget to update the **Email** and **Submission** templates after adding the field to the form.

Adding multiple choice selection with the checkbox group

In contrast to radio buttons, the checkboxes in a group can be checked without changing the state of other checkboxes, so multiple choices are possible. It would not make any sense for the salutation field, but for fields where the visitor can request different types of information this can be useful. Click on the **Add New Field** link, and select **Check Box Group** as **Field Type**. Enter the fields as shown in the following screenshot:

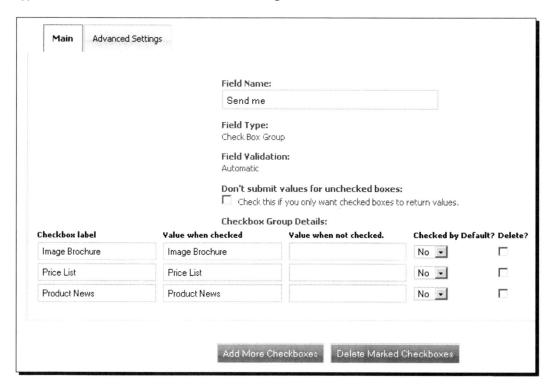

Checkboxes can have different states—checked and not checked. Depending on the state, different values will be sent to you after submitting the form. You can leave the **Value when not checked** field empty. No values are sent if the boxes are not checked.

Keep the number of mandatory entries to the bare minimum, if you actually want people to write to you. The best clients are busy people who won't spend hours on filling in pedantic forms in the first place, but rather choose a provider that spares their time.

Adding a Captcha to the forms

A **Captcha** is a type of test used in forms to ensure that the form is not filled in by a computer. It is an acronym for **Completely Automated Public Turing Test To Tell Computers and Humans Apart**. The process usually involves the page asking a user to enter some characters in the special field. Computers mostly are not able to solve the captcha test, so any user entering a correct solution is presumed to be a human being. You can activate captcha in all CMS Made Simple forms.

Install the **Captcha** module (**Extensions | Module Manager**). In the admin console, choose **Extensions | Catpcha**. There are some options you can use to generate a captcha image. The captcha library **hn_captcha** is used by default. To change the default settings of the image, click on the **options** link beside the field **Captcha Library to use**.

To give your captcha strong security, change the values in the fields—**chars**, **minsize**, **maxsize**, **maxrotation**, and **secretposition**. Add a secret string (something that one cannot guess).

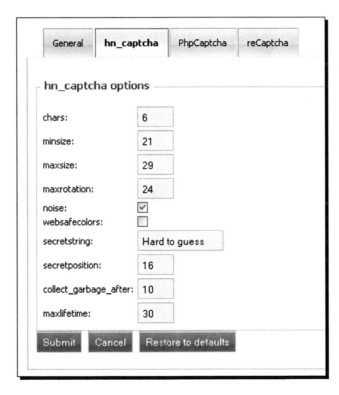

The strength of the captcha will grow depending on how many changes you have made. Some spam programs can read captcha images generated with default values. However, they fail if you place any individual values here. Be sure that you make only slight changes in the fields **minsize, maxsize,** and **maxrotation,** so that the captcha will still be readable to human users. Note that the changes are valid for all forms and modules in CMS Made Simple that use the **Captcha** module.

To activate the captcha for the contact form, open the form in **Extensions | Form Builder**. Choose the **Captcha Settings** tab, and select the box **Use Captcha to protect form submissions**. See the captcha Image added to the bottom of the contact form.

reCAPTCHA has some advantages. This library is supported by a crew responsible for keeping it up-to-date, it is accessible for disabled persons, and it helps to recognize texts of scanned books thus making them available in electronic formats. If you would like to use reCAPTCHA you should sign up at `reCaptcha.com` and add your website so that you can get public and private keys for it. You cannot reuse the same keys for sites on other domains, so you have to add every new site to your account to get a new set of keys.

Sending out newsletters

With CMS Made Simple and the **Newsletter Made Simple (NMS)** module, you can send out newsletters to your customers or any visitors of your website who have subscribed to the newsletter.

You can define one or more user lists, thus separating your customers from the visitors and being able to send different newsletter to each user list. One user can be assigned to one or more lists. You create a template that contains the e-mail subject and text, so you don't need to start each message from a blank page, you can use a template that has already been created. However, you can write newsletters without templates as well.

To send out a newsletter, you will choose an existing message and a list of users that are going to get this message. This will be called a **Job**. The job will be processed manually at the time you activate it.

Install the **NMS** module from the list of available modules in the admin console (**Extensions | Module Manager**). Pay attention to the modules found on the **Dependencies** link before installing the module. These modules should be installed before you attempt to install Newsletter Made Simple.

Time for action – sending mails to registered customers

Let's create our first newsletter that will be sent to the visitors of the website. You have to create one or more test users with different valid e-mail addresses to be able to control how the messages will be delivered. Do not use real e-mail addresses, unless you want them to get test messages at this point.

1. In the admin console, click on **Extensions | Newsletter Made Simple**.

2. Click on the **Create a List** link, and enter the fields, as shown in the following screenshot:

3. Click on **Submit**.

4. Switch to the **Users** tab. At the bottom of the page, click on the **Add User** link, and add two or more users. Assign them to the group **Public Newsletter**, as shown:

5. Click on **Submit**.

6. Switch to the **Messages** tab, and click on the **Compose Message** link. Enter the **Subject** of the mail. Choose **Yes** in the field **This message contains only text**. Select the **Newsletter** page in the list of pages and select **No** for showing in the public archive lists. Enter the **Text Message** that should be sent to the users in the user list for the **Public Newsletter**. You can use placeholders in the e-mail text; these are shown in the **Message Authoring** section.

7. Click on **Submit**.

8. Switch to the **Jobs** tab, and click on **Create Job** link.

9. In the list of messages, select the message you would like to send. Then select the list that contains the users who should get this message.

10. Click on **Submit**.

11. Switch to the **Preferences** tab, and enter the **Admin Email Address** (valid e-mail address) and the **Administrator Name** (the name newsletter's sender).

12. Click on **Submit**.

13. Below the list of the jobs, click on the **Process Jobs** link, and confirm the message that you are going to send the newsletter.

14. Do not close the new window until all messages are sent out. Close the window when you see the message **You can now close this window**, as shown in the following screenshot:

Newsletter Made Simple Batch Processing Window

Processing of output queue finished

Total processing time: 32 **Seconds**

Total Emails Sent (including to admin): **2**

You can now close this window

What just happened?

You have just created a new list of users in the **Newsletter Made Simple** module. This was a public list; it means that the administrator of the website is not the only person who can add users to this list. Making the group public means that any visitor of the website, whether he is a customer or not, can subscribe himself to the list, if the subscription form is added to the website.

Then you created some test accounts. When you compose a new message for the newsletter, you can choose if the message should be sent as HTML or as plain text. If you need any special HTML formatting such as hyperlinks, lists, tables, or images, then you must compose an HTML mail. In this case, you should also compose an alternative text message that will be shown to the customers who are not able to see HTML e-mails in their mail clients. Do not use any HTML tags in the **Text Message** field, just plain text.

For HTML e-mails, you can create templates that contain your company logo and contact information, so that you do not need to add it to each message separately.

In the text message, you can use the following Smarty tags linking to your website:

♦ {$unsubscribe}: A URL that can be used to display a page for unsubscribing

♦ {$preferences}: A URL that can be used to display a user preferences page

♦ {$confirmurl}: A URL that can be used to confirm subscriptions

For these links to work, you have to choose a **Return Page** in the list of pages while composing a message. This page should contain the Smarty tag {NMS}.

You can also display the sent messages as newsletter archive on your website. Any message marked as public will be displayed in this public archive and can be read by every visitor of your website. Please read the next section to see how a public subscriber form for the newsletter can be added to the page or template.

Creating jobs means putting a message and a list of users together. You do not send messages but just create a task. This task will be started when you process the job.

 Public newsletter means that every user of your website can subscribe to the newsletter.

Template	Description
Subscribe	The subscribe form, activation e-mail sent to the subscriber to confirm his e-mail address and message displayed after subscribing on the page.
Confirm Subscribe	The confirmation e-mail sent to the subscriber after he/she has confirmed his e-mail address and message showed on the page when the e-mail is confirmed.
Unsubscribe	The unsubscribe form, subject, and text of the e-mail sent to the user after he has unsubscribed from the newsletter. Text shown on the page after the unsubscribing form is sent and the confirmation e-mail sent to the user when the unsubscribing process is finished.
User Settings	If you have more than one newsletter list that the visitor can subscribe to, then you can also offer a link where he/she can manage his subscription lists. Forms and messages needed for managing these preferences are found on this tab.
Archive Templates	If you would like to display a newsletter archive on the website, you can use the Smarty tag `{NMS action="archivelist"}` on the page. There are two templates that can be used to display an archive: **list view** and **detail view**. You can modify the templates to suit your design on this tab.

Open the **Newsletter** page and place the Smarty tag `{NMS}` into the content of the page. Edit the appearance of the forms in the admin area of the **Newsletter Made Simple** module.

You can adjust the delay between each message that is sent. Messages are grouped into batches (50 messages per batch). After each batch is sent, there is a larger delay. The delays are very important to preserve your web hosting's performance. Sending out many mails has a heavy impact on your web server. The more mails you send at once, the more critical the server performance. You can change the delay on the **Preferences** tab. Use it with care; ask your provider how many mails you are allowed to send per hour and how you can be sure that your mails will not be implied to be spam. To get even better performance, use the `sendmail` method in the module **CMSMailer**.

Displaying videos

Videos have become more and more popular on websites. Everyone can upload videos to YouTube, but only some people know that any of these videos can also be seamlessly integrated into websites. Open any video on YouTube website and look on the panel to the right of it.

There are two fields with the names **URL** and **Embed**. The first field contains the plain link to the video. The second field contains HTML code to display it.

Which field to use depends upon the place of the video on your website. If the video should be shown on every page of your website, you have to copy the HTML code from the field **Embed**, open your page template (**Layout | Templates**), and add the code at the place where the video should be shown on every page.

If the video should be shown in the page content on the single page, you have to open a page for editing in the admin console, and click on **Turn WYSIWYG on/off** below the **Content** field. Find the place in HTML source of the page where the video should be displayed, and add the code from the field **Embed** to this place. Not so comfortable, right? You can work this way if you have HTML knowledge, but what about the editors of the website who do not have any HTML knowledge?

In the WYSIWYG editor, you can activate a simple plugin that helps to implement any video without looking into the HTML source.

In the admin console, click on **Extensions | TinyMCE WYSIWYG**, and choose the **Plugins** tab. Select the plugin with the name **media**, and click **Save plugins**. Then switch to the **Profiles** tab. There are three sections:

◆ **Backend profile settings**: Settings for editors of the website

◆ **Advanced backend profile settings**: Settings for the administrator of the website

◆ **Frontend profile settings**: Settings for the usage of the WYSIWYG editor on the frontend, for example, if your visitors can add news articles to the website

The button for inserting embedded media is called **media** and can be added to any **Toolbar** of any profile depending on your individual needs. For example, to make the button available to the editor of the website and to the administrator in the first line of the toolbar, add the word **media** at the very end of the field **Toolbar 1** in both profiles, as shown in the following screenshot:

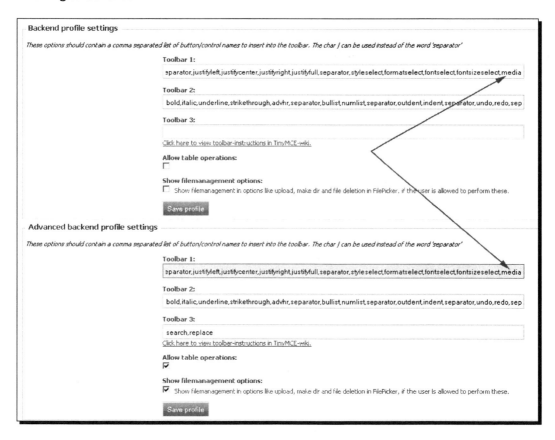

Save each profile and see the button at the end of the first line in the *TinyMCE* editor. Now you or the editor can add any video from YouTube by clicking on the button. The **Type** of the file should be **Flash**; in the **File/URL** field, copy the link from YouTube, as shown in the **URL** field:

The dimensions of the video will be set automatically. Additionally, a preview of the video is shown below. Click on **Insert**, and the video will be added to the page. Now, your editor should only know the link to the video; the rest will be done by the WYSIWYG editor.

You do not need any additional module to insert the video on the page. A lot of functionality is covered by the core CMS Made Simple. Its just waiting to be discovered!

Adding your own player

The method described in the last section would help if you uploaded your videos to YouTube first. But sometimes you would like to upload videos to your own hosting and display them, bypassing services like YouTube or Google Video.

In this case, you have to provide your own video player to be able to display any video to most visitors. If you just uploaded an AVI or MPEG video to the website, you would have to rely on your visitors having the correct browser settings to be able to play the files. Depending on the browser, the visitors may have to decide themselves what program to use to display the video. It is also important to understand that most video programs you use to create or edit your files use decoders (so called codecs). If the visitor of your website is missing the decoder, he will not be able to see the video until he has installed it. Most visitors would not install anything and just leave your website.

To serve most browsers and visitors to your website, you should convert your videos to FLV files and play them with a flash player. The only requirement that the visitor has to fulfill to see the video is the installed flash plugin—no decoders, no other special programs.

There are some free players such as **neolao** that can be found at `flv-player.net`. This video player is free and customizable, but its integration into a CMS Made Simple website can be a bit difficult. Luckily, you have another excellent third-party module that is delivered with the player neolao. The module in question is called **Play**.

After installing the module from the **Module Manager**, you will find its administration area in **Content | Multimedia Player**. The video files for the module must be uploaded with **File Manager** and should be available in the directory `uploads`. On the **Records** tab, you can then assign and group uploaded videos to display them on the website. You can display one file using **Tag to insert in your content**, as shown:

```
{Play record="1"}
```

You will find this Smarty tag beside the name of the file in the admin area of the **Play** module.

To display a list of files, you have to skip the parameter record from the above example and just use the Smarty tag `{Play}`. You can also group your videos and display only videos that are assigned to the same group as follows:

```
{Play group="myvideos"}
```

You can play only FLV files with this player. As explained, you have to convert your AVI files to FLV. If **FFmpeg** is available on your host, then you can use extra features like video conversion from AVI and also automatically created thumbnail pictures from videos. Please contact your provider to figure out if you can use FFmpeg.

You can also create and upload your own thumbnails for each video. They should be uploaded in the same folder as the video file. The name of the thumbnail file should correspond to the name of the video file prefixed by `thumb_` and ending with `.jpg`. For example, for the video file name `video.flv`, you can create and upload the thumbnail file with the name `thumb_video.jpg` to the same folder. Alternatively, you can customize the template of the neolao FLV player (**Content | Multimedia Player**, tab **Players**) or create your own customized template.

Pop quiz – using third-party modules

1. Where do you find the admin area for the **Photo Gallery**?
   a. **Content | Image Manager**
   b. **Content | Gallery**
   c. **Extensions | Modules | Photos**
   d. **Extensions | Modules | Images**

2. What extension is not allowed in the **Gallery** module?
   a. `.jpeg`
   b. `.eps`
   c. `.png`
   d. `.jpg`

3. Which module should be installed first in order to send e-mails with a form created in **Form Builder**?
   a. **Newsletter Made Simple**
   b. **CTLModuleMaker**
   c. **CMSMailer**
   d. **File Manager**

4. When you are editing your contact form, why should you set the value in the field **Send User a Copy of Submission** to **Never**?
   a. The user knows best what he/she wrote, so he/she does not need any notice about that stuff.
   b. Because e-mail submissions can run the web server to its capacity.
   c. Because this will cause an endless loop and can run your web server to its capacity.
   d. Because the user gets your e-mail address and could start a communication bypassing the feedback form.

5. What does the **Submission Template** in **Form Builder** define?
   a. The appearance of the response message after the form was sent.
   b. The appearance of the **Email Template** which is responsible for the look of the sent e-mails.
   c. The appearance of the form before submitting a message.
   d. The appearance of the personal admin area for creating the templates.

6. What is the right statement according to a group of radio buttons and a group of checkboxes?

   a. In a combined group of checkboxes and radio buttons, all alternatives can be activated.

   b. In a group of checkboxes, all alternatives can be activated, in a group of radio buttons, only one can be activated.

   c. In a group of radio buttons, all alternatives can be activated, in a group of checkboxes, only one can be activated.

   d. In a group of checkboxes, a drop-down menu has to be integrated, otherwise you cannot hear music by handling the radio buttons.

7. What is a **Job** in the **Newsletter Made Simple** module?

   a. Everything you are doing in order to send e-mails.

   b. Sending out the prepared e-mails to a mailing list.

   c. Choosing an existing message and an existing list of users that are going to get the message.

   d. Thinking about the different possibilities you have for combining mailing lists and planned messages.

Have a go hero – installing other modules

Now, if you require other features for your website, you should look at the available modules and try them out. Use each module's **Help** to figure out whether you can solve your requirements with it. Do not forget about plugins. They give you small but useful features in cases where the modules will be too much overhead.

A good website is mostly never ready, and you work on it again and again; hide unfinished parts now, and present the first version of your website online, while working on unfinished parts in the development environment.

Summary

We learned a lot in this chapter about how different modules in CMS Made Simple extend the features of your website.

In this chapter, we covered:

- **Gallery**: How to create a photo gallery and create a custom template for the gallery from scratch.

- **Form Builder**: How to create and customize forms like contact or feedback forms on the page, without any deep programming knowledge.

- **Newsletter**: How to import e-mail addresses to the user list of the module **Newsletter Made Simple** and send out messages to existing e-mail lists.

- **YouTube videos**: How to embed YouTube videos in the website. You do not need any special module to show single videos on the page. Discover the core functionality before looking for add-ons.

In this chapter, only some modules were explained. There are many more modules that have very sophisticated functionality and offer extended features for your website. Every week, new modules are developed for CMS Made Simple and updates are made to the existing ones.

In the next chapter, you will learn how to build more functionality from existing modules and even create your own functionalities from scratch.

8
Creating Your Own Functionality

CMS Made Simple has only some rudimental features that belong to the standard installation. Any additional functionality can be installed with other modules, as you have learnt from the previous chapter. However, you often need your own functionality that is not covered by any existing module.

In this chapter, we will:

- ◆ Create a product catalog with custom fields and an individual hierarchy
- ◆ Use the functionality of a module in a way that it was not developed for

So let's get started...

Creating a product catalog

In this section, we will learn how to create a new module. As an example, the product catalog will be created, but in the same way, you can create any kind of catalog such as services, courses, real estate advertisements, or freelancer directory.

Before you create your own catalog module, you should plan its structure very thoroughly. First of all, reflect on the number of levels. Write down how many levels (product categories, subcategories, and so on) you need. For my example, I will create a simple office furniture catalog. I need the following three categories to which the products can be assigned during creation:

- ◆ Desks
- ◆ Chairs
- ◆ Bookcases

This means that for the furniture catalog, a two-level structure is required, such as categories and products. Each product will belong to only one of the categories listed previously.

In the next step, you have to figure out what fields you need to create for one item (product) in your catalog. This is like making a table from your product's list. What columns do you need to separate different information? For my example, I need the following four fields:

- Product title
- Description
- Image
- Price

Now, you can start creating your own module. You are not going to use any special dedicated modules, but you will learn how to create an individual module perfectly fitted for your individual needs. This can be done with **CTLModuleMaker** module that allows the creation of any fully functional catalog-like module.

The example structure of the new product catalog is as follows:

- Desks
  - Computer desk
  - Executive desk
- Chairs
  - Executive chair
  - Guest chair
- Bookcases
  - .....

Install the **CTLModuleMaker** module from the list of available modules (**Extensions | Module Manager**). When the module is installed, its admin area can be found in the admin console (**Extensions | CTLModuleMaker**).

Creating a new catalog-like module

We will now start to create a new individual module. In the admin console, go to the admin area of **CTLModuleMaker** (**Extensions | CTLModuleMaker**), and click on the link **Create a new module**.

Step 1: Basic information about the module

The module wizard will take you through all steps needed to create a new module. In step 1 you are asked to define basic information about the new module.

Step 1 : Basic Module Informations

Enter the name of the module.
This is for internal use only. It should be alpha-numerical, without accents, spaces, or other symbols.

BWProducts

Enter a description for the module.

Manage products catalogue on the website

Enter the module's friendly name. This will be shown in the admin menus.

Products Catalogue

How many levels should there be in the module?

2

In the first field, enter the name of the module. This name will appear in the list of modules (**Extensions | Modules**). It will also be used in the Smarty tag {cms_module module="NAME_OF_MODULE"} later on. It's better to choose a unique prefix for the module name, as shown in the previous example. Do not name it just **Products** (there is a third-party module called **Products**), but **BWProducts**. BW stands for Business World in my example (sure you can use your own prefix).

 The first field is also used to generate URLs for the module items later on. For example, the detailed view of the product will display http://www. mydomain.com/nameofmodule/detail/nameofproduct/5/.

The description of the module will appear on the module **Help** in the section **What Does This Do?**

The friendly name of the module will be shown in the admin menu when the module is installed. In the previous example, the module will be installed in **Content | Products Catalogue**.

We have figured out that we need a two-level structure: categories and products. If you need more levels, then change it here. However, I recommend starting with a simple two-level structure at the beginning and then, if the principle is clear, creating one or more additional levels.

Click on **Next** and proceed with step 2.

Step 2: Creating levels

The products in the module will be assigned to different categories. Categories will help to group different products and make the navigation within the product list easier

Creating the first level (categories)

This step helps you to define categories for the new module, so that the items can be assigned to later on.

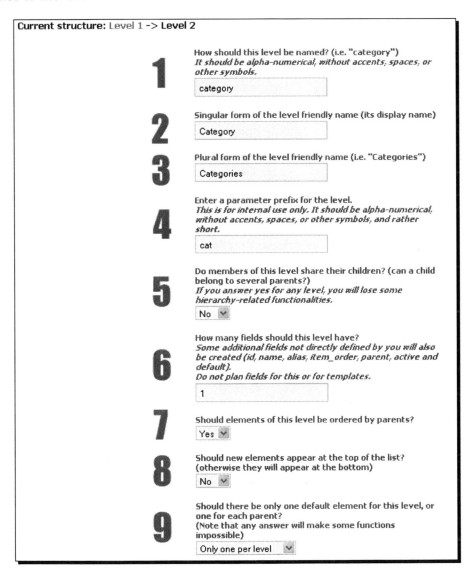

The first and the fourth fields require a technical name and a prefix for the categories. Technical names are not shown to the visitors of the website and should not contain any special characters. On the contrary, the second and the third field is user friendly and can contain special characters. These fields will be used in the admin console. For example, the plural form of the level name will appear on a tab in the admin area of the module, as shown in the following screenshot:

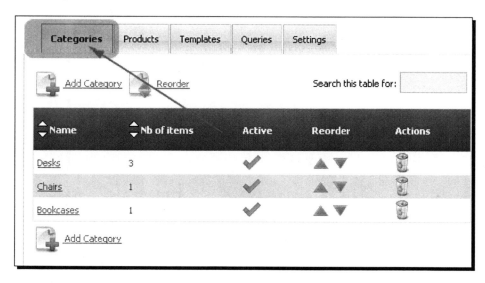

The fifth field deals with the flexibility of the hierarchy. Can a product belong to only one category or to many categories? As an example, imagine a book catalog where a book can belong to more than one category. Historical crime logically belongs to crimes and historical literature at the same time. For the furniture catalog, we do not need such flexibility. In our example, the products can only belong to one category.

In the sixth field, you enter number of fields that are required additionally to the fields automatically added to each level. You can read from the comment of the field what fields will be created. This means that we do not need any extra field for the category title as we will use the field name for it. Additionally, we need the field that stores the description of the category. Therefore, you enter **1** in this field.

The seventh field is not important for the level 1 in the catalog structure as there are no parent elements for the categories.

Where should new categories appear in the list of categories (in the admin area and on the website) by default? Note that you can always reorder the appearance of the category manually in the admin area of the module later on.

The last field is not important for level 1 and can be left as it is. Click on **Next**.

On the last screen, you defined the number of additional fields (see the sixth field in the first image under step 2) that the category should have. Now, you have to give more information about this field on the next screen, as shown in the following screenshot.

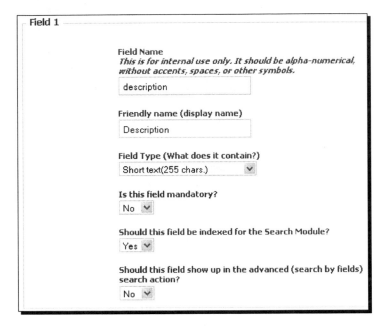

The first field contains the technical name of the field for internal use only. The second field is the friendly name which will be visible to the editors of the catalog in the admin console. Choose **Short text(255 chars.)** for the field type if you feel that 255 characters will be enough for the category description. Setting a field to be mandatory means that you won't be able to create a new category without giving it a description.

Should the content of the field be indexed in the **Search** module of CMS Made Simple? This module is a standard module and was explained in Chapter 5, *Using Core Modules*.

Every module created with **CTLModuleMaker** will get an additional advanced search function, as shown in the following screenshot:

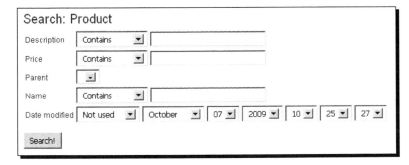

In the last field of the field definition, you can define whether or not you would like to see the field in the advanced search. In the previous example, the field is searchable and therefore displayed at the top of the search function. Click on **Next**.

In the next step, you define what fields will be displayed in the list of categories in the admin area of the future module. The field **name** is mandatory, you cannot delete it from the list, but you can add any other fields from the list of **Possible fields**. Add the field **nbchildren** to the list, as shown in the following screenshot:

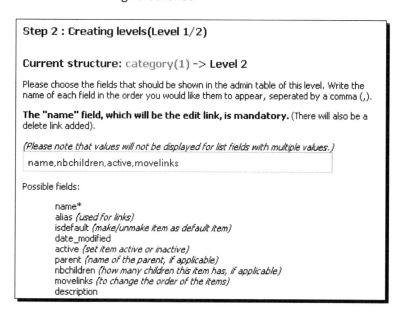

With the fields defined previously, the list of categories in the admin console of the module will look as shown in the following screenshot:

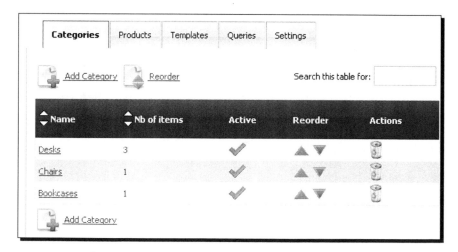

Click on **Next** and proceed with the definition of the products (level 2 in the catalog structure).

Creating the second level (products)

In the following steps, you will be asked for information about your products. You will see that the definition of each level is similar. There are the same fields as for categories where you now provide information about products.

How should this level be named? (i.e. "category")
It should be alpha-numerical, without accents, spaces, or other symbols.

product

Singular form of the level friendly name (its display name)

Product

Plural form of the level friendly name (i.e. "Categories")

Products

Enter a parameter prefix for the level.
This is for internal use only. It should be alpha-numerical, without accents, spaces, or other symbols, and rather short.

prod

How many fields should this level have?
Some additional fields not directly defined by you will also be created (id, name, alias, item_order, parent, active and default).
Do not plan fields for this or for templates.

3

Should elements of this level be ordered by parents?

No ▼

Should new elements appear at the top of the list?
(otherwise they will appear at the bottom)

No ▼

Should there be only one default element for this level, or one for each parent?
(Note that any answer will make some functions impossible)

Only one per level ▼

For the products, we need three additional fields:

   ◆ Description
   ◆ Price
   ◆ Image

The product title will be saved in the mandatory field **Name** and should not be planned here.

The seventh field, which could be ignored for the category level, gets some meaning in the second level. How the products should be displayed in the list of products, whether categorically or alphabetically, and whether they should be displayed independent of the category they are placed in or not.

By category	Alphabetically
Executive Desk	Computer Desk
Computer Desk	Executive Chair
Executive Chair	Executive Desk
Guest Chair	Guest Chair

In the last field, you can define whether there can be only one default product for the whole product list, or one default product for each category. In our example, we do not need any default products, so you can leave the field as it is.

Click on **Next**.

Similar to the definition of the additional field **description** for the category, you are now asked to define the three additional fields for the products.

The first field required for the product is **Product Description**. This field is defined in the same way the category description was defined. I have chosen the field to be **Long text** so that there is no limit to the description length of the product. The field should be searchable both ways, from the standard search field of CMS Made Simple and from the advanced search feature of the module itself.

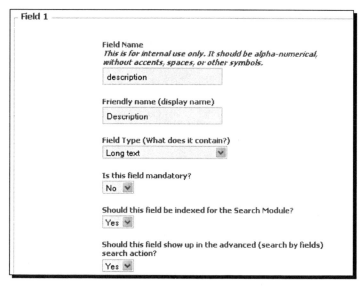

In the next field, the price of the product should be stored. The field must be defined as **Short text(10 chars.)**. If you choose **Number** in the **Field Type**, then no decimal numbers can be stored in it.

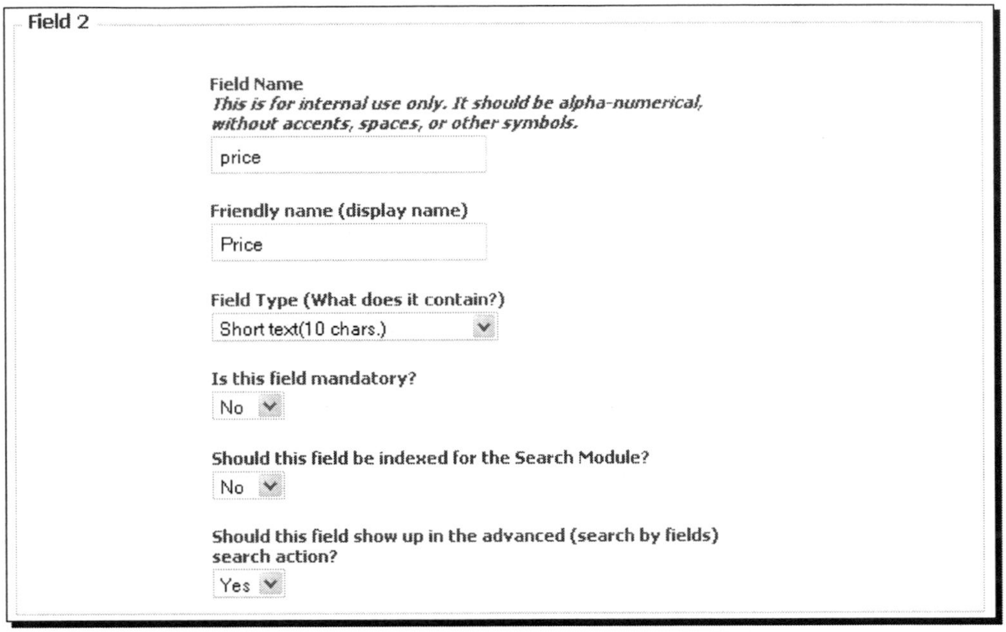

Field 2

Field Name
This is for internal use only. It should be alpha-numerical, without accents, spaces, or other symbols.

price

Friendly name (display name)

Price

Field Type (What does it contain?)

Short text(10 chars.)

Is this field mandatory?

No

Should this field be indexed for the Search Module?

No

Should this field show up in the advanced (search by fields) search action?

Yes

The third field will allow you to upload product images. Once you have changed the **Field Type** to **Image**, additional information will be displayed as shown in the next screenshot:

Field 3

Field Name
*This is for internal use only. It should be alpha-numerical,
without accents, spaces, or other symbols.*

image

Friendly name (display name)

Product Image

Field Type (What does it contain?)

Image

Is this field mandatory?

No

Should this field be indexed for the Search Module?

No

Should this field show up in the advanced (search by fields)
search action?

No

Enter the path of the folder in which the files should be
uploaded.
*This path will be added to the upload folder (empty = root
of the upload folder).*

images/catalogue

Should the uploaded images be resized to a maximum size?
*Enter the size in pixels, format "widthxheight"
(empty = images not resized).*

The resize functions require the gd librairies and will only
work with .jpeg, .jpg, .png or .gif files

500×700

Should the image be cropped when not of the resize
proportions?

No

Should a thumbnail be created, what should be its
maximum size?
*Enter the size in pixels, format "widthxheight"
(empty = no thumbnail created).*

120×120

Should the thumbnail be cropped when not of the resize
proportions?

Yes

Allowed file extensions, seperated by commas. (empty
allows gif/jpeg/jpg/png for images, and anything for other
filetype)

gif,jpeg,jpg,png

The information in the last six fields is only required for the fields where images can be uploaded.

You should enter the name of the folder where the images will be saved after upload. This folder will be created automatically below the `uploads` folder on your web hosting. You can use the `images` folder and then the custom name of the module folder. This will ensure that the images are automatically saved in the `images` folder and thus can be edited online with **Image Manager**.

In the next field, enter the maximum size of the product image to what the image will be resized if it is larger than the size given here. However, sometimes it is not possible to resize the image precisely to the size given in the field without changing the image's proportion. In this case, either width or height will be considered. If you would like to keep the exact size, then the module has to crop the image. If you crop an image, it would mean that a part of the image will be cut off. You can choose the resize method in the field below.

In the same way, you can define the size of the thumbnails. The best resize method depends on your source images and design so a general recommendation cannot be made.

In the last field, you give the extensions that are allowed for the upload. Note that only GIF, JPEG, JPG, and PNG files can be displayed as images in all browsers. Do not allow any other format so that the editors of the products will not be able to upload other files in this field.

Click on **Next**, and define what fields should be shown in the admin console for the list of products:

Current structure: category(1) -> product(2)

Please choose the fields that should be shown in the admin table of this level. Write the name of each field in the order you would like them to appear, seperated by a comma (,).

The "name" field, which will be the edit link, is mandatory. (There will also be a delete link added).

(Please note that values will not be displayed for list fields with multiple values.)

name,price,parent,active,movelinks

Possible fields:

> name*
> alias *(used for links)*
> isdefault *(make/unmake item as default item)*
> date_modified
> active *(set item active or inactive)*
> parent *(name of the parent, if applicable)*
> nbchildren *(how many children this item has, if applicable)*
> movelinks *(to change the order of the items)*
> description
> price
> image

If you defined the fields as shown in the preceding screenshot, your admin console will look as shown in the following screenshot when the module is in use.

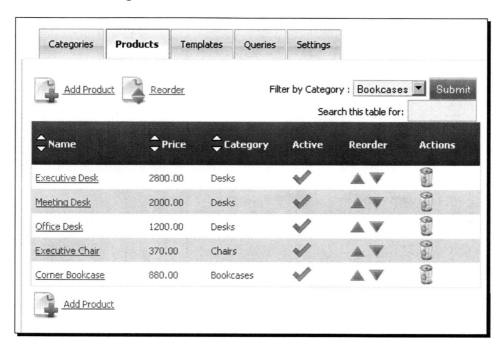

Click on **Next** and answer the final questions before the module is created.

Step 3: Finishing creation and module installation

To display a list of categories or products on your website, the editor of the product catalog will have the possibility to choose between different templates. The question here is about the template for the product detail view.

We have three different categories. If products of the category **Desk** must be displayed in a different way than products of the category **Chairs**, then you need category as a template level. This means that each category must have its own template for the product display. If the template for the product doesn't depend on its category, then leave the value **Only one template** in this field.

Step 3 : Final step (last element before the creation of files...)

What level should determine the template for the final item (final child)?
In addition, there will be for each level a template for the list of it's members. | Only one template ▼ |

Click on **Next**. You have reached the last step and are close to the finish and installation of the new module.

Leave the values in the last step as they are. They deal with file fields (we do not have any), languages (we learn more about translations in Chapter 10, *Advanced Use of CMS Made Simple*), and the module version. The module version is used for revision control and is used to manage changes made to the module afterwards. For example, an initial configuration of the module gets the version 1.0. When the first change to the module is made, the resulting configuration will be marked as version 2.0, and so on. We do not allow visitors to the website to add products, so leave the **Frontend User Management** set to **No** as well.

Click on **Next**. The **CTLModuleMaker** module starts to create all required folders and files. Click on the **Install module** link, and the new custom module will be installed. You can now find it in the admin console **Content | Products Catalogue**.

Additionally, the module can be found in, removed, and installed from the list of modules in **Module Manager** (**Extensions | Modules**).

Configuring the new Products Catalogue module

Add some categories and some products in the admin area of the new module.

Then, open the page **Products** (**Content | Pages**), and add the following Smarty tag to call your module:

```
{cms_module module="bwproducts"}
```

Replace the name in the parameter module by the name of your module. This name can be found in the list of installed modules (**Extensions | Modules**). Open the page, and see the list of products on the page.

The new module also has a **Module Help** section where all parameters that you can use with this module are listed. The help section can be accessed from the **Module Help** icon placed in the module admin area at the top-right of the page.

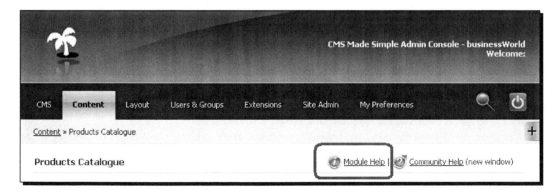

For more help, you may take a look at the FAQ. The link to the FAQ can be found in the module help above the **Copyright and License** section.

Creating the product list template

For modules created with **CTLModuleMaker**, some sample templates are created automatically. However, for each level, you can create an unlimited number of templates by yourself.

Time for action – creating a new list template

Let's customize the appearance of the product list and add products' images as thumbnails to this list.

1. In the admin console, click on **Content | Products Catalogue**, and choose the **Templates** tab.

2. Below the section **Default Templates**, you will find a list of sample templates. Click on the **Add template** link.

3. For the product list with thumbnails, enter the following code snippet in the **Template** field:

```
{if $itemcount > 0}
  <ul>
    {foreach from=$itemlist item="item"}
      <li style="list-style-type:none; float:left;
        margin: 20px;"><a href="{$item->detailurl}">
        <img src="uploads/{$item->image->thumbnail}"
        alt="{$item->name}" /></a>
      <br/>
      {$item->detaillink}<br/>{$item->price} USD</li>
    {/foreach}
  </ul>
{/if}
```

4. Click on **Submit**.

5. In the **Default templates** section, choose the template you just created to be the **Default list template for level "product"**. The list of products should look as shown in the following screenshot:

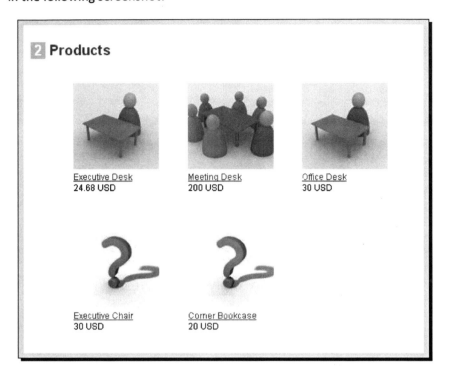

What just happened?

You have created a new template for the list of the products. This template shows not only the products' name but also the small version of the products' image. The small version of the image is represented as Smarty variable `{$item->image->thumbnail}` in the template. All Smarty variables that you can use in the template can be found on the tab **Template variables (Content | Products Catalogue | Templates)** when the template is open for edit. Consider that the fields containing images have even more variables. They are explained in the FAQ for the module in the section titled *How can I retrieve images in the display templates?*

 The inline CSS added to the template is not the proper way to implement styles. It has been made to simplify the example. You should create a new CSS class and store the style definitions in the main stylesheet.

In the same way, you can modify or create a new template for the **Default detail template** that is used to display the detailed view of one product.

With the **CTLModuleMaker** module, you can create any kind of catalog such as products, services, real estate advertisements, courses, and more. Everything that you can categorize can be put in a custom catalog-like module. Remember, that you create an ordinary module that can be removed from the list of modules, exported as XML, and imported into another installation.

Implementing service desk functionality

There are over 300 third-party modules in CMS Made Simple, and this number grows weekly. Some modules do not work as expected, as there is no quality assurance for the third-party modules. However, sometimes you do not need to use a dedicated module to solve your requirements. With some creativity you can divert modules from its intended use to create your own functionality.

There is no sophisticated module for the service desk in CMS Made Simple. However, if you need it to handle support tickets, then you can use the module **CGFeedback**; which was originally created to handle comments for the pages or news articles. Although this module has not been developed to handle support tickets, it can be used to solve the required features with some advanced customization.

Managing visitors' logins

Before you set up the service desk feature on your website, you have to install the module **FrontEndUsers**. The **FrontEndUsers** module is a kind of membership management facility for your website. In our case, members are the customers who can authorize with their access data on the website and the protected content or communicate with you through their personal member area.

Generally, **FrontEndUsers** can be integrated with many other modules such as:

- **News** (Registered visitors can add news to the website)
- **DownloadManager** (Registered visitors can download protected files from the website)
- **Forum** (Registered users can communicate on the boards)
- **NMS** (Mass mail for registered users)

 Website members are not the same as the admin users of your website, which were described in Chapter 6, *Users and Permissions*. They have nothing to do with your admin console (hopefully!).

The module **FrontEndUsers** has a dependency on the module **CMSMailer**. It means that you have to configure e-mail settings, as described in Chapter 2, *Getting Started,* before installing member management on the website. Otherwise, features like sending out forgotten passwords will not work.

To install the module in the admin console, click on **Extensions | Module Manager**, and choose the letter **F** from the **Available modules** tab above the alphabetical module list. Find the **FrontEndUsers** module, and click the **Download & Install** link. The module will be installed and can now be configured.

Open the page **Service Desk** (**Content | Pages**), and add the login form into the **Content** field of the page, shown as follows:

```
{cms_module module="FrontendUsers"}
```

Now, you can see the login form on the page. Let's create a first customer account and log in to the page so that you can test the functionality of the module.

Time for action – creating the first user account

We are going to add the first customer account to the website.

1. In the admin console, click on **Users & Groups |Frontend User Management**.

2. Click on the **User Properties** tab.

3. Click the **Add Property** link and fill in the form, as shown in the following screenshot:

4. Click on **Submit**.

5. Open the **Groups** tab, and click on the **Add Group** link.

6. Fill in the fields, and assign the e-mail field created above to the group, as shown in the following screenshot:

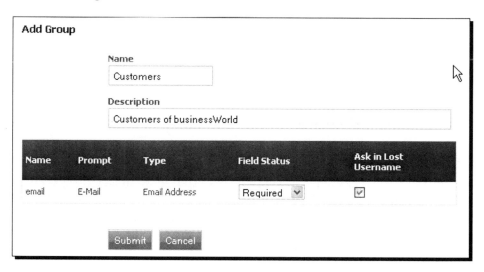

7. Click on **Submit**.

8. Click on the **Users** tab and then on the **Add User** link.

9. Fill in the fields, as shown in the following screenshot (provide a valid e-mail address!), and assign the user to the **Customers** group:

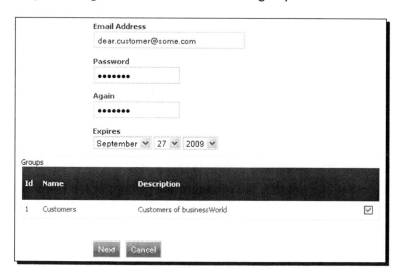

10. Click on **Next**, and enter the e-mail address of the customer again.

11. Click on **Submit**.

12. Log in with the customer data (**Username** = **Email Address** of the customer) on the page **Service Desk** to see how it works. If you are logged in, the page should look as shown in the following screenshot:

Welcome dear.customer@some.com

Sign out

Change My Settings

What just happened?

You have created the first customer account. You have started by adding the user property (a field that contains a customer's e-mail address). This field will be used for sending e-mails such as if the customer forgets his password. By default, this field is also used as the username (you can change it later on). The **Type** of the field must be set to **Email Address**, so that anything entered in this field must be a valid e-mail. You do not need to define user properties such as **username** or **password**. These two properties are already provided for you and cannot be changed or deleted.

 Never use any special characters like dashes in the field **Name** while adding user properties!

You have already created a new user group (**Customers** in our example). The e-mail field has been assigned to the group **Customers** as a required field (**Field Status**), which means that each customer must have a valid e-mail address.

At this point, you have configured the module so that the first customer could be added. All customer accounts have their expiration date, so they are disabled automatically if the date is in the past. The new user has been assigned to the **Customer** group and is now shown in the list of users on the **Users** tab (**Users & Groups | Frontend User Management**).

Useful settings for module FrontEndUsers

As the administrator of the website, you can adjust the settings of the **FrontEndUsers** module. In the admin console of your website, click on **Users & Groups| Frontend User Management**, and select the **Preferences** tab. The following settings should be made:

- ◆ **Email address is username**: Deselect this if the username should be different from the e-mail address. It is better not to use the e-mail address as the username, so the customer can change his username and e-mail address separately.

- ◆ **Allow users to login more than once**: This should be selected. If the user is currently logged in to your website and the session expires in the browser but not on the server, then the user will not be able to log in again. By selecting this box, you allow your customers to log in at any time, even if their session is still open.

- ◆ **Allow duplicate "forgot password" reminders?**: I recommend selecting this as well. Otherwise, if the e-mail with the new password does not reach the user because of mail delivery failure, he will not be able to get a new e-mail.

- ◆ **Use cookies to remember login details**: Select the box if you would like the member to remember his passwords for the website and be automatically logged in each time he visits your website. If you select this box, then you should also fill **The name of the cookie**. Use only English letters and no special characters for the cookie name. This feature requires the PHP function `mcrypt` to be installed on your web hosting. If you see the notice **This uses the mcrypt functions for encryption purposes, and they could not be detected on your install. Please contact your server administrator** below the field, then this feature will not work. You must enable or install the PHP function `mcrypt` on your web hosting first, then contact your provider to get further information.

Save the settings, and add another customer to see how the above settings affect the behavior of the module.

Templates for the FrontEndUsers module

Six templates can be fully customized to suit your design and layout requirements.

Template	Description
Login Template	The default template if the user is NOT logged in.
Logout Template	The default template if the user is logged in.
Change Settings Template	If the user is logged in, then a link **Change My Settings** is shown. Customize this template to change the settings area of the customer.
Forgot Password Templates	If the user is not logged in, there is a link **Forgot Your Password?**. Customize this template to change the form for password recovery.
Lost Username Template	If the user is not logged in, a link **Forgot Your Login Details?** is shown. Customize this template to change the form for the username recovery.
View User Template	This template is used to show user details on the website.

You can find all the templates listed in the table in the admin console (**Users & Groups | Frontend User Management**) on the corresponding tabs. **Forgot Password Templates** and **Lost Username Templates** include verification forms as well.

To see the verification form for **Forgot Password**, click on the link **Forgot Your Password?** below the login form on the website, enter the **Username**, and click on **Submit**. Check incoming mails for the subject **Lost Password** sent out from your website. If you do not get an e-mail (has your customer entered a real e-mail?), then you have to check the configuration of the **CMSMailer** module, as explained in Chapter 2, *Getting Started*.

The text of e-mail messages sent by the **FrontEndUsers** module cannot be changed in the admin area of the module. These messages are stored in the language files and can be edited with **Translation Manager**, which will be explained in Chapter 10, *Advanced Use of CMS Made Simple*.

Creating protected pages

Protected pages can be viewed only by registered members, and as you have already installed the **FrontEndUsers** module, you can continue with creating protected pages.

To protect content pages, you have to install the module called **CustomContent**. The module **CustomContent**, in conjunction with the module **FrontEndUsers**, allows creating protected pages that will be accessible only by logged users. Open **Extensions | Module Manager**, and click on the tab for available modules with the letter **C**, search for the module **CustomContent**, and click on the link **Download & Install**. The module is installed. This module does not have any admin area. Nevertheless, you can access the module help from the list of installed modules (**Extensions | Modules**) by clicking on the module name.

You will find an example in the **How Do I Use It** section, that we are going to alternate for our purpose. The smarty IF condition checks if the user is logged or not and displays different content depending on it.

```
{if $customcontent_loggedin > 0}
  Welcome <b>{$customcontent_loginname}</b><br/>
{else}
  <h1>You are not authorized to view this data</h1>
{/if}
```

If the Smarty variable `$customcontent_loggedin` is greater than 0, then the user is authorized to see the content, otherwise a message that the user is not authorized is displayed. We are going to protect the **Service Desk** page. If the user is not logged in, then no content should be shown on the page except the login form.

Time for action – protecting the service desk

Now, let us protect the **Service Desk** page so that its main content can only be viewed by registered members. If the user is not logged in, only the login form should be shown.

1. In the admin console, open the **Service Desk** page for editing (**Content | Pages**).

2. Click on the **Options** tab, and mark the page to be not cachable and not searchable, as shown in the following screenshot:

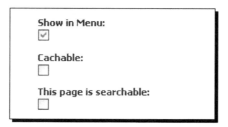

3. Switch to the **Main** tab, and fill in the content field, as shown in the following screenshot:

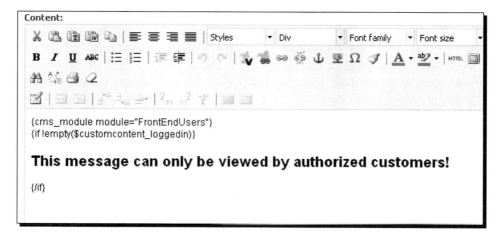

4. Click on **Apply**.

5. View the page as a logged in user as well as a logged out user.

What just happened?

You have protected a part of the page content from being viewed by an unauthorized user. You have set the page as not cachable first. It is important to do it with every page that should be protected or every page that contains the login form. Cached pages would also cache the login status of the user and show him as logged in even if he is logged out.

The page should not be searchable as it would not make sense to show it in the search results to the non-authorized users.

In the **Content** field, the login form (if the user is not logged in) or logout form (if the user is logged in) is displayed. The form will automatically change depending on the user's status. Everything passed between the smarty tags IF is only shown to the logged in users.

In this way, you can protect every page or only a part of the content depending on whether the user is authorized or not.

Creating user area for support requests

A support ticket system is an area where your customers can place their questions about your products or services. This area is private and cannot be seen by website visitors or other customers. When the question is placed in the support ticket area, the support staff can give the customer an answer to it. If the issue is not resolved by an answer, the customer can respond to the answer and the staff answers again. This dialog (questions and answers) is organized as one ticket. If the customer has another question, then he can open another ticket. In the private service desk, the customer can always see the list of his tickets and read the answers given from the staff. A support ticket system is often used in the professional customer care.

To create a support ticket system, you do not need a special support ticket module. Let us see how you can use the feedback module to create service desk functionality. The name of the module in question is **CGFeedback**. This module is developed to allow website visitors to provide comments on individual pages, news articles, products, or other items on your website. We will use the functionality of this module to create a rudimentary support ticket system.

In the admin console, click on **Extensions | Module Manager**, and search on the **Available Modules** tab for the module **CGFeedback**. Click on the **Dependencies** link to figure out what modules should be installed first. You will see the following modules:

- **CGExtensions**
- **CGSimpleSmarty**

Install these modules first, and then install the **CGFeedback** module. The simplest way to use the module is to include the following Smarty tag at the bottom of any page content:

```
{CGFeedback}
```

This will create a comment form and allows visitors to enter comments and ratings about that particular page. To display those comments, you would add another tag below the preceding tag:

```
{CGFeedback action="summary"}
```

These tags can be optionally placed in page templates or in module templates. If nothing else is defined, then the comments are automatically attached to the page where they have been made. If you would like to allow comments on module items like news articles, you should use two additional parameters:

```
{CGFeedback key1="News" key2=$entry->id}
```

There are two parameters, key1 and key2. Each parameter can be filled with different values. In the preceding example, the parameter key1 is filled with the value **News** so that ordinary page comments can be differed from the comments on news article. The second key saves the number ($id) of the news article to be sure that a comment is only shown on the page with this particular news item displayed in detailed view.

When comments are added, they are saved in the database with the values given in both parameters (key1 and key2) like "comment for the news article with particular ID". Why should we not use this functionality to manage comments that are attached to one particular logged user? The first parameter, key1, will separate page comments from tickets. From Chapter 4, *Design and Layout*, we know that there are some Smarty variables that exist in every page. One of those variables is provided by the module **FrontEndUsers** and is called $userid. This variable exists only if the user is logged in and contains the user ID. By placing the following two lines into the page content, you say "save and display comments for the particular logged in user":

```
{CGFeedback key1="Ticket" key2=$userid}
{CGFeedback key1="Ticket" key2=$userid action="summary"}
```

These two lines would show the comment form and the summary view of all comments written by one user. When the user is not logged in, he cannot see the comments, as the variable $userid does not exist for users not logged in. Another user would not see these comments as well, as he has another user ID. Test it by placing these two Smarty tags into the page **Service Desk**. As there is a login form on the page, the complete content should look similar to the following screenshot:

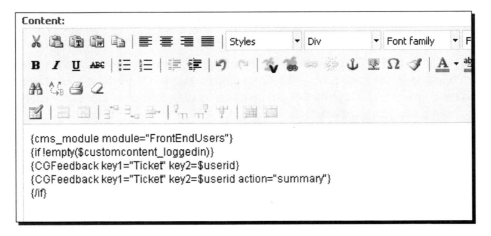

A logged in user can now create comments or, let's say, support tickets, which can only be viewed by himself on the page or by the support staff in the admin console of CMS Made Simple. You can fully customize the template with the comment form, as shown in the following screenshot:

You can delete or replace the legend **Add a Review**. Remove the **Notify me of new comments to this page** checkbox, and rename the field **Additional Comments** field to **Your question** or **Your request**.

To create a new **Comment Form Templates** in the admin console, click on **Content | Calguys Feedback Module**. Select the **Comment Form Templates** tab, and click on **New Template**. Enter **NewTicket** as the **Template Name** and the following code snippet in the **Template Text** field:

```
{if isset($message)}
  <p class="success">{$message}</p>
{else}
  {if isset($error)}
    <p class="error">{$error}</p>
  {/if}
{$formstart}

  <p><label>Title:</label>
  <input type="text" name="{$actionid}title" value="{$title}"/></p>

  <p><label>Your name:</label>
  <input type="text" name="{$actionid}author_name"
  value="{$author_name}"/></p>

  <p><label>Your e-mail:</label>
  <input type="text" name="{$actionid}author_email"
  value="{$author_email}"/></p>

  <p><label>Question:</label>
  <textarea name="{$actionid}comment" cols="40"
  rows="5">{$comment}</textarea></p>

  <p><input type="submit" name="{$actionid}submit" value="Send"/></p>

{$formend}
{/if}
```

Click on **Submit**. Open the page **Service Desk** (**Content | Pages**), and modify the Smarty tag of the comment form as shown in the following code snippet:

```
{cms_module module="FrontEndUsers"}
{if !empty($customcontent_loggedin)}
{CGFeedback key1="Ticket" key2=$userid commenttemplate="NewTicket"
policy="session"}
{CGFeedback key1="Ticket" key2=$userid action="summary"}
{/if}
```

Now, the comment form is displayed with the template **NewTicket**. Additionally, the form is redirected to the same page after the question has been submitted due to the parameter `policy`.

To test the module, create some new tickets with two different customers to see how exactly they are separated, depending on which customer is currently logged in. We will customize templates for summary and detail view later on.

Now, let's see how we can implement the possibility of answering the tickets from the admin console by the support staff.

Adding answer fields to the tickets

We are now going to create two custom fields in the module **CGFeedback**. The first one will contain the name of the support staff answering the ticket. The second field will contain the answer.

Time for action – creating new fields

Support staff should be able to answer to the support tickets and store their names to each answer as well. Let's create the new fields that will contain this information.

1. In the admin console, click on **Content | Calguys Feedback Module**, and select the **Fields** tab.

2. Click on **Add a new field**, which contains the names of the support staff as shown in the following screenshot:

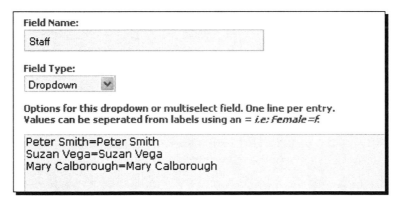

3. Click on **Submit**.

4. Then, add another field that will contain the answer text from the support staff, as shown in the following screenshot:

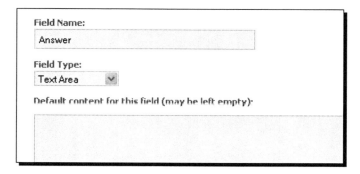

5. Click on **Submit**.

6. In the admin console, open an existing ticket (**Content | Calguys Feedback Module**) for edit and find both custom fields at the edit screen.

What just happened?

You have added two custom fields. From now you can enter an answer to the ticket in the admin console as if you were a support staff. The answer will appear on the website when the detail view template is customized properly. This will be described later in this chapter.

Templates for ticket list and ticket detail view

Before customizing a detail view, let's create a new summary template. The summary view is used below the ticket submission form to show a list of all tickets submitted by one customer on the page **Service Desk**. The title of each ticket is linked with the detailed view of the ticket, where the answer from the staff is shown.

Time for action – customizing list of tickets

The appearance of the list of tickets created by the customer and shown to him should be changed to meet our needs.

1. In the admin console, click on **Content | Calguys Feedback Module**, and choose the **Summary Templates** tab.

2. Click on **New Template**, and enter **TicketList** as the **Template Name**.

3. Add the following code into the **Template text** field:

```
{if isset($comments)}
  {foreach from=$comments item="one"}
    <p><strong>Ticket No {$one.id}: <a href="{$one.detail_url}"
      title="{$one.title}">{$one.title}</a></strong><br/>
      <small>{$one.created|date_format:"%a %d %b %H:%M"} |
       <a href="mailto{$one.author_email}">{$one.author_name}</a>
      </small>
    </p>
    <div class="feedback_item_data">
      {$one.data}
    </div>
  {/foreach}
{/if}
```

4. Click on **Submit**.

5. To use this template for the list of tickets, open the page **Service Desk (Content | Pages)**, and modify the Smarty tag for the summary view of tickets, as shown in the following code snippet:

```
{cms_module module="FrontEndUsers"}
{if !empty($customcontent_loggedin)}
  {CGFeedback key1="Ticket" key2=$userid commenttemplate=
    "NewTicket"
  policy="session"}
  {CGFeedback key1="Ticket" key2=$userid summarytemplate=
    "TicketList"
  action="summary"}
{/if}
```

6. Click on **Submit**.

7. The template displays a list of all tickets with their number, title, and content, as shown in the following screenshot:

Ticket No 16: Custom service
Mo 28 Sep 21:34 | Max Mustermann

It there any service located in my area? I could not find any partner on your website.

Ticket No 13: Product instruction in other languages?
Mo 28 Sep 20:15 | Max Mustermann

I need a product instruction in Russian and German. Can you provide me with translations? Thank you.

What just happened?

You have created a new template for the list of tickets in the customer area. To keep the example clean, I have removed the page navigation from the summary template, but you can copy it back from the **Sample** template if you like.

In the next step, change the detail template for the ticket detail view. In the admin console, click on **Content | Calguys Feedback Module**, and choose the **Detail Templates** tab. Click on **New Template**, and enter **TicketDetail** in the **Template Name** field. In the **Template Text** field, enter the code suggested as follows:

```
<h3>Ticket No. {$onecomment.id}: {$onecomment.title}</h3>
<p>{$onecomment.created|date_format:"%a %d %b %H:%M"} |
  <a href="mailto:{$onecomment.author_email}">
    {$onecomment.author_name}
  </a></p>
  <div class="feedback_item_data">
    {$onecomment.data}
  </div>
{if isset($onecomment.fields)}
   {foreach from=$onecomment.fields key="name" item="field"}
   {assign var=$name value=$field.value}
  {/foreach}
  {if !empty($Answer)}
     <p><strong>Staff Answer</strong><br/>
  <small>{$onecomment.modified|date_format:"%a %d %b %H:%M"} |
    {$Staff}</small></p>
  <div>
    {$Answer}
  </div>
  {/if}
{/if}
```

Click on **Submit**. To use the created template for displaying tickets with staff answers, you have to set the template as default. Open the list of detail templates (**Content | Calguys Feedback Module**, **Detail templates** tab) and click the icon with a red cross in the **Default** column to use the template **TicketDetail** by default.

This template will display the customer's question and the answer of the staff (if any) in the detailed view of the ticket, as shown in the following screenshot:

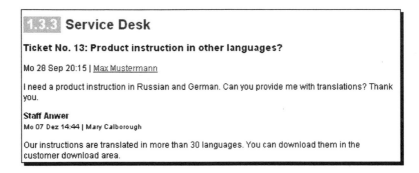

Enabling dialog within tickets

At this point, the customer can submit his question and wait for the response from the staff. But what happens if the ticket is answered and the customer would like to reply to this answer? There is no possibility of doing it at this point. However, this feature can be easily added as well.

What we need is another comment form placed in the detailed view of the ticket. It is usually possible to place Smarty tags in the module templates as well, so that the detail template for the ticket calls another form template of the same module and another summary template.

Edit the template **TicketDetail** to add another comment form and another summary list to it at the very bottom of the template.

```
{CGFeedback key1="Dialogue" key2=$userid key3=$onecomment.id
action="summary" sortorder="ASC"}
<hr/>
{CGFeedback key1="Dialogue" key2=$userid key3=$onecomment.id
policy="session"}
```

Save the template, and see the detail view of the ticket on the page. Now the customer can reply to answers given by the support staff or just add some more information missed in his question.

This dialog form has three keys: `key1`, `key2`, and `key3`. The first key separates tickets (1. level) from the dialog within the ticket, the second key still tracks the user ID, and the third key has got a reference to the ticket. In this way, you say "save the comment **as an answer** from the particular customer to the particular ticket".

To give a finishing touch, create a template for the dialog form and a template for the dialog summary view. The dialog form does not need any special title as it will get the title of the ticket and gets **Re:** as prefix for the ticket title. It will also be prefilled with the values from the ticket. Create a new comment form template, and add the following code snippet into it:

```
{if isset($message)}
  <p class="info">{$message}</p>
{else}
  {if isset($error)}
  <p class="error">{$error}</p>
  {/if}
  {$formstart}
  <input type="hidden" name="{$actionid}title" value="Re:
  {$onecomment.title}"/>
    </p>
  <p><label>{$mod->Lang('prompt_your_name')}:</label>
    <input type="text" name="{$actionid}author_name"
      value="{$onecomment.author_name}"/>
  </p>
  <p><label>{$mod->Lang('prompt_your_email')}:</label>
    <input type="text" name="{$actionid}author_email"
                value="{$onecomment.author_email}"/>
  </p>
  <p><label>Question:</label>
    <textarea name="{$actionid}comment" cols="40"
            rows="5">{$comment}</textarea></p>
  <p><input type="submit" name="{$actionid}submit" value="{$mod
>Lang('submit')}"/>
  </p>
  {$formend}
{/if}
```

Save the template with the name **TicketDialogue**. In the detail view of the ticket (template **TicketDetail**), adjust the Smarty tag at the bottom to use the new form template as shown in the following code snippet:

```
{CGFeedback key1="Dialogue" key2=$userid key3=$onecomment.id
action="summary" sortorder="ASC"}
<hr/>
{CGFeedback key1="Dialogue" key2=$userid key3=$onecomment.id
policy="session" commenttemplate="TicketDialogue"}
```

With the last step, you show answers from the staff to the customer, so that the entire conversation within the ticket is displayed. Create a new summary template (**Content | Calguys Feedback Module**, tab **Summary Templates**) with the following code snippet:

```
{if isset($comments)}
  {foreach from=$comments item='one'}
  <p><strong>{$one.title}</strong><br/>
    <small>{$one.created|date_format:"%a %d %b %H:%M"} | <a
        href="mailto:{$one.author_email}">{$one.author_name}</a>
  </small>
  </p>
  <div class="feedback_item_data">
    {$one.data}
  </div>
  {if isset($one.fields)}
    {foreach from=$one.fields key='name' item='field'}
      {assign var=$name value=$field.value}
    {/foreach}
    {if !empty($Answer)}
      <p><strong>Staff Answer</strong><br/>
        <small>{$one.modified|date_format:"%a %d %b %H:%M"} |
            {$Staff}</small>
      </p>
    <div>
      {$Answer}
    </div>
    {/if}
  {/if}
  {/foreach}
{/if}
```

Save the template with the name **DialogueList**. In the detail view of the ticket (template **TicketDetail**), adjust the Smarty tag at the bottom to use the new summary template as shown in the following code snippet:

```
{CGFeedback key1="Dialogue" key2=$userid key3=$onecomment.id
action="summary" sortorder="ASC" summarytemplate="DialogueList"}
<hr/>
{CGFeedback key1="Dialogue" key2=$userid key3=$onecomment.id
policy="session" commenttemplate="TicketDialogue"}
```

Now, the basic service desk functionality is complete. The customer can submit his questions in his private area, the questions can be answered by the support team from the admin console of CMS Made Simple, and the customer can reply to the answers.

Use the functionality for the **Admin Notifications** already implemented in the module, so that the support staff are informed if a new ticket is opened or a new reply is added.

In the admin area of the module **Calguys Feedback Module** (tab **Fields**), you can create a new custom field that allows one of the following values: **Opened, Waiting for Response,** or **Closed**. Use the field type **Dropdown** to define it. This field can be set by the support staff while working on the ticket and shown in the summary view of the tickets, so that the customer can see what the current status of the ticket is.

You have seen how you can use the module that is not dedicated for creating a service desk to set up the required features. Be open-minded and experiment with the modules. Even if their description is not exactly what you need, you can use it in your way, as shown in this section.

Pop quiz – creating your own functionality

1. Why should the **Allow users to login more than once** box be selected when setting preferences in the **FrontEndUsers** module?

    a. When the user is currently logged in and the session expires in the browser and not on the server, the user would not be able to log in again.

    b. You should give users with a dual personality a chance to log in at least twice at the same time.

    c. A lot of users are working on different computers (private, office, and so on), so they can log in from more than one computer.

    d. When this box is not checked, it is not possible to generate a new password (or regenerate the username) when the user once forgets it.

2. What is the right statement according to the following Smarty tags used in protected pages?

    ```
    {CGFeedback key1="Ticket" key2=$userid}
    {CGFeedback key1="Ticket" key2=$userid action="summary"}
    ```

    a. These tags show the summary view of all comments written by all registered users.

    b. These tags show the comment form and the summary view of all comments written by one user.

    c. These tags show the summary view of all comments written by all users, who are currently visiting the website.

    d. These tags show the comment form and the summary view of all summaries of professional books written by all users having the same ID.

3. What is the advantage of using a support ticket system?

   a. The website will get more visitors because of the fact that ticket systems are modern and the users are projecting this fact to your whole site.

   b. The user can have a non public discussion with the service staff concerning his/her needs and problems.

   c. The user gets tickets for the champion league for a special price.

   d. The user can have a public discussion in the forum concerning his needs and problems.

Have a go hero – creating your own functionality

Before you say that there is no module that can cover my requirements and start to develop one, try to figure out if your requirements can be solved with on-board means. A lot of modules are just categorized catalogs of something, so they can be created with help of the module **CTLModuleMaker**. And, as you have seen, try to see your requirements more abstractly and reflect on using other modules to solve your functionality before starting to develop from scratch.

Summary

We learned a lot in this chapter about implementing our own functionality not covered by any ready-made module of CMS Made Simple.

Specifically, we covered:

◆ **Module Maker**: Creating some entirely new custom modules with catalog-like content.

◆ **Custom Area**: Enabling the login functionality on the website and creating rudimentary service desk functionality with the feedback module.

Now that we've learned about how to create our own functionality, you can follow a workshop on how to realize basic e-commerce solution with CMS Made Simple. If you do not need any e-commerce functionality, you are now ready to place your website online because by this time, your website is fully functional.

9
E-commerce Workshop

CMS Made Simple is, as its name suggests, a content management system. In a CMS, data can be defined as almost anything—documents, movies, pictures, phone numbers, scientific data, and so on. CMS is generally used for storing, controlling, revising, and publishing content. They are not explicitly designed for e-commerce or community needs. For sophisticated online shops without any content management features, it is better to get a dedicated e-commerce application. The same applies to the typical community features like forum or chat.

*However, if your website is heterogenic, then it is not just a content management system and has a mix of various features. You can use additional modules for basic functionality of other applications. In CMS Made Simple, there are some community modules such as **Forum Made Simple (FMS)** and **Shootbox Made Simple**, and a number of modules that cover basic e-commerce features.*

*A number of additional e-commerce modules for CMS Made Simple can be confusing at the beginning. Actually, there are different solutions such as e-commerce suite, **Shop Made Simple (SMS)**, and the **Cataloger**. These different solutions are not compatible with each other in any way and cannot be used together on one website.*

In this chapter, you will learn about a solution made of nine modules that offers the widest functionality. This suite can be enriched by a number of additional modules to get even more features. Often users of CMS Made Simple wonder why there are so many modules that are required to get a basic online shop. It is a philosophy of CMS Made Simple to act like a Lego system, where you can build your required solution without installing a big package having a bunch of features that you will never use.

This solution is made of nine modules that are listed as follows:

- **CGExtensions**
- **CGSimpleSmarty**
- **Products**
- **Cart**
- **FrontEndUsers**
- **SelfRegistration** (optional)
- **CGPaymentGatewayBase**
- **Orders**
- **PaypalGateway** (optional)

Two of them are optional. The **SelfRegistration** module will allow your buyers to register with the website during the checkout process. The last module, **PaypalGateway**, should be installed if you use **PayPal** service to instantly collect payment from the website. For this workshop, I will use products from the official CMS Made Simple shop that can be found at `http://www.cafepress.co.uk/cmsmadesimple`. I also assume that you already know how to install modules and customize module templates with HTML, CSS, and Smarty.

Module Products

The **Products** module will be the heart of your e-commerce solution . This module is the place where products that you would like to sell in your shop are saved. Generally, it is possible to use any other module for the solution, but this would imply that you have to make some heavy modifications to your templates and, probably, the PHP code of the modules.

With the **Products** module, you can manage:

- Products
- Product attributes that will have an impact on the price (like size or color)
- Categories
- Product hierarchy
- Custom fields

This module is the basis for all other modules that you will use later on. After all, you cannot start a shop if you do not have any place to store the products.

Install the **Products** module with the **Module Manager**. Pay attention to the **Dependencies** section of the module before installing it. There are two (**CGExtensions** and **CGSimpleSmarty**) modules that provide convenience APIs, reusable forms, and Smarty tags for use in other modules. If you are not a programmer, you probably will not need to do anything with these modules besides adjusting some preferences if you ever need them. In the workshop described here, you just need to install them.

Time for action – adding the first product

After the **Products** module is installed, we will display it on the page **Shop** and add the first product to it as follows:

1. Create a new content page **Shop** (**Content | Pages | Add New Content**).

2. Add the Smarty tag {Products} into the field **Content** of the page. If you see the page in browser, it will not show anything at this time as you have not added any product to the shop so far.

3. In the admin console of CMS Made Simple, click on **Content | Product Manager**.

4. Under the **Products** tab, click on the **Add A Product** link and add your product as shown in the following screenshot:

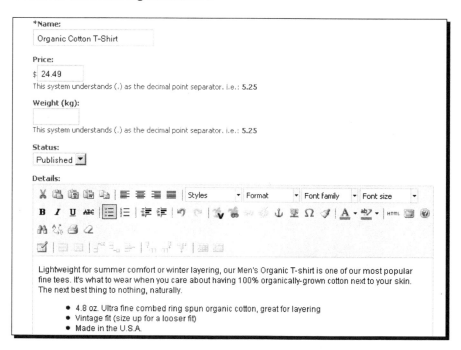

5. Click on **Submit** and see the **Shop** page on your website.

What just happened?

You have added the first product to the **Products** module. This product is displayed on the page with the **Price** and **Weight** (we can delete this field later on). Click the product link to see the detailed view of the product. The template looks very technical, but with some HTML, CSS, and Smarty knowledge you can change its look and feel later on. Let's concentrate on the functionality of the module first and not on the design.

Add some more products in the **Product Manager** and see the list of products on the **Shop** page. Pay attention that the detailed view of every product is displayed in the same way. In the **Products** module, there are some fields like **Price** and **Weight** already defined. But you will need to add your own fields.

Creating custom fields

Usually one or more pictures of the product can be found in an online shop. However, there is no special image field where you can upload the product picture. Luckily, you can add as many custom fields as you need. In the next step, you will create a custom field, where the image of the product can be uploaded. In the admin area of the **Product Manager,** choose the tab **Field Definitions** and click on the link **Add A Field**.

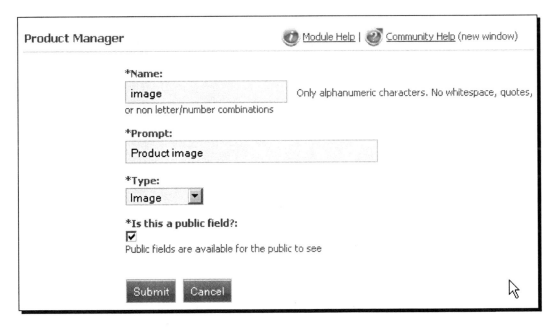

Name is a kind of technical field that is not displayed to your visitors. You should not use any special characters or spaces in the name of the field. Use only letters and numbers, no dashes, slashes, or anything else non-alphanumeric.

The **Prompt** field is the label of the field that you will see in the admin area of the **Product Manager** during adding or editing products. You can use any characters in this field.

The **Type** of the field should be **Image**. By selecting this type you ensure that the field is displayed as a field for file uploads in the admin area. This field will also be validated, so that only images can be uploaded here. Additionally, thumbnails for the uploaded images (small preview versions) will be created automatically after upload.

Let the field be public by selecting the checkbox for **Is this a public field?** It means that the content of the field (the image itself) will be shown to the visitors of your shop. If you make it private, only the administrator of the website can see the field in the admin area of the module.

Save the field. This field is automatically added to the detail template on the page and the editing view of the product in the admin area of the **Product Manager**. To test the field, open any product for editing in the admin area, find the field **Product image (Prompt)**, and upload an image for the product using this field.

Control the display of the field in the detailed view of the product on the website. The small preview version of the product is added to the section **Custom Fields** of the detailed view. We still do not care of how it looks like, but how it works. We will change the detailed view of the product when we are ready with all the custom fields and the product hierarchy.

Image already exists

When you try to upload the same image twice you will get an error saying that the image has been already uploaded. To control what images are already saved for the product and delete them, open **Content | File Manager** in the admin console. Find the folder `Products` and then the folder name `product_[ID]`. The ID of the product is displayed in the list of products in the admin area. Click on this folder and remove the images already uploaded. Now, you can upload the same image in the admin area of the **Product Manager**.

Define your own fields

Create as many custom fields as you need to display and manage the product. With the **Type** of the field you decide how the field is displayed in the admin area. The output of the field on the page can be fully customized and does not depend on the type.

If you need a **Product Number** field, create a new custom field (**Text Input**) with maximum length of 12 characters and make the field public. Then edit each of your products and enter a number in this field. You can adjust the order of the fields under the **Field Definitions** tab. Again, this order only applies to how the admin area for the product management looks; the output on the page can be completely different.

Creating a product hierarchy

Next, let us create a product hierarchy. In the official shop that I am trying to reproduce here, there are four hierarchy items:

- **Shirts (short)**
- **Shirts (long)**
- **Home & Office**
- **Mugs**

You should understand the difference between product categories and product items in the **Product Manager** module. Product categories are kind of tags for the products. It is not possible to arrange them in the hierarchy. However, you can assign one product to multiple categories if you like. In contrast to the categories, a product can belong to only one hierarchy item. That means the structure above should be implemented as a hierarchy and not as categories. One product cannot be a shirt and a mug at the same time.

We will use categories later on to mark the products as:

- **New**
- **Popular**
- **Discounted**

Categories will allow you to make one product both new and discounted at the same time. A hierarchy would not, as multiple assignment is not possible.

In the admin area of **Product Manager**, click on the **Product Hierarchy** tab and create four hierarchy items displayed in the first list. It is your choice if you want to add any description or image to the hierarchy or leave it empty.

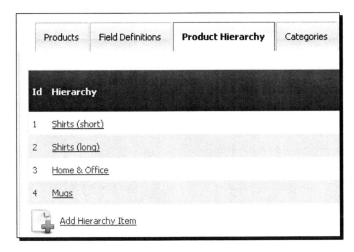

Once the hierarchy is created, go through your already created products and assign them to the proper hierarchy item. The hierarchy can now be displayed in the sidebar navigation on the page. Open the main page template (**Layout | Templates**) and find the section with sidebar navigation. Add the Smarty tag for the product hierarchy shown as follows:

```
{Products action="hierarchy"}
```

Customizing product templates

The display of the product hierarchy template is very technical. Let's customize all the templates for the module. There are three of them:

- **Summary Templates**
- **Detail Templates**
- **Hierarchy Report Templates**

Let's start with the **Hierarchy Report Templates**. This template defines how the hierarchy in the sidebar is displayed. In the admin area of the **Product Manager**, click on the **Hierarchy Report Templates** tab and find the list of existing templates for the hierarchy. The template **Sample** is the one that is used by default. You can customize this template or create your own by clicking on the **New Template** link. I choose the second way. It is generally advisable not to change sample templates, but create your own and set them as default. This way you can delete anything from the custom template and use the **Sample** template for reference if you need parts removed from the custom template. For the template name, I chose **My Shop**. However, you can use any name you wish.

In the **Template Text** field, the sample template code is already suggested. Leave this code as it is and submit the new template. Now you see two templates in the list. Make the template **My Shop** the default one by clicking on the red cross in the **Default** column. Let's see what we have in the template and what we actually need. Open the new template for editing:

Smarty variable	Description
{$hierarchy_item.name}	The name of the hierarchy item.
{$hierarchy_item.id}	The ID of the hierarchy item.
{$upurl}	The URL to the parent hierarchy item. Only applicable if there are more than one hierarchy levels.
{$mod}	The object containing all the information about the module **Products**. In the template the object is used to get translations:
	{$mod->Lang('parent')} returns the translation for the key parent from the translation file.
	You can replace this variable with your custom text if your website is monolingual and the language of the website will be never changed.

Smarty variable	Description
{$parent}	This array supposes to hold the information about the parent item. However, it is not assigned in the current version of the module and cannot be used.
{$child_nodes}	The array that contains information about all child hierarchy items. The information in this array is:

- {$child_nodes.id}: ID of the hierarchy item
- {$child_nodes.name}: Name of the hierarchy item
- {$child_nodes.description}: Description of the hierarchy item
- {$child_nodes.parent_id}: ID of the parent hierarchy item
- {$child_nodes. image }: The name of the image file for the hierarchy item
- {$child_nodes. thumbnail}: The name of the thumbnail file for the hierarchy item
- {$child_nodes. long_name}: The full name of the hierarchy item (including the names of all parents)
- {$child_nodes. extra1}: The value saved in the Extra Field 1
- {$child_nodes. extra2}: The value saved in the Extra Field 2
- {$child_nodes. downurl}: The URL for this hierarchy item

Smarty variable	Description
{$hierarchy_image_location}	Path to the folder where images for the product are saved.
{$hierarchy_item}	An array that contains the ID of the actual item hierarchy.

From the preceding table, you can now combine the HTML and Smarty tags and create your own template. Create a list of hierarchy items for the sidebar with the sample template as shown in the following code snippet:

```
{if isset($child_nodes) && count($child_nodes)}
  {foreach from=$child_nodes item='node'}
    <h3>
      {if isset($node.downurl)}
        <a href="{$node.downurl}
title="{$node.name}">{$node.name}</a>
      {else}
```

```
        {$node.name}
      {/if}
    </h3>
      {if !empty($node.description)}
        <div>{$node.description}
        </div>
    {/if}
  {/foreach}
{/if}

<!-- This tag will be automatically added to the page content.
     It uses the default summary template for products. -->
{Products hierarchyid=$hierarchy_item.id}
```

This template goes through each hierarchy and displays its name as a HTML heading <h3>. It will also show a description field of the hierarchy item below the heading. The last Smarty tag in the template shows the summary list of the products limited to the hierarchy item selected in the sidebar. The template of this summary list is the default summary template. The products summary list will automatically replace the page content.

Before you customize the summary template, open it (**Content | Product Manager**, tab **Summary Templates**, template **Sample**) and find out what the major parts of this template are. It consists of:

- Drop-down list of categories
- Page navigation
- List of products with the add-to-cart functionality for each product

At present, you can see only the list of products, no categories, no page navigation, and no cart functionality.

Displaying the drop-down list of the categories does not work in the actual version of the module the way it is added to the sample template:

```
{if isset($catformstart)}
  {$catformstart}
  {$catdropdown}{$catbutton}
  {$catformend}
{/if}
```

It is still possible that this functionality will be added in a later release of the module. At present, you can completely delete this part or replace it with the Smarty tag shown as follows:

```
{Products action="categorylist"}
```

The output of the category list can be changed by customizing the **CategoryList Templates** in the admin area of the **Products** module. In my example, I have added the categories to the sidebar just above the hierarchy item as shown in the following code snippet:

```
{Products action="categorylist"}
{Products action="hierarchy"}
```

The second line of code in the last example already exists in your template. The first line adds the links to the different categories that have assigned products. In the brackets behind the name of the category, the number of assigned products is shown. If you have assigned some products to categories, it should look as shown in the following screenshot:

New(2)
Popular(1)
Discounted(1)

Shirts (short)

Shirts (long)

Home & Office

Mugs

To define how many products should be shown on one page and to see how the page navigation for the product list looks like by default, add the parameter `pagelimit=""` to the Smarty tag `{Products}`. We have placed this tag in the page **Shop** at the very beginning of the workshop. Open the page (**Content | Pages**) and add the parameter to the tag as shown in the following code:

```
{Products pagelimit="2"}
```

Be sure that the whole number of products is greater than the value set here. Otherwise, you will not see the page navigation and cannot customize it. The page navigation in the module **Products** does not support SEO friendly URL, so if you do not have many products, you can completely delete the navigation from the template and do not limit the number of products per page. The number of products shown on one page is limited to 100000 products, if you do not limit it explicitly. But I would not recommend displaying more than about 20 products per page. It is not user friendly and will significantly impact the performance of your shop.

The last part in the template is the cart functionality. The **Products** module does not contain any cart functionality. There is another module that is perfectly integrated into it. The module in question is called **Cart** and will be installed in the next step. We cannot change the display of the **Cart** module at this time, so we will leave the tag as it is.

The last question is how to display the product image in the summary list of products. In the **Summary template,** you will find a Smarty comment made by the developer of the module saying **The summary template has access to custom fields via the $entry->fields**. The values of the custom fields can be generally accessed by the following lines of code:

```
{$entry->fields.image->value}
{$entry->fields.number->value}
```

The part of the code in bold corresponds to the technical name of the field. To get thumbnails of the images automatically created by the module during the upload use:

```
{$entry->fields.image->thumbnail}
```

So let's put it together and create a complete template for the summary view of products including custom field containing the thumbnail of the product. Create a new summary template and name it **My Shop**. Add the template code as shown in the following code snippet:

```
{Products action="categorylist"}
  <ul class="products-summary">
    {foreach from=$items item=entry}
      <li>
        <a href="{$entry->detail_url}">
          <img src="{$entry->file_location}/{$entry->fields.image
>thumbnail}" alt="{$entry->product_name}"/></a>
          <br/>
  <a href="{$entry->detail_url}">{$entry->product_name}</a>
<br/>
          {$currency_symbol}{$entry->price}
      </li>
    {/foreach}
  </ul>
```

Save the template and set it as default. The variable in bold in the template is the custom field containing the image of the product. I have named the field **image** as I have created it. If you have chosen another name, you have to adjust it here.

The list of products can be styled with CSS. To display the products one by one, open the stylesheet used in your main template (**Layout | Stylesheets**) and add the following style definitions to it:

```
ul.products-summary
{
  list-style: none;
}
ul.products-summary li
```

```
{
  float: left;
  padding: 15px;
  text-align: center;
}
```

This is just an example; you are free to add any styles that will fit into your own design.

The size of the thumbnails created while uploading product images can be changed in the tab **Preferences (Content | Product Manager)**. On this page, scroll down to the section **Image Handling Settings** and adjust the values as you like.

If you have used my templates so far, your summary template and hierarchy should look as shown in the following screenshot:

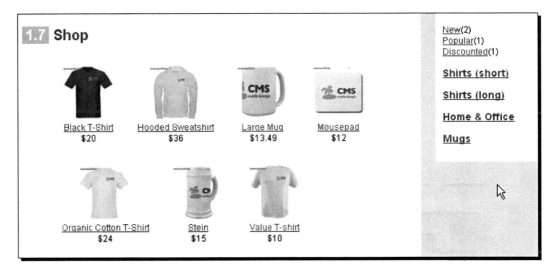

The last step will be customization of the detailed view of the product. Create a new template called **My Shop** under the **Detail Templates** tab in the admin area of the **Products** module. Then set the template as default.

In the detail template, you will find a section for the product attributes. We did not discuss it so far. The products can have different attributes, like size or color for the t-shirts. These attributes may or may not have an impact on the price. For each product, the attributes are added separately. It does not make sense to add size or color to the mouse pad, if we have only one model.

Let's create the attribute for the color of the long t-shirt. Assume that we have two colors available: white and grey. The color does not change the price of the product. In the admin area of the **Products** module, click on the **Products** tab. In the list of products, at the end of each line there is an icon for **Edit Attribute Sets**. Click on this icon in line with the product to which you would like to add attributes.

On the next screen, click on **Add Attribute**. Enter the name of the attribute. This name contains the generic term like **Color**. In the **Label** field enter the name of the attribute in the same way as it should appear on the website. As the color of the t-shirt does not change the price of the product, enter 0 in the field **Price Adjustment** and click on **Update**. Add another label for the color **Grey**. It should look as shown in the following screenshot:

Click on **Submit** once you have entered all possible values for this attribute. See the detailed view of the product with defined attributes. All possible values are listed in the template. When you install the **Cart** module later on, you will not only be able to display the attributes, but add them to the cart as well. The price will be automatically adjusted in the cart view.

You should now be able to customize the detail template yourself.

Follow these steps:

1. Create a new template and do not overwrite the sample one. The **Sample** template can be used for future reference if you delete any part from your custom template.

2. Analyze the template. Try to figure out its major parts and usage of other modules in it.

3. Write down all the Smarty variables used in the templates in a table as shown previously for the **Hierarchy Report Templates**.

4. Figure out, what values are saved in these variables. If the variable contains an array, use the Smarty modifier `print_r` to get all array values from it. For example, `{$entry|print_r}` will output all the values contained in this variable.

5. Use HTML and Smarty to markup the template.

6. Add stylesheet definitions to change the appearance.

Creating detail view for product

Follow the list above and create your own template for the detailed view of the product. Delete everything you do not need in the template; for example, the **Weight** field. Assign custom fields (**Product image** and **Product number**) the same way you did in the summary template. Check the values of the variables with the modifier `print_r` if you are not sure what you have to use.

My detail template looks as shown in the following screenshot:

The template code I have used for the detailed template is shown in the following code snippet:

```
<div class="products-detail">
  <img align="left" src="{$entry->file_location}/{$entry
  >fields.image->value}" alt="{$entry->product_name}"/>
  <h1>{$entry->product_name}</h1>
  <h2>{$currency_symbol}{$entry->price}</h2>
<div>{$entry->details}</div>
```

```
{* print out attributes *}
{if isset($entry->attributes)}
  {foreach from=$entry->attributes key='name' item='attribset'}
    <p><strong>{$name}:</strong>
      {foreach from=$attribset key='label' item='adjustment'}
        {$label} ({$currency_symbol}{$adjustment}),
      {/foreach}
    </p>
  {/foreach}
{/if}
  {* include the cart *}
  {if isset($cart_module_tag)}
  {eval var=$cart_module_tag}
{/if}
</div>
```

You are now ready to add cart functionality to your solution.

Module Cart

This module will add simple cart functionality to the **Products** module. Once installed, the **Cart** module will be automatically displayed in the detailed view of the product. The visitor of the website will then be able to put one or more products in the basket along with the desired quantity. There are other modules that you can use instead of the **Cart** module, like **GiftBaskets**. For our example **Shop,** it is enough to use the simple functionality of the **Cart** module.

Install the module **Cart** from the list of available modules in the **Module Manager**. The admin area of this module will be added to **Extensions | Cart** in the admin console of CMS Made Simple.

Time for action – connecting products and cart

If you now look at your **Shop** page and open a detailed view of any product, you will discover that there is still no cart functionality in it. The reason for it is that the **Products** module does not know that the **Cart** module has been installed and is ready for use. Let's connect two modules.

1. Open the admin area of the **Products** module (**Content | Product Manager**).

2. Click on the **Preferences** tab.

3. Select the **Cart** module from the field **Cart Module**.

4. Click on **Submit** and open detailed view of any product. You should see the button **Add to My Cart** in the detailed view of the product. If the product has some attributes additionally to the quantity field, then the attributes are displayed in a drop-down field besides it.

What just happened?

You have told the **Products** module what module has to be used for cart functionality. Test it and add some products to the cart right now. The products will be added, but there is no possibility to display the content of the cart for the visitor yet.

Create a new content page called **Cart** and add the following Smarty tag as the content of the page:

```
{Cart action="viewcart"}
```

Save the page, then open the admin area for the **Cart** module (**Extensions | Cart**) and switch to the **Preferences** tab. Select the newly created page in the list of pages, so that the visitor is automatically redirected to the page after he has added the product to it.

There are four templates that you can customize for the module:

Template	Description
AddToCart	This template controls how the quantity field, the button **Add To My Cart** (shown in the previous screenshot) and optionally product attributes with price adjustment will look.
MyCart	This template is used to display the cart status. It is displayed at the place where the Smarty tag {Cart action="mycart"} is placed. It shows the number of items currently saved in the cart and a link to the cart page.
Viewcart	This template is used for extended display of all products saved in the cart. It shows all products with their quantities and prices and the total order price. Additionally it offers the possibility to start the checkout order process if the module **Orders** is installed.
Product Summary	This template is used to format the output used for each product summary in the **Viewcart** template. It allows you to customize the product label based on the attributes, product name, and price.

The Smarty tag {Cart action="mycart"} can be added to the navigation of the website, like the link to the Basket in the official shop (http://www.cafepress.co.uk/cmsmadesimple) we are trying to reproduce. It would appear as shown in the following screenshot:

There is nothing else you should know about the **Cart** module. The next step will be to integrate the checkout process.

Module Orders

This module is designed for processing orders from the cart. This module handles billing and shipping addresses from the customer and either uses an external payment gateway (such as PayPal) to handle the payment process or performs manual e-mail-based invoicing. This module can also optionally collect credit card information and store it in the database for later offline processing.

 Even if the module offers the possibility, never collect credit card information in a low security shared hosting environment!

The **Orders** module keeps track of all orders, and allows for the specification of items like tracking numbers and confirmation numbers and sending e-mails to the customers related to a particular order.

The functionality of the module can be extended with even more modules that allow configuring different taxes, shipping costs, and promotion actions (like discount or promotion coupons).

This module has a lot of dependencies:

- **CGExtensions**
- **FrontEndUsers**
- **Products**
- **CGSimpleSmarty**
- **CMSMailer**
- **CGPaymentGatewayBase**

From this list of dependencies, you can learn that it is based on the functionality of the module **FrontEndUsers**. This means that your website's customers must register before they can start the payment process on your online store. There is no possibility to turn off this registration process and it is required for the checkout step.

Install all modules listed in the preceding dependencies list, then install the **Orders** module.

Time for action – adding the checkout step

To enable the checkout process provided by the **Orders** module follow these steps:

1. Create a new content page (**Content | Pages | Add New Content**) and name it **Checkout**.

2. Add the following Smarty tag to the **Content** field of the **Checkout** page:

   ```
   {Orders}
   ```

3. Save and view the page in the browser. This page will display either the billing form if the user is logged in or the warning message if the user is not logged in or does not belong to special user group.

4. To connect the **Cart** module with the new **Checkout** page, in the admin console click on **Extensions | Cart.**

5. Select the tab **Viewcart Form Templates** and click on the **Sample** template (or your own template, if you have created one).

6. At the very end of the template in the **Template Text** field, add the following line of code:

   ```
   {cms_selflink page="checkout"}
   ```

    The parameter page should contain the page alias of the page where the Smarty tag {Orders} has been added to the content.

7. Open your shop and add one or more products to the cart, find a link to the page **Checkout** at the very bottom of the screen.

What just happened?

You have connected the module **Cart** with the module **Orders** by placing a link from the cart view to the checkout process. To test the link, add some products to the cart and click the **Checkout** link at the bottom of the cart view. If you are not logged in, you will see the following message:

The user is not logged in (or not a member of the required group)

This message can be found in the template of the **Orders** module. But first, let's see an overview of the templates delivered with this module. In the admin console, click on **Content | Order Manager** and find the **Templates** link above the list of orders:

Template	Description
Billing Form	This template controls the first step in the order processing. It displays the form where the customer can enter billing address and one or more shipping addresses.
Payment Form	This template controls the second step in the order processing and is used to display the payment form for manual e-mail-based checkout process. You will need this template if you do not use any payment services such as PayPal, EMoney, eWay, or Authorize.Net.
Confirm Order	This template controls the third step in the order processing and is used to display any information the customer entered in the first and optionally second step, so that the customer can confirm the shipping and invoice addresses or go back and correct them.
Invoice	This template is used in the admin area of the **Orders** module to print out the invoice or to send it via e-mail to the customer.
Gateway Complete	This template is used to display the status message after the payment has been made with any third-party service such as PayPal, EMoney, EWay or Authorize.net.
User Email	This template is used to customize the e-mail with order confirmation sent to the customer when the new order has been submitted.
Admin Email	This template controls the layout and content of the e-mail that is sent to the authorized administrator of the store when a new order is submitted.
Message	There is no sample template for the messages. Here you can define your custom e-mail notifications that can be manually sent to the customers from the admin area of the module. An example of such message can be an e-mail notification that is sent when the order is shipped.

Now, we know where to start and how to proceed with customizing of the templates according to our requirements and payment configurations. Let's give the customer the possibility to register with or login to the website to be able to complete the checkout process.

Integrating the login screen

The message that indicates that the customer is not logged in is saved in the template **Billing Form** (the first step in the checkout process).

 The user is not logged in (or not a member of the required group).

This is not very user friendly. Whether the user is registered or not we should give him a possibility to log in or to register on this page as shown in the following screenshot:

Already registered?

Username
Password

☐ Remember me on this computer
Sign in
Forgot Your Password?
Forgot Your Login Details?

New customer?

Register

The login form for registered customers can be displayed with the module **FrontEndUsers**. This module was discussed in the section *Managing visitors' logins* in Chapter 8, *Creating Your Own Functionality*. If you have not installed the module yet, use the **Module Manager** to do so and see the login form on the website. The link to the page where the customer can register will be provided with the **SelfRegistration** module discussed further.

In the admin area of the **Orders** module, click on the **Templates** link and create a new template with the name **My Shop** on the **Billing Form** tab. Scroll down to the very bottom of the suggested template text and find the last ELSE condition:

```
. . .
{else}
  {* user is not logged in, gotta make him *}
  <h3 style="color: red;">{$Orders
>Lang('error_notloggedin')}</h3><br/>
{/if}
```

This is the place where the message that the user is not logged in is shown. Replace this section with the login screen of the module **FrontEndUsers**, as shown in the following code snippet:

```
. . .
{else}

  <h1>Already registered?</h1>
  {FrontEndUsers}

{/if}
```

Save the template and do not forget to set it as **Default** to see changes on the website. Registered customers can now log in to start the checkout process.

But, what about customers who do not have an account? They should be able to register themselves with our website. As it gets a bit complicated I have created the following flowchart:

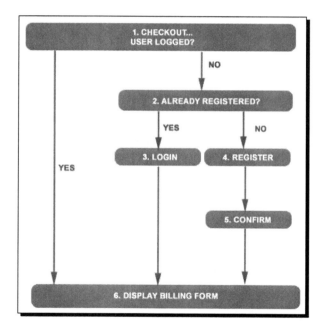

The billing form checks if the visitor is logged in or not. If yes, he can fill in the billing information; if not, the login form of the **FrontEndUsers** module (step 3) is displayed. The steps 4 and 5 in the workflow should assist new customers by allowing them to register. These steps can be accomplished with the **SelfRegistration** module. Read the next section to see how the module can be configured.

Before you continue be sure that:

- The **CMSMailer** module is configured and is able to send out messages (refer to Chapter 2, *Getting Started*).

- There is a user property of type **Email Address** in the module **FrontEndUsers** (**Users & Groups | Frontend User Management**, tab **User Properties**).

- There is a user group that has the above user properties associated as **Required** (**Users & Groups | Frontend User Management**, tab **Groups**).

You can read how to configure the **FrontEndUsers** module in Chapter 8, *Creating Your Own Functionality*.

Integrating customer registration

This module is designed to allow visitors of the website to register themselves. It optionally sends a confirmation e-mail with an activation link that must be clicked before the registration is complete. Once the registration is complete, a user account is created in the module **FrontEndUsers**.

Install the **SelfRegistration** module from the list of available modules in the **Module Manager**. For the registration page, create a new content page **Register** and add the following Smarty tag into the content of the page:

```
{SelfRegistration group="Customers"}
```

Pay attention to the part in bold in the above code. The value of the parameter group should exactly reflect the name of user group in the module **FrontEndUsers** (**Users & Groups | Frontend User Management**, tab **Groups**). Please read Chapter 8, *Creating Your Own Functionality* to see how the **FrontEndUsers** module should be configured if you do not have any user groups so far.

Open the **Register** page of your website and sign in yourself as a new customer with the **SelfRegistration** module to see how the module works by default. There are some preferences in the module that can make the registration process user friendly. In the admin area of the **Self Registration** module (**Users & Groups | Self Registration Module**), click on the **Preferences** tab.

The **SelfRegistration** module offers registration with an e-mail verification step or optionally single-step registration without any confirmation. If you do not need the e-mail verification, you should deselect the option **Require the user to confirm registration via email** on the **Preferences** tab of the module. The three settings considering the final message work different depending on what registration method you have chosen.

Setting	With verification	Without verification
Don't display the final message after registration	Prevents the registration form to be replaced by the confirmation message after the form is submitted.	Prevents the registration form to be replaced by the final message after the form is submitted.
PageID/Alias to redirect to after registration is complete	N/A	Redirects to the given page, but replaces the whole content of the page with the final message.
PageID/Alias to redirect to after verification step is complete	Redirects to the given page, but replaces the whole content of the page with the final message.	N/A

According to the workflow, let's add a link to the registration page for the new customers (step 4). In the billing template of the **Orders** module, open the template for the **Billing Form** again, scroll down and add a link to the registration page for the new customers as shown in the following code snippet:

```
. . .
{else}

  <h1>Already registered?</h1>
  {FrontEndUsers}

  <h1>New Customer?</h1>
  {cms_selflink page="register"}
{/if}
```

Pay attention to the parameter `page`. It should contain the alias of the page where the registration form is displayed. Customize the **Registration Template 1** of the **SelfRegistration** module that displays the registration form. Generally, there are two templates. The first one is for the registration form and the second one (**Post Registration Template**) contains the message informing the customer that his registration should be confirmed through a link sent to his e-mail address. Other templates that you can customize are as shown in the following table:

Templates	Description
Registration Template 2	This template contains the form where the username, verification code, and password will be added to complete registration.
Confirmation Email	Contains the subject of the verification e-mail, the plain text and the HTML version of the e-mail sent out after the customer has registered.
Final Message	The message is shown to customer after the registration process is completed. To build the workflow suggested previously (step 5) add link to the billing form in this template, so that the user can carry on with the checkout process. It is also advisable to tick the option **Login user after registration**, so that the login step can be skipped after registration.
Lost Email	This template contains a form for the customers who have registered but did not get verification e-mail. This template is shown at the place where the Smarty tag `{SelfRegistration mode="sendmoremail"}` is shown.

When the user registers with the website and e-mail verification is required, the temporary user account is saved in the **SelfRegistration** module (not **FrontEndUsers**!). After e-mail verification is complete, new user account is automatically moved to the **FrontEndUsers** module. At the same time the temporary account is deleted from the **SelfRegistration** module.

There is a limit of 250 temporary accounts in the **SelfRegistration** module. When the number of 250 non-verified accounts is reached, no registration is possible. Therefore you purge from the **SelfRegistration** module by using the option on the **Preferences** tab.

After the module **SelfRegistration** is configured and all required templates are customized, you can go through the whole manual e-mail-based checkout process.

I suggest that you use the workflow to test all three cases:

- The visitor is registered and logged in
- The visitor is registered, but not logged in
- The visitor is not registered

I recommend that you customize the final message in the **SelfRegistration** module and add two links to assist the user in his further steps. Link to the **Checkout** page to continue the checkout process and to the **Shop** page to continue shopping.

Module Paypal Gateway

This module is used by the **Orders** module to checkout orders using **PayPal Website Payments Standard** mechanism. In other words, this module allows the order to be paid through the PayPal website. This payment option can be used either additionally to the manual e-mail-based invoicing delivered with the **Orders** module or as a substitute for manual processing.

Using this module the customer will be redirected to the PayPal website where the order and all payment details are displayed. He has to log in to his PayPal account to confirm the payment. After the payment is made, the PayPal will automatically redirect to your website.

There are several ways PayPal returns payment data to you after the payment is completed. The **Paypal Gateway** module supports two methods:

◆ **Payment Data Transfer (PDT)**

◆ **Instant Payment Notification (IPN)**

PDT is a way to confirm the payment with the redirection URL from the PayPal website after the payment is complete. However, the payment can be confirmed in the **Orders** module this way only if the customer is patient and does not close the browser or navigate away before redirection is completed. If the redirect breaks for some reasons, you won't know about the payment and will have to complete the order manually in the admin console of CMS Made Simple.

IPN is independent of the customer's action. It communicates with your website in the backend. If the customer closes the browser or navigates away, you will still receive notifications from PayPal about the payment. IPN also has a built-in retry mechanism. If there's a problem reaching your website, PayPal will retry to inform you about payments for several days. IPN works parallel to the order process and can be slightly desynchronized. It is possible that the customer may return to your page before IPN informs you that the order is paid.

These two methods can be used together to combine their advantages.

Install the module **Paypal Gateway** from the list of the available modules in **Module Manager**. The admin area of the module is placed in **Extensions | Paypal Gateway**. Click on the **Preferences** tab. There are some fields that are required for module usage, which are shown in the following screenshot:

While testing e-commerce solutions you are naturally not going to use your real PayPal account. The suggested **Paypal URL** points to the official testing environment of the PayPal service. This environment simulates the payment process without making real money transfers.

This environment can be found on `http://sandbox.paypal.com`. It acts the same way as the real PayPal website does.

Time for action – creating test accounts

Before you use this environment, you have to register a developer account on `http://developer.paypal.com` and create two test accounts.

1. Open `http://developer.paypal.com` in your browser and click on **Sign Up Now**.

2. Fill in the fields and click **Agree and Submit**.

3. Log in to your developer account with your e-mail and password.

4. Click on **Create a preconfigured buyer or seller account**.

5. Select **Buyer (Use to represent your customer's experience)** and fill in the field with any test data. Click **Create Account**.

6. Create another account, but this time choose **Seller (Use to represent yourself as the merchant)** as the **Account type**.

7. After both accounts are created, click on **Test accounts** on the left hand side. You should see an overview of the test accounts as shown in the following screenshot:

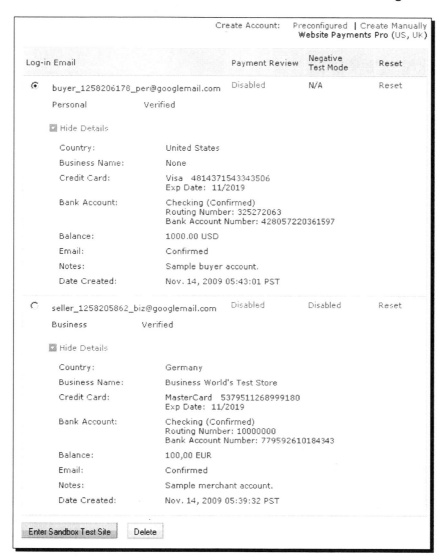

What just happened?

You have created two test accounts, one for the buyer and one for the seller. The easiest way to create such accounts is to choose the preconfigured ones. Now, you can log in with the buyer account on `http://sandbox.paypal.com` and act as if you were your own client. You can purchase anything without having to pay real money.

You can also log onto `http://sandbox.paypal.com` with the seller account to configure it. You have to activate the PDT and IPN features for the account, get your PDT identity token, and make some more settings on your PayPal account, so that instant payment works with the module **PayPal Gateway**.

Configuring PayPal's seller account

Click on the **Profile** link in the seller account. There are four sections that you have to customize to set up PayPal payment with the website.

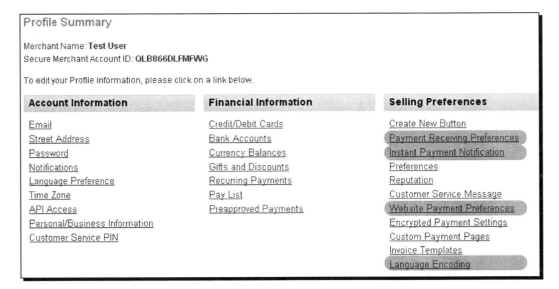

Payment Receiving Preferences

First of all, decide if you would like to manually accept payments made in other currencies. This applies only if the default currency of your PayPal account is different to the currency set in the **Products** module on the **Preferences** tab. For example, if your PayPal currency is Euro but on your webpage you offer the products in USD. Generally, PayPal does not convert any currency automatically. This means that all payments made in other currencies are on hold until you accept them in your PayPal account manually. Once the payment is accepted the order status is set to **Paid**. If you would like to convert currencies automatically and accept payments in any currency, you have to deselect the setting **Block payments sent to me in a currency I do not hold**.

Secondly, you can block all payments with the status **Pending**. This will reject all payments that are not completed instantly after the payment confirmation. Consider that the **Paypal Gateway** module is able to handle pending payments if IPN is activated.

Instant Payment Notification

We remember that instant payment notification is able to communicate with the website in the backend. It notifies the **Orders** module about payment, even if the payment was pending first and accepted later. All that PayPal needs to know is the notification URL. This URL waits for the instant payment notification, handles the answer from the PayPal website and updates the order status automatically.

This notification URL is concealed in the module **Paypal Gateway**. To get it, perform the following steps:

1. Add a product to your cart.

2. Click on **Checkout** and fill the billing form.

3. Click on **Submit**.

4. At the bottom of the confirmation page you see the button **Checkout w/Paypal**.

5. Open the source view of this page in your browser and look for the hidden input field with the name `notification_url` that looks like the following code snippet:

    ```
    <input name="notify_url"    value="http://yourdomain.com/index.php?
    mact=PaypalGateway,cntnt01,ipn,0&amp;cntnt01order_id=15&amp;cntnt0
    1mycustom=05db2efd49ce4195d97efe01d4df00f4&amp;cntnt01returnid=59"
    type="hidden">
    ```

6. You have to copy the value of the field and paste this URL to the PayPal merchant account.

7. Click on **Instant Payment Notification** in the **Profile** of the seller account in PayPal and edit the IPN Settings. Enter the notification URL you have copied from the hidden field above and click on **Receive IPN messages (Enabled)**. Save the settings.

Website Payment Preferences

Click the **Website Payment Preferences** link, turn on the **Auto-Return** option, and enter any URL of your website in the field **Return URL**. It does not matter what you enter here as this URL will be overridden by the **Paypal Gateway** module. Then turn on **Payment Data Transfer** and save.

Pay attention to the yellow information message at the top of the PayPal website after you have changed the above setting:

> You have successfully saved your preferences. Please use the following identity token when setting up Payment Data Transfer on your website.
> XXXXXXXXXXXXXXXXXXXXXXXXX-XXXXXXXXXXXXXXXXXXXXX

This is your generated PDT identity token that you need to save in the **Paypal Gateway** module on the **Preferences** tab.

Language encoding

On this page you should adjust the language encoding. CMS Made Simple uses UTF-8 encoding by default. Click on the **More Options** button and select **UTF-8** in the **Encoding** field. Leave the same encoding for IPN and save.

Now you have all the information required to configure the **Paypal Gateway** module. In the admin area of the **Paypal Gateway** module, click on the **Preferences** tab and enter your custom values gained from PayPal sandbox environment. The **Business Email** field in the **Paypal Gateway** module contains the generated e-mail address of the seller account. The following screenshot shows my custom values:

Next, connect the **Orders** module with the **Paypal Gateway** module. In the admin area of the **Orders** module, click on the **Preferences** tab and scroll down to the **Payment Gateway Settings** section. Choose the **Paypal Gateway** module in the list of payment modules and click **Submit**.

Test your order process now. Pay attention to the **Email** field in the billing form, it must be filled in for the PayPal payment. After the payment is made, you have to control the payment status in the seller PayPal account. It should be completed. In the admin console of CMS Made Simple, click on **Site Admin | Admin Log** and see the communication protocol with the PayPal website. For each order completed with PDT and IPN you should have five messages, as shown in the next screenshot:

User	Item ID	Item Name	Action
webmaster	0	PaypalGateway	Received successfull transaction reply for 12Y48348G3951362M
webmaster	0	Orders	Order status changed to "Pending" on 16
	0	PaypalGateway:ipn	IPN Transaction 12Y48348G3951362M successful. Status: Completed
	0	Orders:gateway_event	Handled Async Transcation 12Y48348G3951362M for order 16
	0	Orders	Payment received for order 16.

The reason for the order being pending is the activated IPN feature. The module sets the order to pending status until the IPN message is received from the module. So, the result of these five messages above is a completed and paid order in the admin console of CMS Made Simple.

Once you have tested the module, you should configure your real PayPal account as explained previously, gather all required information like PDT identity token from the real account, and change the PayPal URL to `https://www.paypal.com/cgi-bin/webscr`.

Optional modules for the e-commerce suite

There are some more modules that you can use together with this e-commerce suite to enrich the functionality:

- **Flat Rate Taxes**: Allows you to apply flat rate taxes to any or all products in the module **Products**.

- **warehouse taxes**: Calculates taxes for a product based on the US state the warehouse is in, and the US state the customer is situated.

- **FlatRateShipping**: Provides an interface to set up some simple weight shipping rules, and to calculate the cost of shipping based on its total weight.

- **Destination Based Shipping**: Allows the calculation of flat shipping costs based on destination country, and number of items. It does not consider weight in calculations.

- **PriceBasedShipping**: Allows the calculation of shipping costs based on the pre-tax total order price.

- **Promotions**: Allows you to create and manage promotions/sales in the order process. A sale will consist of a start date, end date, a discount or offer, and a set of conditions. Conditions can include total order amount, coupon code, subset of products based on category or hierarchy or user group. Offers can be a percentage off the total order price or a product item, a fix amount reduced from total order price, or a free product given with the order. Discounts will be applied in the order process and shown up as a line item in the invoice.

- **GiftBaskets**: This module is another **Cart** module for the e-commerce suite. You can use it instead of the standard **Cart** module. This module allows the creation of many different gift baskets, with different shipping addresses, and allows you to add different items in each.

- **EMoney Payment Gateway**: This is a payment processing gateway module which works with the ETS Corporation payment authorization system (https://www.etsms.com/ASP/home.htm).

- **Authorize.Net AIM**: A payment gateway that interacts directly with Authorize.net using their AIM protocol.

- **Attachments**: This module requires some programming knowledge to create functionality like related products, so that you can attach some products to others and display them as related products on the detailed view of the product.

Pop quiz – e-commerce workshop

1. CMS Made Simple is a content management system and cannot be used as e-commerce solution.
   a. True
   b. False

2. The **Products** module allows you to ...
   a. Manage products on the website
   b. Add order functionality to the website
   c. Create customer accounts and track their orders

3. To track the orders in the admin console of CMS Made Simple, you need the module:
   a. **Cataloger**
   b. **Orders**
   c. **Users**
   d. **Paypal Gateway**

4. If you would like to test PayPal functionality on your website, you can use a so called sandbox environment. What is true about the PayPal sandbox?

   a. It charges your real PayPal account.

   b. It can be used to create a seller account for testing purposes.

   c. It can operate only with USD as currency.

   d. It is not free

5. E-commerce solution described in this chapter requires that the customer creates an account before purchasing:

   a. True

   b. False

Summary

In this chapter, you learned how to set up basic e-commerce functionality with CMS Made Simple. Even if CMS Made Simple does not pretend to offer fully sophisticated e-commerce features, it offers the most wanted features with delivered modules.

Be sure that you do not use CMS Made Simple for pure e-commerce websites. It is better to use a dedicated e-commerce solution for an online shop rather than CMS Made Simple. However, if your website has a mix of features such as a blog, a shop, a forum, and so on, then you can use third-party modules to implement these features.

Specifically, we covered:

◆ The **Products** module that allows you to create and edit products for the online shop. This module is a basis for the e-commerce suite.

◆ The **Cart** module that adds simple cart functionality to the **Products** module. It saves its data in the browser session and connects the module **Product** with the module **Orders**.

◆ The **Orders** module that starts the checkout process for the items added to the cart. This module saves all orders in the admin area and allows tracking and updating order status for the administrator of the website.

◆ The **SelfRegistration** module that allows your website's visitors to register with your website before making payment. We have also created a small workflow to see how the module is integrated in the checkout process.

◆ The **PayPal Gateway** module that accepts instant payments from the PayPal website and keeps you informed about the status of the payment.

Now that we've learned how to realize a complete website including e-commerce functionality, we're ready to proceed with advanced topics that require basic PHP knowledge, which is the subject of the next chapter. By this time your website is fully functional and can be published, so that you do not need any extended topics from the next chapter to have a complete website.

10

Advanced Use of CMS Made Simple

This chapter includes some tips for advanced webmasters who are creating websites with CMS Made Simple. You do not need to read the entire chapter; you can just pick up the sections that are most important to you.

In this chapter, we will:

- ◆ Learn how to develop multilingual websites with CMS Made Simple
- ◆ Create additional layout control possibilities for the editors of the website
- ◆ Make some search engine optimizations
- ◆ Work with user-defined tags and the event manager to implement our own functionality or define custom workflows

You will need basic PHP knowledge to follow instructions in this chapter. So let's get on with it.

Localization and translation

The admin console of CMS Made Simple is translated in over 20 languages. As you already know from Chapter 2, CMS Made Simple is distributed in two versions. The base version contains just the English language files, while the full version includes all language files.

If you need only one language in addition to English (English cannot be uninstalled), you can download the base package and then the required language files. Language files can be found on the official CMS Made Simple website (http://www.cmsmadesimple.org/), in the **Downloads | CMSMS Release** section at the bottom of the page (you will only need the file corresponding to your release). To include any language in the base installation, download and unpack the base installation file first, then download the required language file corresponding to the base release number and unpack it as well. Merge the contents of the base folder with the contents of the language file folder by copying the language folder over the base files. Then install CMS Made Simple as usual.

Users with access to the admin console of the website can select their preferred language in their personal accounts (**My Preferences | User Preferences**). For the base installation, only **English** is shown in the field. If you have installed any additional language, then it will be shown in the drop-down field **Language** as well. This setting does not affect the website language used for visitors to the website.

To set up the website language, in the admin console, click on **Site Admin | Global Settings**, and change the **Default language for the frontend**. If no language is set there, then CMS Made Simple uses English as the default language (**en_US**). This setting will automatically change the default text for some modules on the website, for example, the label of the search button in the **Search** module or some labels in the **News** module.

In the preceding screenshot, see the difference between the labels for **Category** (**Kategorie** in German), **Posted by** (**Erstellt von** in German), and so on. This will help to define most labels displayed by the modules that are translated into your language. However, this would only help if your website is not multilingual and uses only one language.

Configuring dates

From time to time, CMS Made Simple must output dates and times. Especially, for news articles, the proper date format is important.

The general date format can be changed in the admin console (**Site Admin | Global Settings**) in the field **Date Format String**. The date format should be entered according to the PHP format function `strftime` (`http://www.php.net/manual/en/function.strftime.php`). There are some examples shown in the following table:

Date format string	Output
`%Y-%m-%d`	2009-05-20
`%a %d %b %Y`	Wed 20 May 2009
`%a %d %b %H:%M:%S %Y`	Wed 20 May 15:53:40 2009

The first column is built according to allowed parameters (please see the last link for an explanation). The second column shows the result on the page. Enter parameters from the first column in the **Date Format String** field to get the results shown in the second column.

The month and weekday names depend on the `locale` setting of your server. On some servers, you can change the language used to output dates. Setting the locale will also affect currency, decimal separators, and other outputs dependent on the language. In CMS Made Simple, open the `config.php` file and find the line with `$config['locale']`. It depends on your server, what value you enter here. For German month names on a Linux server, try changing the line as shown:

```
$config['locale'] = 'de_DE.UTF8';
```

Making multilingual websites

Multilingual websites are created in more than one language. Every language has its own translated navigation, content, and probably translated news articles. We do not speak about automatic translation of the websites that are made by Google or any other tool. Automatic translations are awful. They are often not readable by human beings and make no sense. In this section, you will learn how to create a real multilingual website where the entire content is translated by human translators.

You can use the **Babel** module to manage multiple languages for the website and navigation. Install the module the same way you install other modules for your website (**Extensions | Module Manager**).

After installation of the module, set up the page structure for the website to suit your desired languages, for example:

1. English

    1.1. Our company

    1.2. Announcements

    1.3. Contact Us

2. German

    2.1. Unternehmen

    2.2. Aktuelles

    2.3. Kontakt

The root language pages (1. and 2.) should be defined as pages with the content type **Section Headers**. You can give them any title you want. For the page alias, I suggest using the two-letter ISO 639-1 code system such as *en* (for English), *de* (for German), and *fr* (for French). The page alias will be used in the website URL like `http://www.yourdomain/en/ our-company` or `http://www.yourdomain/de/kontakt`.

In order to display the menu correctly (that is, not to display language header pages and pages belonging to other languages), you have to add the parameter `start_level="2"` to your top menu tag in the main template (**Layout | Templates**). Open the template, and adjust your top navigation, as shown in the following code snippet:

```
{menu number_of_levels="1" start_level="2"}
```

This would ensure that only second level pages belonging to the selected language are displayed in the top navigation. If you use the sidebar navigation, you should change the number of levels here as well by reducing the number of the start level:

```
{menu start_level="3"}
```

When the page structure is created, click on **Extensions | Babel: Multilingual site** in the admin console. For each language you have integrated in the page structure, click on the link **Add Language**, and enter the appropriate information, as shown in the following screenshot:

The **Root page associated with the language** should be one of the section headers you have created for each language. The **Default page for redirection to this language** should be the start page for each language (not the section header from the preceding field). For the **Language code**, you can use any five character code, but in order to provide good compatibility with the modules, you should use the same language codes as CMS Made Simple. Use the drop-down list on the top-right of the admin area to prefill the form with default values.

Click **Submit**, and be sure that you have activated the language in the **Active** column. Add all desired languages the same way.

To display a language menu, use the following tag in the main template at the place where the links to different languages should be displayed:

```
{babel action="menu"}
```

Editing language entries

In the admin area of the **Babel** module, you will find a link for editing the language entries for each language. Language entries are strings that exist for each language but hold different text (or HTML code). For the label of the *search* button in the **Search** module, you would definitely like to have different descriptions such as:

- *Search* for English
- *Suche* for German
- *Recherche* for French, and so on.

Open the **Babel: Multilingual Site** module in the admin console, and click on the **Edit language entries** link. Click on the **Add a new language entry** link at the top-right corner of the module's admin area. This is the place where you can define your personal translation for each language. The entry name is a general key that will be used to get the right translation. In our example, we would like to translate the label of the search button, so the key for the translation can be *search* button. In the fields below, enter the translation for each defined language, and click on **Submit**.

Customize the label for the search button in the template of the module **Search** (**Extensions | Search**, tab **Search Template**), and replace the tag {$submittext} with {babel show="search button"}, as shown in the following code snippet:

```
{$startform}
<input type="text" class="search-input"
  id="{$search_actionid}searchinput"
  name="{$search_actionid}searchinput" size="18" maxlength="50"
  value="{$searchtext}" {$hogan}/>
<input class="search-button" name="submit" value="{babel show="search
  button"}" type="submit" />
{if isset($hidden)}{$hidden}{/if}
{$endform}
```

This would show the proper label translation on the search button considering the currently selected language. You can replace the variable {$searchtext} the same way. Create a new language entry in the **Babel** module for the search text, translate it, and then replace the variable {$searchtext} in the search template with the corresponding tag {babel show="[KEY]"}.

The hierarchy solution

The **Babel** module uses the page hierarchy to know which page is equivalent in other languages. In our example, the page *2.2. Aktuelles* is the German equivalent of the English page *1.2. Announcements*, as it has the same position in the hierarchy of the German branch.

In other words, should the pages in other language be ordered differently, all would be messed up.

1. English
    1.1. Our company
    1.2. Announcements
    1.3. Contact Us
2. German
    2.1. Aktuelles
    2.2. Unternehmen
    2.3. Kontakt

In this example, the *Aktuelles* page has the first position within the German branch, so it is the equivalent of the first page in English, even if it is not logically.

The page structure must be identical for each language. This means that all pages must be an equivalent in other languages or the link to the other language will not be shown in the language menu on this specific page. If your structure is not identical and some pages are not translated, then use the method displayed below.

Adding flags as the language menu

You can add small flag images for each language on your website. Free images can be downloaded from http://www.famfamfam.com/lab/icons/flags/. Upload the required images into the folder /uploads/flags/. In the main page template (**Layout | Templates**), insert links to the start pages of each language as small flag icons, as shown in the following code snippet:

```
{cms_selflink page="our-company" image="uploads/flags/lang_en.gif"
    alt="English" imageonly=1}
{cms_selflink page="unternehmen" image="uploads/flags/lang_de.gif"
    alt="Deutsch" imageonly=1}
{cms_selflink page="enterprises" image="uploads/flags/lang_fr.gif"
    alt="Français" imageonly=1}
```

You can replace the tag {babel action="menu"} with the last code snippet. In this case, you do not need to have the same structure for each language. However, the above flags always point to the start page of another language and not to the page equivalent in the other language, whether it exists or not.

Separate news articles by language

In our example, not only the labels must be translated. In the page templates, we show news articles on each page. It does not make sense to display news articles in English to the German visitors of the website and vice versa. It would be better to separate the news automatically by language.

The easiest way is to create new categories in the **News** module and to change them depending on the language. With the **Babel** module, a new Smarty variable $page_lang is added to each page, so you can create Smarty conditions with this variable as follows:

```
{if $page_lang == "en_US"}
{news category="General" number="5"}
{elseif $page_lang == "de_DE"}
{news category="Allgemein" number="5"}
{/if}
```

The last code snippet assumes that two news categories were created, namely, **General** and **Allgemein**. Depending on the language the visitors choose, the news articles from only one or another category is shown in the template. The editor of the news only needs to choose the right category while adding news articles in the admin console.

 Use the language entries of the **Babel** module to replace language strings such as **Category** and **Posted by** in the news templates according to the currently displayed language.

CMS Made Simple translation center

Translations for CMS Made Simple, core modules, and third-party modules are made in the **Translation Center**, which is the official translation tool for modules and for the core CMS Made Simple. All translations are made by the users of CMS Made Simple and everyone can participate in translation projects by placing a request to join the project in the CMS Made Simple Forge (`http://dev.cmsmadesimple.org`). Register with CMS Made Simple Forge, search for the language in question, and click on the **Request to Join Project** link or contact one of the **Project Admins**.

When your application is approved, you can enter the Translation Center (`http://translations.cmsmadesimple.org`). You will see your language on the first screen. Click on it, and you will find a list of modules on the left-hand side. Choose the module that you would like to translate, and a new page will be opened where translations can be made. You do not need any special knowledge to take part.

An example for the Russian Translation Center is as shown in the following screenshot:

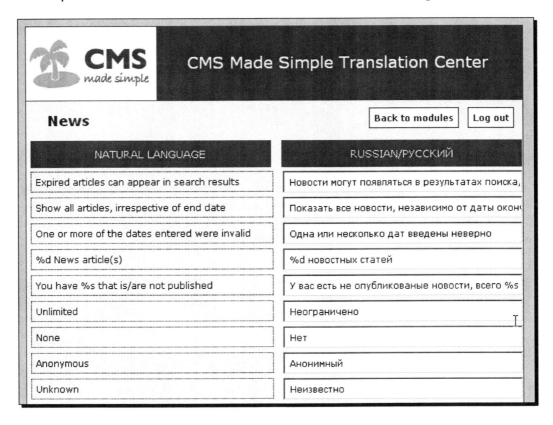

On the left-hand side, you see English words and phrases that have to be translated. Translations are made on the right-hand side of the window. If the translation has not been made, then both columns are identical and contain English. You can replace the English text in the right column by the translation into your language and submit. That's all! The more the users participate in translations, the better the translation will be.

 If you want to participate and your language doesn't exist in the Forge, create a project and inform the CMS Made Simple Forge admin, then the language will be added to the Translation Center.

The translations made here will be available to all users with the next release of CMS Made Simple or with the next release of the core or third-party modules. If you need the translation right now or if you would just like to customize the existing language to your needs, then you have to add or change the language files manually on your server.

Translating modules in your installation

Language files for the modules are always saved in the same folder /modules/MODULE_ NAME/lang/ext. Only the default English translation is placed directly in modules/ MODULE_NAME/lang in the file en_US.php. Open the file to see how it is organized.

All language files are built the same way for each language. They consist of a single PHP array $lang.

```
$lang['key'] = 'Custom language translation';
```

Search for the file with the required language in /modules/MODULE_NAME/lang/ext, and open it for editing. If the file is not there, then it means that the module has not been translated yet. In this case, you can just copy the file en_US.php into the folder /modules/ MODULE_NAME/lang/ext and rename it to the language you need. For German, you would name the file de_DE.php, for French fr_FR.php, and so on.

The file can be edited with a simple text editor like Notepad or WordPad. However, this way of translation requires some basic PHP knowledge. Be aware that the custom changes made in these files may be overwritten with the next release of the module or CMS Made Simple, so be sure that you create a backup file with the changes made somewhere apart from your installation.

Let's see how you can translate your own module, **BWProducts** (created in Chapter 8, *Creating Your Own Functionality* with **CTLMakerModule**), into other languages.

Time for action – custom translation of the module

You have created a new module and need a German translation for it.

1. With an FTP browser of your choice, for example, FileZilla, connect to your web hosting.

2. In the `modules` folder, look for the folder that contains your module; in our example, it is `bwproducts`.

3. Download the file `en_US.php` from the folder `modules/bwproducts/lang` to your local disk.

4. Rename the file to `de_DE.php`, and make your translation with any text editor.

5. Upload the translated file `de_DE.php` to the folder `modules/bwproducts/lang/ext`.

What just happened?

The language of the module is taken from the global settings of the website (**Site Admin | Global Settings**, field **Default language for the frontend**). If the language file for the module is not found, then CMS Made Simple will automatically use the file `en_US.php`.

You have created a new file for your language, renamed it according to the ISO language naming conventions, translated it into your language, and uploaded it to the right folder. That's it. You do not need to translate everything in the file. Set your custom translation to some keys and see how the translations are overtaken in the module.

In the same way, you can adjust existing language files if you like.

Additional content and controls for editors

Often websites are edited by people who are not well-versed in HTML. However, you would like to give them as much control as possible, even if they do not have any special knowledge. There are some concepts in CMS Made Simple that help you and your editors.

You can add more than one content block to the website if your layout requires physical separation of the content on one page. And you can use page attributes to give editors more control over the layout and the style of the website as well.

Additional content blocks

A page can have one or more content areas or content blocks. The first one must be {content}, otherwise there will not be any content area for the editors in the admin console. To add more content blocks to your template, use the Smarty tag {content block="block name"}. This block will appear as a text area when you edit a page, and its content will be shown at the same place when the page is displayed to the visitor.

You can also make a content block with only one line, instead of a full text area, by using the parameter oneline=true.

Time for action – adding a content block for subtitles

Let's see how you can define an additional content block for subtitles.

1. Open the main template of your website (**Layout | Templates**).

2. Add the following code between the title and content of your page:

   ```
   <h1>{title}</h1>
   <h2>{content block="Subtitle" oneline="true" wysiwyg="false"}</h2>
   {content}
   ```

3. Open any page based on this template (**Content | Pages**), and find the **Subtitle** field above the **Content** field.

4. Enter the subtitle, save the page, and view the page in the browser. You should see the text entered as a subtitle below the page title.

What just happened?

You have added an additional content block to the template. In this way, the editor of the page can enter structured data that is exactly placed in the template. The tag for the additional content block is shown as an input field in the admin console, and its content is displayed on the website at the place where it is defined in the main template.

You can read about more parameters in the **Help** section for the tag {content} in the admin console (**Extensions | Tags**).

Extra page attribute

Another way to give more control over the layout of the page to the editor without any special knowledge is using extra page attributes. When you open any page for editing, you will find three fields on the **Options** tab, which are as follows:

1. **Extra Page Attribute 1**
2. **Extra Page Attribute 2**
3. **Extra Page Attribute 3**

These fields can hold any information and can be evaluated and used in templates. For example, if you would like to hide the news summary on some pages, you can use one of these fields, fill it with defined values, and then check the field value in the template.

Time for action – using extra page attributes

Let's see how you can hide the news summary on the **Contact Us** page.

1. Open the **Contact Us** page (**Content | Pages**) for editing.

2. Switch to the **Options** tab, and enter **nonews** into the field **Extra Page Attribute 1**.

3. Save the page.

4. Now in the admin console, open your main template (**Layout | Templates**).

5. Find the Smarty tag {news}, and add an IF function as shown:

```
{if $node->extra1 != "nonews"}
   {news ...}
{/if}
```

6. Check the **Contact Us** page to see the changes.

What just happened?

Extra page attributes are a simple way to give additional control over the layout of the website to the editor of the website. He should only know what he must enter into the field **Extra Page Attribute 1**. In the template, you evaluate whether any value is saved in the field and control what content should be shown or not on this specific page.

The values entered in the extra page attributes can be retrieved in the template with $node->extra1, $node->extra2, and $node->extra3.

The fields can also be used to display any additional information on the website like the article author or anything else that you would like to handle in your template separately from the main content. In this case, you can use the following Smarty tag:

```
{page_attr key="extra1"}
```

Search engine optimization (SEO)

Nowadays, it is not enough to have a website alone. Even the most beautiful and useful page is meaningless, if it cannot be found in search engines. And just being present in the search engines does not answer a purpose of getting new customers. You should care about the ranking (the place) your page has in the search results, when the most important key words or phrases representing your business are entered.

In this section, you will find important information that will help you to improve your search ranking and get the most from your website.

Before you start to optimize your website made with CMS Made Simple, you should know that search engines are greedy for any kind of text on your website. They are not interested in CSS, JavaScript, or any other beautiful technology. The most important point to start with is writing good unique content. If you copy content from other pages, you will not succeed. Having unique content is the key for search engine optimization. Unique content is also very important for the visitors of your website. The more interesting the content, the higher is the possibility that the visitor will turn to a customer and the visitor may probably recommend your website to other people.

Title of your website

The most important part of your website in the eyes of a search engine is the title of the page. It is the text that is found between the HTML tags `title`. In Chapter 4, *Design and Layout,* you had created a new template and had added the title, as shown in the following code snippet:

```
<head>
<title>{title}- {sitename}</title>
```

The Smarty tag {title} is exactly what you enter in the field **Title** while creating or editing the page. The title must be short enough (not more than 70 characters) and should include search keywords and phrases that match this particular page (not the entire website). The title should be unique for every page that you create in your website.

This last requirement is easy to follow with content pages, but what about generated pages like news articles or products? If you examine the URLs of the detailed view of news, you will see that that the title does not match the news article, but holds the title of the page where it is displayed.

You can customize the title of the generated pages with a simple trick. In the admin console, click on **Content | News**, and choose the tab **Detail Templates**. Open the template for edit, and at the very top of the template, add the following line of code:

```
{assign var="pagetitle" value=$entry->title|escape:'html':'utf-8'}
```

This line will generate the Smarty variable $pagetitle that contains the title of the news article. To add the customized title to the main template, open it (**Layout | Templates**), and replace the entire HTML title tag with the following code snippet:

```
{if isset($pagetitle) && !empty($pagetitle)}
<title>{sitename} - {$pagetitle}</title>
{else}
<title>{sitename} - {title}</title>
{/if}
```

This piece of code checks if the Smarty variable $pagetitle is defined and is not empty. If so, then the news title is used within the HTML tag title. If not, then the normal page title is taken. You should ensure that the very first line in your main template contains the following line:

```
{process_pagedata}
```

Without this line, the trick will not work. In this way, the title of every generated page can be changed. From now on, you should customize the detail templates of each module, and add the following line of code at the very top of the module's detail template:

```
{assign var="pagetitle" value=PAGE_TITLE}
```

Replace PAGE_TITLE with the Smarty variable that contains the desired page title. In the **News** module, this was $entry->title. In the modules created with **CTLModuleMaker**, the line will look like:

```
{assign var="pagetitle" value=$item->name}
```

Different titles on every page of your website are very important for the search engine optimization. They are also important for the visitors of your website, as the title of the page is used on the browser tab and as a description of the website when the visitor adds the page to their favorite links or bookmarks it.

Meta tags

Meta tags used to be a very important part of the search engine optimization. Nowadays, the only important tag is the meta tag for description:

```
<meta name="description" content="Find the best tips on this website" />
```

Description meta tags must include a readable description of the actual page (not of the whole website). It can contain any words or sentences and is displayed in search engines below the page title in the search results.

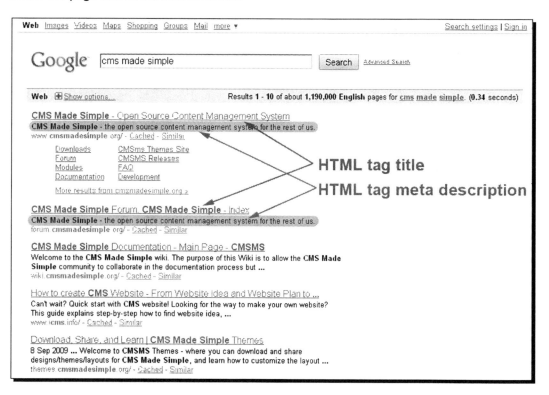

The description has to be attractive to the visitor, encouraging him to visit your website and not the one above or below yours in the search results.

There are two places where you can add meta tags to your website. In the admin console (**Site Admin | Global settings**, field **Global Metadata**), you add meta tags that will appear on every page. Be careful! Do not add a meta tag for the description here. This tag must be unique for every page if you would like to achieve the best search engine ranking.

To add a specific description to one page, open the page for editing in the admin console (**Content | Pages**), and switch to the **Options** tab. Add the description meta tag into the field **Page Specific Metadata**, the same way you would do it in plain HTML.

```
Page Specific Metadata:
<meta name="description" content="Put the description of the website here!" />
```

Do not copy the same meta tag to every page, it does not make any sense for search engine optimization. The description meta tag should be different in every page.

The method just described is suitable for editors with some basic HTML knowledge. However, if the editor of your website does not have any HTML knowledge, you better give him a special field where the description of the page can be added and then automatically pasted into the template at the right place.

Open your main template (**Layout | Templates**). Add the following line of code into the head section of the template, right below the Smarty tag {metadata}:

```
<meta name="description" content="{description}" />
```

Then, open any page for editing, and switch to the **Options** tab, fill in the description of the website in the field **Description (title attribute)**, and the meta tag will be generated the right way.

If you have a lot of pages and would like to have a description generated automatically, then you can also use the special third-party tag called autometa (http://dev.cmsmadesimple.org/projects/autometa). This tag creates meta tags for keywords and descriptions on the fly, if they are not found in the page metadata field. Keywords are taken from the **Search** module, which should be installed. The meta tag description includes the first characters of the page content.

Meta tag keywords

There is a discussion on the use of meta tag keywords still being important or not. I do not add any keywords to my websites anymore, as I cannot see any difference in the ranking of websites with or without keywords. However, they cannot do any harm, and if you would like to use meta keywords, then add the following lines in the head of your main template (**Layout | Templates**), below the Smarty tag {metadata}:

```
<meta name="keywords" content="{content block='Keywords'
  oneline='true' wysiwyg='false'}" />
```

This code uses additional content blocks described in the previous section, and adds a new field named **Keywords** to the page editing window in the admin console. The field can then be filled by the editor of the website and will be automatically placed at the right place in your template.

Using SEO markup in templates

This is not really a CMS Made Simple trick. However, this tip is very important for search engine optimization. Use the HTML tag `<h1>` in your template, and pay attention to the words you use in your title. The best way is to place the title of every page within an `<h1>` tag in your main template, as shown in the following code snippet:

```
<h1>{title}</h1>
{content}
```

Do not use any other HTML tag for the title, as the search engine will not pay enough attention to titles formatted like:

```
<div class="title">{title}</div>
{content}
```

Use words and search phrases that are relevant and important for your business in `<h1>` tags, especially on the start page. If you use a title like *Welcome!* on the start page, then you say to the search engine that the word *Welcome* is extremely important for your business. You see, that does not make sense, as you would not like to be found if someone searches for *Welcome*, but for the products or services you offer.

Use headings in the module templates as well, for example, for the detailed view of news article. The best way is to place the news title in `<h1>` or `<h2>` tags as well:

```
<h1>{entry->title}</h1>
```

It is recommended that you have at least one `<h1>` tag and some `<h2>`-`<h6>` tags in one page. In the WYSIWYG editor, you can use the format drop-down to automatically select headings 1 to 6, as shown in the following screenshot:

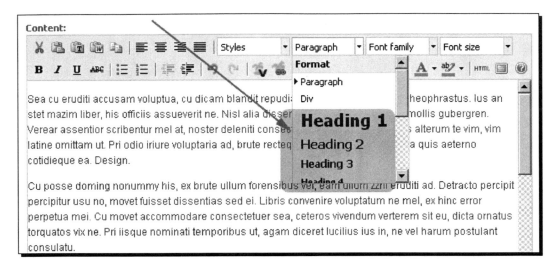

Using SEO markup in pages

While writing content for your website, use HTML `strong` tags to emphasize words or phrases relevant to your business, products, or services. The more text you have, the better for search engines. However, a search engine does not use any logic and is not human. If it sees 800 words on the page, it can not differentiate between important and unimportant words. To help it identify, place important words in between `strong` tags. But do not use a lot of them. One per paragraph is more than enough; do not exaggerate, as it would harm your search engine ranking rather than help. In the WYSIWYG editor, you can use the **B** button to format anything in strong tags:

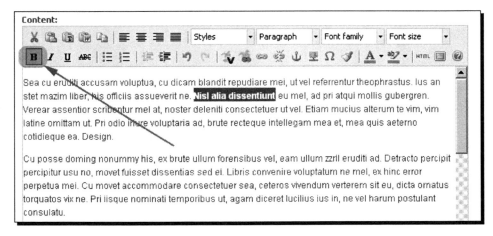

Use internal links in your text to other pages. It means, link your own pages if it makes sense. You should link search words and phrases instead of phrases like *click here*.

When adding images to your website, never forget to fill in the HTML attributes `alt` and `title`. Search engines use these attributes for finding and matching pictures in the special image search. With a WYSIWYG editor, the two fields are shown right below the **Image URL** tag:

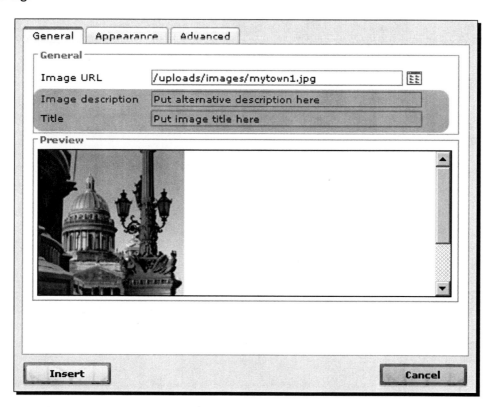

Using keywords in page alias and image files

Using keywords in page aliases that are used to create unique URLs for the website is a simple way to improve its search ranking. A page alias is generated by default from the title of the page, but you can change it afterwards. In the admin console, open any page for editing, and switch to the **Options** tab. Find the **Page Alias** field, and change it to suit your desired search words or phrases.

Do not change the alias often, especially if the page is already linked to other websites. If you change the alias, the page will not be found. If you still need to change the alias of a good linked page, without losing references, change it. Then create a new page with the content type **Internal Page Link**, give the page the old alias, and choose as the destination the page with the new alias. Do not show this page in the menu. The old link will still work and redirect the user to the new page alias.

It is also better to use search keywords in the names of the image files.

Search engine friendly URLs

Search engine friendly URLs are website addresses that do not contain any dynamic components in them, and thus are better readable for humans and search engines. Compare the following two URLs:

`http://youdomain.com/index.php?page=products`

`http://yourdomain.com/products`

Which is better? A search engine will find the second version more attractive and will better index your website. Some pages with query strings in the address (as in the first example) are never indexed, while some will take longer to be indexed. After setting up your website with CMS Made Simple, you will find that the URLs of your pages are built in the first way. We should rewrite them to achieve better results with the website.

The search engine friendly URLs are also better readable by people. If you do not care about the search engines, then think about the visitors of the website. How easy is it to type or write down the address of the specific page if we do not use the second rewritten version? Imagine your visitor would like to recommend the page. He/she would do it without any difficulties with search engine friendly URL and may fail with the first example.

Time for action – turning on search engine friendly URLs

Let's see how search engine friendly URLs can be enabled in CMS Made Simple.

1. Open an FTP browser of your choice (for example, FileZilla), and find the folder doc in your installation.

2. Copy the `htaccess.txt` file from the doc folder into the root directory of your CMSMS website (at the same level as the `config.php` file).

3. Rename the file `htaccess.txt` to `.htaccess` (pay attention to the period at the front of the filename).

4. In the next step, open the `config.php` file for editing, and find the section *URL Settings*.

5. Change the line for rewriting URLs, as shown:

   ```
   $config['url_rewriting'] = 'mod_rewrite';
   ```

6. Open your website, and see how the links in the navigation look. They should be search engine friendly now.

What just happened?

To enable search engine friendly URLs on your website, you had to complete two steps. In the first step, you moved the file `htaccess.txt` into the root directory of your website. You then renamed the moved file to `.htaccess` (period at the beginning belongs to the filename). `.htaccess` is the name of a configuration file that allows you to control the web server. The file is placed in the root directory and overrides some of the default settings of your server.

The default `htaccess.txt` is suitable for most servers. However, sometimes you may encounter difficulties. For example, not all web hosting providers accept the following setting:

```
Options +FollowSymLinks
```

In this case, you will get an error 500 (internal server error) after turning on search engine friendly URLs. To solve the issue, comment out the following option as shown:

```
# Options +FollowSymLinks
```

If your website is placed in a subfolder, like `http://www.yourdomain.com/folder`, then you have to adjust the `.htaccess` file. Find the line `RewriteBase /`, and change it to the name of the folder where your website is placed. In our example, it would be:

```
RewriteBase /folder
```

In the second step, you modified the file `config.php`. With these changes, you have told CMS Made Simple that `.htaccess` is placed in the root directory, and you are going to use these new settings to rewrite URLs.

With CMS Made Simple, you can even simulate a static address like `http://www.yourdomain.com/products.html`. In this case, the address of the pages will look like static HTML files. Open `config.php`, and find the line `$config['page_extension'] = '';`. If you change it to `$config['page_extension'] = 'html';`, then all URLs of your website will look like static HTML pages.

If you still get an internal server error (error 500), please check the following known issues:

- Your hosting company does not support `mod_rewrite`. Ask your provider if the module `mod_rewrite` is available on your web hosting.
- You have installed CMS into a subdirectory, for example, `http://yourdomain.com/mycms`. In this case, you have to edit the `.htaccess` file, and replace the line `RewriteBase /` with `RewriteBase /mycms` (change the name after the slash to your subdirectory).

Avoiding duplicate content

Duplicate content refers to the pages whose content completely matches other pages. Normally, you do not create such pages consciously. However, there are some examples for non-malicious duplicate content:

- Printer-only version of the page
- Pages that are linked using multiple URLs
- Mobile versions of the website, and so on.

CMS websites with generated pages are extremely vulnerable to being penalized by search engines for duplicate content.

 Google says: As a result, the ranking of the site may suffer, or the site might be removed entirely from the Google index, in which case, it will no longer appear in the search results.

There are some steps you can take to prevent duplicate content issues that have been described in the following sections.

Consequently use domain with www or without www

Normally, your website can be reached at `http://yourdomain.com` or `http://www.yourdomain.com`. Even if the same content is shown on both addresses, it is technically possible to serve different contents on both addresses. Search engines know it, and can skip your website from the index if both versions are reachable and serve the same content.

First of all, decide what your preferred domain version is. Then check what address has been given during the installation of your website. Open the file `config.php` in your FTP browser, and search for the following line:

```
$config['root_url'] = 'http://yourdomain.com';
```

Adjust the line to your preferred domain version if it does not match, and save the file on your web hosting. In the next step, open the file `.htaccess`, and add the marked lines as shown in the following code snippet, if your preferred domain name includes www:

```
RewriteEngine on
RewriteBase /

# Redirect to canonical domain name with www
RewriteCond %{HTTP_HOST} ^yourdomain\.com$ [NC]
RewriteRule ^(.*) http://www.yourdomain.com/$1 [L,R=301]
```

In the other case (your preferred domain name is without www), add the lines as shown in the following code snippet:

```
RewriteEngine on
RewriteBase /

# Redirect to canonical domain name without www
RewriteCond %{HTTP_HOST} ^www\.yourdomain\.com$ [NC]
RewriteRule ^(.*) http://yourdomain.com/$1 [L,R=301]
```

Now, all links in your website navigation should point to the correct version. If you enter a wrong version in the address bar of the website, it would immediately redirect to the right one.

Avoid publishing of print versions of your pages

If you use the **Printing** module on your website to offer a printer friendly version of your content, then you should block it from search engines.

In the admin console, click on **Extensions | Printing**, and click on the **Print template** tab. Add the following meta tags to the head section of the template:

```
<meta name="robots" content="noindex,nofollow" />
```

This meta tag can control the behavior of search engine crawling and indexing and applies to all search engines. `noindex` prevents the page from being indexed, and `nofollow` prevents the search engine from following links from this page.

Use tag for canonical URLs

If you use search engine friendly URLs, then the pages of your website are available through different URLs. Say you have a page called **FAQ** placed under the page **Client Center**. This page can be accessed through three different URLs:

- http://www.yourdomain.com/client-center/faq
- http://www.yourdomain.com/index.php?page=faq
- http://www.yourdomain.com/faq

All these URLs actually call the same page. How can we inform the search engine that there is only one "main" URL that should be considered? There is a link tag, which can be placed in the head section of HTML:

```
<link rel="canonical" href="http://www.yourdomain.com/client-
    center/faq">
```

This tag tells the search engine what the main or canonical URL of the page is. All other versions of the page would be treated as non-canonical and thus not considered by the search engines. In CMS Made Simple, you can generate a canonical URL in your main page template (**Layout | Templates**) as shown in the following code snippet:

```
{if isset($canonical)}
<link rel="canonical" href="{$canonical}" />
{elseif isset($content_obj)}
<link rel="canonical" href="{$content_obj->GetURL()}" />
{/if}
```

Place the code in the head section of your HTML template and save it. From now on, the canonical URL of every page will be generated automatically in CMS Made Simple.

Creating XML sitemaps for search engines

Sitemaps are a way to tell search engines about the pages on your website which otherwise they might not discover. In its simplest terms, an XML sitemap—usually called a sitemap—is a list of the pages on your website. Creating and submitting a sitemap makes sure that search engines know about all the pages on your site, including URLs that may not be discoverable by a normal crawling process.

XML sitemaps can be created with the **SiteMapMadeSimple** module. After installation, this module creates a file called sitemap.xml in the root of your website and tells the search engine which pages can be found on the site and when the page was last changed. An XML sitemap is automatically updated every time you make changes to the pages or page structure.

You can submit your sitemap to major search engines such as Google, Yahoo!, Bing, or Ask. For minor search engines, you can extend the `robots.txt` file placed in the root directory of your website. Add the following line at the very bottom of the file:

```
Sitemap: http://www.yourdomain.com/sitemap.xml
```

Adjust your domain name in the example.

Visitor statistics

Now, when the website is published, you would probably like to know how many visitors you get per day, week, and month. In this way, you can control your efforts in search engine optimization and gain additional information about what the visitors of your website look for or which content is the most interesting to them. The module provides information on how the visitors find your website and where they come from. You can also see what browser and screen resolution the visitor used.

There are a lot of web analysis tools that you can use on the website. There is even a special third-party module that you can install to see the statistic of your website directly in the admin console. The module is called **Statistics**. This module not only makes the visitor statistics available in your admin console, but also shows a visible counter on the website.

You can also use external website analysis tools such as Google Analytics or even both (the module **Statistics** and Google Analytics) if you want to compare the results. Google Analytics provides you with special JavaScript code that you must add to the main template of your website (**Layout | Templates**). It is important to know that only pages that include this code are tracked in the statistics. By placing it in the main template, the code is automatically called with every page, and thus the entire website is covered.

Always include JavaScript code in the Smarty tag `{literal}` to avoid the code being interpreted as Smarty code. For example:

```
{literal}
  alien JS code
{/literal}
```

User-defined tags

User-defined tags are a simple way to insert some PHP code into your site. With the default installation of CMS Made Simple there are two example tags already created, which are as follows:

- `{custom_copyright}`
- `{user_agent}`

You will find them in the admin console. Click on **Extensions | User Defined Tags**, and then on one of the tags displayed there to see simple PHP code implemented.

To use a user-defined tag in the page, just put its name enclosed in curly brackets into the page content or template. For example, you can add the tag {custom_copyright} to the footer section of your template, as shown in the following code snippet:

```
{custom_copyright} businessWorld
```

The tag will automatically display the year 2004, a dash, and then the actual year, so that you do not need to change the template to adjust the year afterwards.

To create a new user-defined tag, you need some basic PHP knowledge. Write your code in any PHP editor, create a new user-defined tag, and paste your PHP code into it (leaving <?php and ?> out). Then call the user-defined tags with Smarty tag in your page or templates.

How to make a user-defined tag

Like most things in CMS Made Simple, adding a new user-defined tag is simple, if you have some PHP knowledge. Let's create a simple PHP countdown script.

Time for action – creating your own user-defined tag

Imagine you would like to countdown the number of days till the New Year on the start page. The days should be counted automatically and displayed at the place where the user-defined tag is added in the content.

1. In the admin console, click on **Extensions | User Defined Tags**.

2. At the bottom of the page, click on **Add User Defined Tag**.

3. Enter **countdown** as the name of the new user-defined tag and the following code snippet into the field **Code**:
```
$target = mktime(0, 0, 0, 1, 1, 2011);
$diff = $target - time();
$days = floor($diff/86400);
echo $days;
```

4. Click on **Submit**.

5. Open any page of your website, and add the user-defined tag, shown as follows:
```
It is {countdown} days until 1. January 2011
```

6. Click on **Apply**, and see the result on the page.

What just happened?

You have created your own user-defined tag (UDT) in CMS Made Simple. This tag automatically shows the number of days until the date given in the first line of the PHP script (January 1, 2011).

Then, you have used the tag in a sentence on the page. Instead of the tag `{countdown}`, the number of days is shown at the place where you have added the tag.

The name of the tag is technical information and can only contain letters, numbers, and underscores, just like the names of PHP variables. The name is what you will have to type in curly brackets to add it into a page. So be descriptive, but do not make it too long.

You do not need any `<?` or `<?php` tags when you paste the code into UDT, just skip them. If you make a syntax mistake in your PHP code, then you will not be able to save the code. However, the following error will be displayed, so that you know you have to correct your PHP code.

Invalid code entered.

Parse error: syntax error, unexpected '}' in /var/www/ html/businessworld /admin/edituserplugin.php(103) : eval()'d code on line 5

Parameters for tags

User defined tags get really useful when you start to add parameters to them. You can pass parameters to the PHP code this way:

```
{countdown date='05-01-2011'}
```

In this way, you can specify the countdown date directly in the UDT instead of writing it in the code, so that that there is no need to customize PHP code again and again.

In PHP code, you can get the parameter with the help of the special array `$params`, which is always defined and contains all parameters passed. In the next example, the passed parameter `date` is used in the countdown script:

```
$date = explode('-', $params['date']);
$target = mktime(0, 0, 0, $date[0], $date[1] , $date[2]);
$diff = $target - time();
$days = floor($diff/86400);
echo $days;
```

Test this tag the same way as before, but instead of using `{countdown}`, use `{countdown date='05-01-2011'}` or any other date in the format MM-DD-YYYY.

These are basic principles of writing user-defined tags. You can do some useful things with a little imagination, so just think about what you can do if you know a little PHP.

How to get the page information in UDT

You can pass any variable to the UDT including objects created by CMS Made Simple. You can show variables and objects that exist in the page with the following code:

```
{get_template_vars}
```

If you add the above tag to the template, then you will find out that the page has an object called $content_obj. This object contains all the information about the actual page and can be passed to UDT as well.

Let's assume we need some additional navigation that looks like the tracing path of the visitor on the website. It means that we would like to display the last three pages that the visitor has seen. This navigation has to be built automatically and saved in the visitor session.

Create a new user-defined tag and call it trace. Add the PHP code shown in the following code snippet:

```
$pagetitle = $params['page']->Name();
$pageurl = $params['page']->GetURL();

$_SESSION['trace'][$pagetitle] = $pageurl;

if (sizeof($_SESSION['trace']) > 3) {
    array_shift($_SESSION['trace']);
}

$trace = array_reverse($_SESSION['trace']);

foreach ($trace as $title => $url) {
    echo '<a href="'. $url .'">'. $title . '</a><br />';
}
```

This code assumes that the parameter page has been passed to it ($params['page']) and this parameter contains the page object. We can call the user-defined tag as shown in the following code snippet:

```
<h4>Last 3 pages you have visited</h4>
{trace page=$content_obj}
```

I suggest that you add the tag to the page template below the site navigation. Every time the user opens a new page, the information about it is passed to the UDT. The page parameter contains the page object, and can be used with page content methods (Name() and GetURL()). Please see CMS Made Simple API for more information.

The last three pages that the visitor has seen are saved in the session variable and are now temporarily displayed below the sidebar menu.

Understanding events

In the last section, you learned to create user-defined tags. To execute the PHP code in the tags, you had to place it in the page or the template. With **Event Manager**, you can execute the code when certain events occur. An event can be the creation of a new page or even deleting a user in the admin console. There are over 50 events already defined in CMS Made Simple, and every module can have additional events.

Examples for executing user-defined tags on events are as follows:

- Sending an e-mail to the administrator of the website if any page is updated
- Replacing certain parts of the page before displaying it on the website
- Deleting associated stylesheets if the template is deleted

CMS Made Simple triggers events such as **ContentEditPost** or **DeleteTemplatePre**, when the specified action occurs. You create one or more user-defined tags with custom functionality and assign them to the event. This means that the assigned functionality will be executed when the event is triggered. The event sends the actual data to the user-defined tag (if there is any), and this data can now be used in any way in your PHP code.

See the list of events already added to CMS Made Simple in the admin console (**Extensions | Event Manager**). For every event, there is a brief description of when the user-defined tags appended to it will be executed.

This functionality allows anybody with a bit of PHP knowledge to extend core or module functionality. For example, it should now be easy to send an e-mail to the administrator if the page is modified by the editor. For the next example, the **CMSMailer** module should be configured properly, as explained in Chapter 2, *Getting Started*.

Time for action – sending mails after page update

To enable CMS Made simple to send e-mails to the administrator when a content page is updated, perform the following steps:

1. In the admin console, click on **Extensions | User Defined Tags**.
2. Click on the **Add User Defined Tag** link.

3. Name the new tag `buzzer` and the code as shown:

```
global $gCms;
$cmsmailer = $gCms->modules['CMSMailer']['object'];
$cmsmailer->AddAddress($cmsmailer->GetFrom(),$cmsmailer->GetFromName());
$cmsmailer->SetSubject('Admin buzzer');
$cmsmailer->SetBody('The page <i>' .$params['content']->mName.'</i> has been changed.');
$cmsmailer->IsHTML(true);
$cmsmailer->Send();
```

4. Click on **Submit**.

5. In the admin console, click on **Extensions | Event Manager**.

6. Find the event called **ContentEditPost**, and click the edit button on the same line.

7. Select the **buzzer** tag from the drop-down field, and click **Add**.

8. Now, change any page to test the admin buzzer function. You should receive an e-mail notification with the page name changed.

What just happened?

We have used the **CMSMailer** module of CMS Made Simple to send an e-mail notification. In this way, we consider all individual settings made in the module and ensure that e-mails are sent properly.

The PHP code added to the tag is a slight modification of the sample code added to the **Help** section of the **CMSMailer** module. It sends mails to the e-mail address configured in the module in the field **From address**. We have also used the name of the changed page in the e-mail notification. This was possible because an event provides us with the object `$params['content']` that contains a reference to the affected page and all information about the page.

Then, you have assigned the user-defined tag to the event **ContentEditPost**. This event is sent after the page is edited and submitted (it is not enough to just **Apply** changes, you must **Submit** them).

Integrating jQuery in navigation

CMS Made Simple uses plain HTML, CSS, and Smarty in all templates. This means that you can use any jQuery effect in your templates as well. jQuery is a JavaScript framework and has a lot of plugins.

To use the plugins, you have to separate HTML, CSS, and JavaScript and put them at the appropriate place in CMS Made Simple. HTML markup is saved in templates, whereas CSS is saved in stylesheets and then assigned to the template. JavaScript can be placed globally (**Site Admin | Global Metadata**), so that it is available on the whole page. Alternatively, it can be placed in the page template. In this case, it will be available in all pages using this template. If you need JavaScript only in one page, then you can add it to the **Page Specific Metadata** field in the **Options** tab.

Let's see how you can integrate a jQuery drop-down menu on your website. Examples and instructions for this effect can be found at `http://www.dynamicdrive.com/style/csslibrary/item/jquery_multi_level_css_menu_horizontal_blue/`.

Time for action – integrating jQuery in navigation

The instruction on the link above explains how you can use this jQuery plugin in the pure HTML website. Let's see how you can integrate the plugin in CMS Made Simple.

1. Save the files `jquerycssmenu.css` and `jquerycssmenu.js` from the address given above to your local disk.

2. Upload the file `jquerycssmenu.js` into the folder `uploads` on your web hosting.

3. In the admin console **Add a Stylesheet (Layout | Stylesheets)**, call it **JQueryCSSMenu**, and copy the whole content from the file `jquerycssmenu.css` into the **Content** field.

4. Click on **Submit**.

5. In the list of stylesheets, click the blue CSS button beside the new created stylesheet.

6. Select your main template from the drop-down field, and click on **Attach to this Template**.

7. Open the main template of your website, and add the following code snippet in the head section:

```
{literal}
<!--[if lte IE 7]>
<style type="text/css">
html .jquerycssmenu{height: 1%;} /*Holly Hack for IE7 and below*/
</style>
<![endif]-->
{/literal}
<script type="text/javascript" src="http://ajax.googleapis.com/
ajax/libs/jquery/1.2.6/jquery.min.js"></script>
<script type="text/javascript" src="uploads/jquerycssmenu.js"></
script>
```

8. Create or replace the top navigation in the main template with:

```
<div id="myjquerymenu" class="jquerycssmenu">
  {menu template="minimal_menu.tpl"}
  <br style="clear: left" />
</div>
```

9. Click on **Apply**, and see the drop-down menu of your website.

What just happened?

This was a very basic example of how to integrate jQuery into your website. First, you have to figure out what JavaScript files are needed for the plugin and upload them to your web hosting. Then create a new stylesheet, copy all styles into it, and attach the new stylesheet to the template. If images are used in the stylesheet, then upload them to the web hosting as well and adjust the image path in the stylesheet.

Then open your template and add JavaScript to the head section of the template. Any scripts should be enclosed in the Smarty tags `{literal}{/literal}`. This tag allows a block of data to be taken literally. This is typically used around JavaScript or stylesheet blocks where curly braces would interfere with the curly braces of Smarty tags. Anything within `{literal}{/literal}` tags is not interpreted, but displayed as it is.

In the last step, you add the required CSS classes and IDs to the HTML markup of the template. This method works for any jQuery plugin you would like to integrate. Another example for integrating jQuery into the **Gallery** module was explained in Chapter 7, *Using Third-party Modules*.

Pop quiz – advanced use of CMS Made Simple

1. If you change the language of the admin console, it would have an impact on:
    a. All user accounts in CMS Made Simple.
    b. On the language displayed to the visitors of the website.
    c. Only to this user account.
    d. Nothing. You have to choose the language once during installation and cannot be changed later.

2. If you would like to participate in making translations for CMS Made Simple, you have to:
    a. Join the official developer team of CMS Made Simple.
    b. Join the translation project of your language in Forge.
    c. Translate on your local installation and upload translations to CMS Made Simple forum.
    d. Pay the community to get needed translations.

3. Meta tags are important for search engines. What meta tags are used by the major search engines like Google, Yahoo and Bing?

   a. `descr<meta name="iption" content="" />`

   b. `<meta name="refresh" content="" />`

   c. `<meta name="robots" content="" />`

   d. `<meta name="author" content="" />`

4. Assume you use the tag `{title}` in the tag `<title>` in your template. What will be affected if the title of the page is changed?

   a. Alias of the page

   b. Menu text of the page

   c. Heading of the page

   d. The name in the title bar of the browser

5. How can you prevent different URLs of the same page being treated as duplicate content?

   a. Consequently use domain with or without www.

   b. Avoid publishing print version of your websites.

   c. Use canonical tag for canonical URLs.

   d. Use `<meta name="robots" content="noindex" />` in all your pages.

6. Why should you use search engine friendly addresses?

   a. The RAM memory of your computer gets overloaded by opening more than seven pages without friendly URLs (they are too long).

   b. The URL is optimized for search engines.

   c. You should not use them at all because you have to create for every search engine a special one and so create duplicated content.

   d. The page is loaded much quicker

7. User-defined tags are written in:

   a. Pure HTML

   b. Pure HTML and CSS

   c. JavaScript

   d. PHP

8. Some jQuery plugins cannot be integrated in CMS Made Simple:

   a. true

   b. false

Have a go hero – make search engine optimization

Make search engine optimizations for your website before you publish it. It is better to start with a clear and optimized website from the very beginning. Double-check page titles, menu texts and words represented as internal links in the content of the page. Control if one page can be reached with different URLs and use a canonical tag to help the search engines to understand which URL is the main one. Create an XML sitemap for search engines and monitor the statistics of your visitors to figure out what pages are the most popular, thus figuring out what contents of your page can be extended.

Consider that your website is made primarily for visitors and not for search engines. Search engines are just carriers that bring visitors to your website. And whether the visitor likes your website or not lies in your responsibility.

Summary

In this chapter, we learned advanced subjects that are not necessarily a part of every website.

Specifically, we covered the following topics:

- **Localization and translation**: You need this section if the primary language of the website is not in English or if you are going to create a multilingual website.

- **Additional content and controls for editors**: This section helps to understand what you can do if you have a sophisticated layout or would give website 'editors' more control.

- **Search engine optimization**: You learned how you can optimize the website for search engines.

- **User-defined tags and Event Manager**: If you have some basic PHP knowledge, you can even implement your own PHP scripts into CMS Made Simple and still stay upgradable.

- **Implementing jQuery effects**: You learned how you can implement simple jQuery functionality into the top navigation of the website.

Now that we've learned how to realize these sophisticated features, read the next chapter to see what tasks you have as a website administrator during the lifetime of the website.

11
Administration and Troubleshooting

Once the website you have created is ready and running, you have to take a closer look at the tasks you have as a webmaster during the lifetime of the website. Depending on the nature of the website, you must regularly make backups if you or your customer continuously add and edit the content or change the design. It is also recommended to watch the development of CMS Made Simple and make updates to keep the website secure and be able to use the newest features.

This chapter helps you administer your CMS Made Simple website once it is running. In this chapter, we will see how to:

- Take a backup of your website
- Move it to another web host
- Upgrade your installation or modules
- Optimize the performance
- Secure and protect your website in the most efficient way
- Get help from the community

You are not supposed to read the whole chapter. You can start reading from any section, as they do not depend on each other. *Upgrading CMS Made Simple* is the part that you will probably need when a new release of CMS Made Simple is published.

I strongly recommend that you read the *Troubleshooting* section and devote 10 minutes of your time to the question *How can I get a quick answer in the free support forum?* There are some useful tips on how to get the best answer in the shortest period of time.

Getting system information

As the website administrator, you should know how to get the system information for your website or your customer's installation. This information helps you to understand how the server, where CMS Made Simple is installed and configured, gives you the first indicators when you encounter problems while running CMS Made Simple or any of its modules.

In the admin console, click **Site Admin | System Information**. The information page is divided into three sections:

- ◆ **CMS Install Information**
- ◆ **PHP Information**
- ◆ **Server Information**

In the first section you see the version of CMS Made Simple installed and all enabled modules with their versions as well.

```
CMS Install Information:

                    CMS Version
                    1.6.6

                         Installed Modules

                    CMSMailer
                    1.73.14

                    FileManager
                    1.0.1

                    MenuManager
                    1.6.2

                    News
                    2.10.3

                    nuSOAP
                    1.0.1

                    Printing
                    1.0.4

                    Search
                    1.6.1

                    ThemeManager
                    1.1.1

                    TinyMCE
                    2.5.5
```

Below the list of modules, you will find the **Config Information** section that gives you an overview of all values set in the file `config.php`. Any value that you see in this section can be changed in this file, except the file permissions.

Behind the paths' values, you see a green tick or red cross. CMS Made Simple checks the permissions of your files and informs you if the permissions are not set properly. You should adjust the file permissions if you encounter any issues with CMS Made Simple or any of its modules. Setting permissions is dependent on the installed operating system. If you are not sure how to do it, then ask your hosting provider or use a common search engine to figure it out. File permissions are not something specific to CMS Made Simple, but to the operating system.

In the second section, you will find individual PHP settings on your server. Pay attention to any setting that is followed by a red cross (failure) or a yellow exclamation mark (warning).

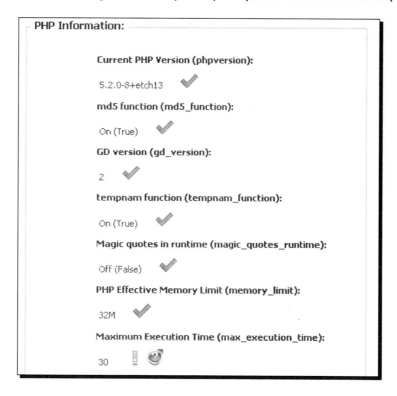

Failures should be corrected as soon as possible. Warnings can be ignored if you do not have any issues when running CMS Made Simple, but you should correct them if something does not work as expected. In the following table, you will find some required and recommended settings for CMS Made Simple. Required settings are mandatory. Recommended settings can make your system run smoother and solve some issues.

Setting	Minimum and recommended values
Current PHP Version (phpversion)	5.0.4 or greater
GD version (gd_version)	version 2
Magic quotes in runtime (magic_quotes_runtime)	On (True)
PHP Effective Memory Limit (memory_limit)	minimum 16 MB recommended 24 MB or greater
Maximum Execution Time (max_execution_time)	minimum 30 recommend 60 or greater
PHP Safe Mode (safe_mode)	Off (False)
Session Save Path (session_save_path)	This path should be writable (green tick)
PHP register_globals (register_globals)	Off (False)
Maximum Post Size (post_max_size)	minimum 2M recommend 10M or greater
Maximum Upload Size (upload_max_filesize)	minimum 2M recommend 10M or greater

The third section on the **System Information** page gives you an overview of your server's configuration. If you are the website administrator, then you should be able to answer at least three questions about your system:

- What operating system is used on your server?
- What server software (and which version) is installed on your server?
- What database (and which version) is used for a CMS Made Simple installation?

All these questions can be answered if you look at the information given here thoroughly.

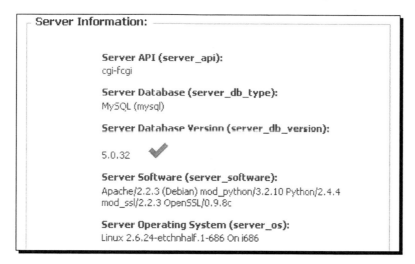

From the preceding screenshot, I can say that this installation of CMS Made Simple is installed on Linux (**Server Operating System**), Apache server version 2 is installed (**Server Software**), and this server uses the database MySQL 5.0.32 (**Server Database + Server Database Version**).

It is important to know how your server is configured to be able to get help if you encounter issues. There are a lot of varieties of applications' versions and configurations, so nobody can guess exactly how your individual hosting is configured. Keep that in mind while getting free help from the community.

Backing up your website

Backing up means making copies of your files and database. You need to backup regularly in case something goes wrong on your web hosting. Your data could be lost due to some hosting issues or through webmaster mistakes. Therefore, it is important to have backup files to be able to restore your website.

To backup a website made with CMS Made Simple, it is not sufficient just to copy all the files found on the server with FTP. Those files are only a small fraction of your website. The most important part is the database where all your text and designs (except image files) are stored.

In CMS Made Simple, you have two modules (one is used for file backups and one for database backups). You would probably not be able to use the modules on free web hosting or on the hosting with strong restrictions. To check if an easy backup of your website with the following described modules is possible, try to install the first module to backup files.

Backing up website files

Website files are the files that you upload to your FTP directory. Most of them are delivered from the team of developers and have been copied to your web space before installation. In the uploads directory, you will find files, like images, that have been uploaded by the editors. If you have installed additional modules, then you will find files for these modules in the modules folder.

To backup files, you can download everything from your FTP to the local disk. However, depending on your connection and the total number of files, this can take a lot of time.

Time for action – creating a backup with the module

If you would like to archive the files before downloading them, then you can use the **FileBackup** module.

1. In the admin console, select **Extensions | Module Manager**.

2. Click on the **Available Modules** tab, and look for the letter **F** above the alphabetical module list.

3. Find the **FileBackup** module, and click on the **Download & Install** link in the same line. If there are restrictions on your web hosting, then you will see the following error:

 You cannot use this module, since you don't have the tar command installed on your server.

In this case, you will have to backup your website manually. If the installation of the module **FileBackup** was successful, then you can start configuring it.

4. In the admin console, go to **Site Admin | File Backup**.

5. Click on the **Preferences** tab. In the admin area you see the following message:

 Please check and save the path to tar binaries before using FileBackup.

6. Click **Save**. (This module tries to recognize the required path automatically). If the message does not disappear, then you have to ask your hosting provider what the path to tar binaries on your web hosting is and enter the path into the field **Path to tar binaries**.

7. Switch to the **Backup Files** tab.

8. Click on **Backup Files**.

9. Wait until the complete list of folders is displayed and you see the message **Task completed** at the end of the list. Below this message, you will see the backup file containing all your website files.

10. Click on the backup file, and save it to your local disk.

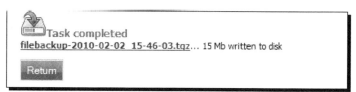

What just happened?

You have created an archived backup of all website files and have saved the archive to you local disk. You should create a new backup file and save it separately from the current installation. For example; on the local disk, anytime you install a new module, upgrade the whole system or one module or upload new images. Do it regularly. You will save a lot of time in case of emergency.

All backup files will also be saved in your installation. You will find them using any FTP browser (for example, **FileZilla**) in the folder /admin/backups on your web hosting.

 Make sure you delete the backup files after downloading to your local disk. Otherwise, anybody could go to http://www.yourdomain.com/admin/backups/ and download your backup, containing the file config.php with your database settings and password.

It is recommended to clear the cache folder before creating a file backup as CMS Made Simple creates a lot of temporary files to speed up the website. These files must not to be saved with the backup as they will be generated automatically once CMS Made Simple is installed and running. To clear the cache folder in the admin console, click on **Site Admin | Global Settings**, select the **Advanced Setup** tab, and click the **Clear** button below the **Clear Cache** label.

In fact, the best solution would be to set up some automation if the files are changed frequently. You should contact your ISP to determine whether it is possible to backup the file automatically.

Backing up database

With the next step, you backup your database. In other words, you create a dump of the database. Dumps hold all the actual data of the installation: page structure, page content, complete design, and any data saved in the modules like **News**.

A database backup has the same importance as a backup of the files. If you just backup the files, then you do not backup any changes on the website such as new pages or new modules.

Time for action – creating a database backup

Let's see how to create a backup of the database along with the file backup. You need the **MysqlDump** module to create a database dump from within your admin console in CMS Made Simple.

1. In the admin console, click on **Extensions | Module Manager**

2. Click on the **Available Modules** tab, and then the letter **M** above the alphabetical module list.

3. Find the module **MysqlDump**, and click on the **Download & Install** link in the same line. If there are any restrictions on your web hosting, then you will see the following error.

 You cannot use this module, if don't have MySQL installed on your server.

This error means that you cannot use the module to create a database dump this way and should do it manually (refer to the next section). If the module installation was successful, then you can create a database dump right now.

4. In the admin console, click on **Site Admin | MySQL Dump**

5. Switch to the **Preferences** tab.

6. Click **Save.** (Usually the path to **mysql binaries** is recognized automatically.) If you still see the message **Invalid path to MySQL utilities**, then you have to ask your hosting provider for the proper path to mysql binaries on your web hosting, and enter the path into the field **Path to mysql binaries**.

7. Switch to the **Backup Database** tab.

8. Click the **Backup database** button. Wait till a list of tables appears, and find the link to create a database dump at the end of the list.

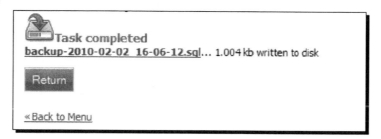

9. Save the file to your local disk.

What just happened?

You have created a backup of your database. This backup includes all your database tables and should be made regularly, ideally every time changes are made to the site's pages or the modules.

Similar to the file backup, you will find all database backups with any FTP client (for example, FileZilla) in the folder /admin/backups on your web hosting.

Manual backup

If you are not allowed to install the modules on your web hosting due to some restrictions (often made on the free web hosting), then you should backup you files manually.

For the file backup, open any FTP browser (for example, FileZilla), navigate to your installation folder, and copy all the files from the web hosting to your local disk. Remember that the files contain only a small part of your website. You should create a database dump to save all your content, design, and module data.

Backing up database with phpMyAdmin

phpMyAdmin is a free open source tool intended to handle the administration of MySQL databases. It is normally installed on every web hosting. Contact your provider to figure out the link to phpMyAdmin on your web hosting, and your login credentials if you are not sure. This tool helps you to create database backups.

Time for action – creating a backup with phpMyAdmin

The steps described here are only needed if you have no possibility to backup the database with the module described previously.

1. Log in to phpMyAdmin on your server (contact your provider to figure out the details as they can differ between web hosts).

2. Upon login, select **Databases** on the major screen:

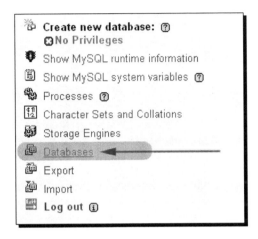

3. Select the database used for a CMS Made Simple installation. If you are not sure, then open the `config.php` file and find the line `$config['db_name']` that contains the name of the database.

4. Click on the database name in the list.

5. On the next screen, you will see the list of all tables in this database. Click on the **Export** tab at on the top of the list, as shown in the following screenshot:

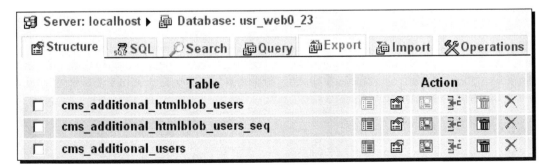

6. In the left box, you can see all the tables selected. At the top of the screen, find the checkbox **Save as file**, and select it. Click the **Go** button.

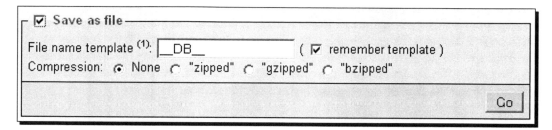

7. You will be prompted to download a file. Save the file to your computer. Depending on the database size, this may take a few moments.

What just happened?

You have manually created the backup file (or dump) of your database. Ensure that you create a new backup of the database every time you make changes to the page structure, install new modules, and add new content to the pages or the modules.

Make a backup regularly; you will need it in the case of an emergency. This backup can also be used if you move your installation from one server to another.

In fact, just making regular backups is not enough. Ideally, you should test the recovery scenario at least once because many things can go wrong:

◆ Incomplete copies of files

◆ Incomplete database backup

◆ Corrupted backups

It's catastrophic when your website crashes and you end up with a useless pack of files you believed to be backups.

Move CMS Made Simple to another web hosting

This section helps you understand how to move an entire CMS Made Simple application to another hosting service.

Step 1

Consider this step for busy websites that accept data from visitors, like **Comments** or **FrontEndUsers**. Enable the **Site Down Message** to prevent somebody from using the website while you are moving it to another hosting service. In the admin console, click on **Site Admin | Global Settings**, and select the **Sitedown Settings** tab. Write the message that the visitors to the website will see if they try to use your website during the transfer, then tick the **Enable Site Down Message** checkbox, and click **Submit**. From now on, visitors to the website will see the **Site Down Message** instead of the website.

Step 2

Clear the `cache` folder. CMS Made Simple creates a lot of temporary files to speed up the website. These files must not be saved with the backup as they will be generated automatically once CMS Made Simple is installed and running. To clear the `cache` folder in the admin console, click on **Site Admin | Global Settings**, select the **Advanced Setup** tab, and click the **Clear** button below the **Clear Cache** label.

Step 3

Create a database backup, as described in the preceding section. Import the database on the new host using phpMyAdmin. Log in to phpMyAdmin on the new host, and select the database intended for use of CMS Made Simple. Click on the **Import** tab, and select the file with the database backup in the field **Location of the text file**. Click **Go**. The database is imported to the new host.

Step 4

Copy all the files from your old site to your new site using an FTP client (for example, FileZilla). After the files are transferred, remember to check the permissions for the folders on the new site to ensure that they are set correctly. Check the permissions on the following folders:

- `/tmp/templates_c`
- `/tmp/cache`
- `/uploads`
- `/uploads/images`
- `/modules`

They should be writable. Contact your provider if you are not sure how to do it.

Step 5

In the last step, you have to open and modify the files `config.php` and `.htaccess`.

In the file `config.php`, check and adjust the following sections:

- Database Settings
- Path Settings
- Image Settings

Update them with the database access credentials and paths applicable to the new server.

The path settings are not always that obvious. In your FTP browser, it might show something like `/cmsmadesimple`. However, the real path on the server might be something like `/home/user/html/cmsmadesimple`. If you have the wrong path, then look at the error messages when you try to access your site after transfer. This message will give you a hint as to the real path settings. Contact your provider for help if it is still unclear.

The `.htaccess` file should only be modified if you change the domain name. However, if you did not make any changes to the file due to the search engine optimization, leave it as it is.

Try to log in to the admin console of CMS Made Simple on the new hosting. If everything looks good, then disable the **Site Down Message** and see the page up and running.

Upgrading CMS Made Simple

The CMS Made Simple development team improves the application constantly; therefore new versions are released regularly. You should ensure that you upgrade your system consequently. Upgrades are important for several reasons.

- **Free community support**: You will probably get no help for old releases, as there are only a few users who will still be working with the old version. The development team will not fix any issues in old versions, as a lot of issues are already solved in newer releases, and you are always encouraged to install the latest version.

- **Features**: In new releases, new features are implemented. If you work with an old version, then you have to reinvent the wheel if you need something already developed and existing.

◆ **Third-party modules**: Developers of additional modules release new versions, including new functionality and corrected bugs. Newer versions of the modules often assume that the newest version of CMS Made Simple is installed. Sometimes, the feature you need is already implemented in the last version of the module, but you are not able to install it due to the outdated version of CMS Made Simple.

◆ **Security releases**: Not only are errors corrected in new releases and new functions added, but from time-to-time, security holes are discovered. In this case, exploits are quickly spread throughout the internet. Exploits are generally sequences of commands that take advantage of a bug in order to take control over your system. If you do not upgrade, then your system becomes extremely vulnerable, your data could be damaged or lost, and nobody would take responsibility for it except you.

◆ **Stability and performance**: New releases often include improvements in performance. Even if you are not interested in the features included in new releases, your website can gain speed just by upgrading.

If a new version has been released, then you will see a message saying **You have 1 unhandled notification** in the admin console below the main menu. The message appears only once a day! Click on the plus sign beside the message, as shown in the following screenshot:

You have **1** unhandled notification ▬

⚠ Core *Notice:* A new version of CMS Made Simple is available. Please notify your administrator.

Let's see how to upgrade your installation to the newer version.

It is important to create a backup of your database and all the files on the web hosting before every upgrade (please refer to the section *Backup your website*). If something goes wrong, you can always return to the previous version and start upgrading again. Having no backup means having no possibility to go back in case of an emergency.

Open the link `http://cmsmadesimple.org` in the browser, and select **Downloads | File Releases** in the main menu on the top of the page. The list of releases is shown. If you are not sure what version of CMS Made Simple is currently installed on your web hosting, then open the admin console; you can see in the footer area at the very bottom of the page what version is used on your website.

In the downloads section, find the newest release, and choose the file named `cmsmadesimple-full-diff-[YOUR.CURRENT.VERSION]-[NEW.VERSION].tar.gz`. For example, to upgrade from version 1.6 to 1.6.5, you have to choose the file `cmsmadesimple-full-diff-1.6-1.6.5.tar.gz`. Save the file to your local disk and extract it.

If you cannot find the upgrade file from exactly your version to the current one, then you will have to download the last full version above the one installed (for example, 1.6) and proceed with these instructions using that version first.

Before copying the files to the web server, you should probably set up a **Site Down Message** (**Site Admin | Sitedown Settings**). Now open any FTP browser, and upload all the files from the extracted folder to your web hosting. Overwrite the existing files and directories. You have to overwrite these existing files with the newer versions.

After uploading the new files, check if a folder called /install has been created in the folder where CMS Made Simple is installed. If so, then enter in your browser http://www.yourdomain.com/install/upgrade.php (substitute the domain with yours). This will automatically update your database to the newest version. Do not forget to delete the install folder after upgrade. If a folder named install was not created, then you have finished the upgrade at this point.

Check the version in the footer area of the admin console. It should display the new version now.

You then have to upgrade the modules. In the admin console, click on **Extensions | Module Manager**, and see if some modules have to be upgraded on the **Available Upgrades** tab.

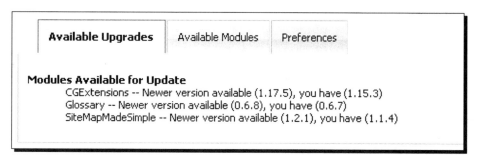

If there are some upgrades shown, then look for the modules on the **Available Modules** tab, and click on the **Upgrade** link beside the module name.

Sometimes, the notification for the new version is not displayed in the admin console. This is due to the security settings of your web hosting. Another possible way of being informed about a new version in this case is subscribing to the official RSS feed from the CMS Made Simple blog or (if you are a registered member in CMS Made Simple Forum) to subscribe to the board **Announcements**.

Remember that upgrading your system is not difficult if you do it regularly. Go with the development to get the best free support and to be sure that your system is secure and stable.

Optimizing (performance tuning)

Like every system, CMS Made Simple can be optimized and tuned for the best performance. The tips described in this section can significantly speed up your system. However, I recommend applying these instructions only if you encounter any performance issues.

Before you start to optimize your system, you should know how the system performs without any optimization. CMS Made Simple has built-in performance measurement. If you open any page generated by CMS Made Simple in a browser and then see the source code of the page, you will find HTML comments at the end of every page, shown as follows:

```
<!-- 0.267839 / 38 / 5834456 / 6113588 -->
```

This comment can be broken into four parts:

1. The page was generated in 0.267839 seconds by CMS Made Simple.
2. 38 SQL queries were needed to generate pages.
3. 5834456 bytes of memory were used.
4. The peak memory usage was 6113588 bytes.

You should save this comment to control the amount of resources that can be saved using optimization tips, given in the following sections. Every time you make an optimization, compare the new numbers on the same page with the previous ones.

Compression

This option allows the output from your server to be compressed before being sent to the browser. In simple words, the page is zipped, and instead of sending HTML, the server sends a much smaller ZIP file. The smaller the file, the faster the website can be loaded. The browser is able to decompress the zipped page automatically, so that neither you nor your visitor should care about it.

Compression can be turned on in the file `config.php`. Open the file and find the line:

```
$config['output_compression'] = false;
```

Turn on the compression by setting it to `true`:

```
$config['output_compression'] = true;
```

This may provide a significant performance increase on some sites. However, it is not needed for Apache servers that have **mod_deflate** enabled. Please contact your provider if you are not sure. Consider that enabling this feature will significantly increase the CPU and RAM usage on the server side, and this can even slow down the website if the server is very busy.

Persistent connections

CMS Made Simple is based on the database. Therefore, for each page loaded in the browser, a connection to the database is needed. There are two concepts on how CMS Made Simple connects to the database. Normally, for each page, the new connection to the database has to be established. A persistent connection is a concept which is designed to improve performance for some applications. Instead of the connection being established for each page, it is opened once and then kept for the application's lifetime.

In the file `config.php`, you can define how CMS Made Simple should connect to the database. Open the file and search for the following line:

```
$config['persistent_db_conn'] = false;
```

Change the line to:

```
$config['persistent_db_conn'] = true;
```

This would ensure that the connection to the database is not closed after the page is loaded but is kept open. The next time the page is requested, the server checks whether there is an opened connection and uses it for the new page. In this way, the time for establishing the new database connection is saved.

 This setting is not allowed by all providers. Please contact your provider to figure out if you can use persistent connections on your web hosting.

CSS in global settings and static CSS

Another place where you can save time is in the generation of the stylesheet for the page. If you open your page in the browser and see the page source, then you will see that the links to stylesheets are actually references to the PHP file `stylesheet.php`:

```
<link rel="stylesheet" type="text/css" href="http://yourdomain.com/
stylesheet.php?cssid=59" />
```

However, it is not necessary to generate stylesheets with every page again and again. You can cache them when you are ready with the design of the website and do not plan to change it.

In the admin console, click on **Site Admin | Global Settings**, and switch to the tab **Advanced Setup**. Find the field **Maximum amount of time (seconds) stylesheets can be cached in the browser**, and enter any value other than 0, as shown in the following screenshot:

Maximum amount of time (seconds) stylesheets can be cached in the browser:

604800

This parameter should be set relatively high for static sites, and should be set to 0 for site development

It depends on how often you will update the stylesheet in the future. If you do not plan to change it in the future, then go for a high value like 2592000 seconds. This means that the stylesheet will be cached for a month.

1 hour = 3600 seconds
1 day = 86400 seconds
1 week = 604800 seconds

Be sure that you change the value back to 0 if you change the stylesheet, as you will not see any changes on the page with the old cached version.

These performance tips can speed up CMS Made Simple. However, you will get more effective results if you tune the server where CMS Made Simple is installed and not only CMS Made Simple itself. Server tuning assumes that you have full access to the server and basic Linux administrator knowledge.

How to secure your installation

In this section, you learn how to secure your CMS Made Simple installation. We will not discuss how to secure the web hosting server as this is a stuff for the web hosting provider. If you host your website on your own, then you should know how to secure the server in general. If you host on a shared hosting or a managed server, then your provider would do it for you and you don't need to worry about it. Let's see what the provider will not do for you.

The first rule for a secure website is to upgrade CMS Made Simple and its modules regularly. Every time a new version of CMS Made Simple is released, run the upgrade as soon as possible. It is especially important for security releases that we close security holes. Upgrading is very easy. Please refer to the section *Upgrading CMS Made Simple* to read about how to perform upgrades.

System verification

A CMS Made Simple installation consists of its files and a database. The database holds page structure, page content, design, and any module data and can change daily on busy websites. In contrast to the database, files are a kind of static part of the website. They are changed only if you:

- ◆ Upgrade CMS Made Simple
- ◆ Upgrade any module
- ◆ Install new modules
- ◆ Remove modules from the installation
- ◆ Intentionally or unintentionally make changes to the files on your own

Sometimes files can be changed by malicious programs or hackers if you do not secure your system enough. So how can you be sure that the system files are not changed and everything is still okay.

CMS Made Simple uses a checksum verification to prove that the files on your web hosting have not been changed. A checksum is a text string computed from a file for the purpose of detecting accidental changes that may occur during its transmission or storage. These checksum strings are generated for each file that originates from the core CMS Made Simple and can be downloaded from `http://dev.cmsmadesimple.org/project/files/6`. A checksum file is generated for each release of CMS Made Simple.

Depending on your version (base or full, and release), choose the right `checksum.dat` file, and save it to your local disk. Open it in a text editor to see what is inside.

```
3ad39cc13942818630935b56dc8af619 *./index.php
6f8ae75cfde0c5a81dc09f35ea40f7a6 *./preview.php
d53ee56d1c123a1ed04326ca3406e744 *./favicon_cms.ico
. . .
```

You will find a long list of checksum strings followed by the filenames and their paths. In CMS Made Simple, you can automatically validate all files in the admin console (**Site Admin | System Verification**). This function will compare the checksum strings of the original files with the files on your installation. Normally, your files should not have any changes if you have not made any upgrades to the system so far.

The only acceptable errors are missing files from the `install` folder, as you had to delete this directory for security reasons. You may also be told that various `index.html` files in the `tmp` folder are missing or invalid. This is not critical. Missing the file `SITEDOWN` is also not critical.

Every time you run an upgrade of CMS Made Simple or any of its modules, you should create a new checksum file. In the admin console, open **Site Admin | System verification,** and click the **Submit** button in the **Download Checksum File** section. This function allows you to generate a checksum file for the current installation and save it on your local computer to be verified later. This should be done just prior to rolling out the website, and/or after any upgrades or major modifications. The integrity of the data can be checked at any later time by comparing the checksum file with the stored files.

Using this function can assist in finding problems with uploads, or exactly what files were modified if your system has been hacked. If you suddenly encounter strange issues and suspect that your system has been attacked, then you should make a system verification first to see whether there are any changed files. If the checksums do not match, then the data was certainly altered (either intentionally or unintentionally).

 The original checksum file from http://dev.cmsmadesimple.org only verifies the core CMS Made Simple and the core modules that are delivered with CMS Made Simple. Any additional modules that you've added are not verified.

You can see the errors, as shown in the following screenshot:

1 Files Not found
Files Not found:
./tmp/cache/SITEDOWN

2 Files failed md5sum check:
./tmp/templates_c/index.html
./tmp/cache/index.html

According to the preceding explanation, these errors are not critical. If you get other failures, it is up to you to interpret what has happened. If you are sure that you have not changed any files, then somebody else has done it to damage your website. In this case, download the original release from CMS Made Simple, extract it, and replace the changed files with the original.

Replacing the files is the first step. If your system has been hacked, it means that there is still a security hole that can be used again and again to damage your system. Please read and implement the following sections to see how you can protect your system.

Usernames and passwords

Check how strong the combination of administrator's username and password on your installation is. Do not use admin, administrator, or any other simple words like these for the username, as they are very easy to guess. Secondly, use strong passwords for the administrator account. Password strength estimates how many trials an attacker of your website would need on an average to guess your password.

There are some tips for choosing good and secure passwords:

- Include numbers, special characters, upper and lowercase letters, and punctuations in the password

- The password length should be around 12 to 14 characters

- Avoid any password made of a word that can be found in the dictionary

- Avoid using relative or pet names or biographical information like your own birth date or a wedding date

Pay attention to an editors' username and passwords as well. Assist them in choosing strong passwords and advise them to keep the passwords in mind and never write them down. You and your users should not use the same password on other websites on the internet.

If you post some news article with the admin account on the website, then the username is revealed on the website in the default news template. It would be better not to show the username at all or replace it with the user's first and last name.

To replace the username with real name, create a new user-defined tag (**Extensions | User Defined Tags**), call it *realname*, and add the following code snippet:

```
global $gCms;
$db = $gCms->db;
$query = "select first_name, last_name from ". $gCms->config['db_
prefix'] . "users where user_id =?";
$row = $db->GetRow($query, array($params['user']));
echo $row['first_name'].' '.$row['last_name'];
```

This code will return the user's first and last name from the user account. It assumes that the parameter `user` with the user ID is provided. To use the user-defined tag in the template, in the admin console, click on **Content | News**, and switch to the **Summary Templates** tab. Open the template for editing, and search for the Smarty variable `{$entry->author}`. Replace the variable with the Smarty tag `{realname user=$entry->author_id}`. Save the template, and see the changes on the website. Apply the same changes to the **Detail Templates**.

Hiding admin directory

Every CMS has an admin URL. In CMS Made Simple, this URL is http://www.yourdomain.com/admin. This URL is defined by default, so that any experienced CMS Made Simple user can get the login screen to your admin console. The more information you reveal to the hacker, the more vulnerable your system is. In CMS Made Simple, you can easily change the URL of the admin console, so that one cannot guess where the "entrance" is.

Open your FTP browser and rename the folder admin to something that cannot be guessed easily (for example, private4me or hide2safe). Then, open the file config.php with any FTP browser of your choice and find the line

```
$config['admin_dir'] ="admin";
```

Change the line to the name you have given to the folder admin. If your admin directory is now named private4me, then change the line shown as follows:

```
$config['admin_dir'] ="private4me";
```

From now on, the URL to your admin console will be http://www.yourdomain.com/private4me. If you enter the standard admin URL in the browser now, then you will get the error 404 (Page not found) instead of the login screen. In combination with a strong username and password, this would give additional protection to your admin area. An attacker must guess the admin URL first, before he tries to manipulate the username or password information.

When you rename the admin folder to something else, the default verification checksum file will not work. This file will still look for the admin folder, will not find it, and then give you an error for each file within this no longer existing folder. Therefore, directly after renaming of the admin folder, create a new custom verification file (**Site Admin | System Verification**), and save it to your local disk. In this way, you hold the current status of the system, considering the renamed admin directory.

When upgrading CMS Made Simple, before copying upgrade files to your current installation, rename your folder back to admin, perform the upgrade, and restore the custom name of the folder again.

File permissions

If your installation is on Linux server (please check **Site Admin | System Information, Server Operating System** if you are not sure), then you should know how file permissions can be configured to secure your system. A Linux server needs to know two things about the file:

- What can be done to a file?
- Who can do it with the file?

The first question can be broken down to three actions: **read, write**, and **execute**. Reading a file means just opening the file and looking at its contents. Writing means changing, replacing, or deleting the file. The last option checks if programs or scripts are allowed to be executed.

The second question can be broken into three types of user: **owner, group**, and **public**. The owner of the file is the user who has initially created it. The group is not important for our needs and will be treated the same way as public. Public is every other user on our server who is not the owner of the file.

With Linux permissions, we combine the preceding information and say who is allowed to do what with each file. You can imagine a permission matrix shown as follows:

Permission	Owner	Group	Public
Read	4	4	4
Write	2	2	2
Execute	1	1	1

You see that there are theoretically 27 possible combinations for the permissions of only one file. Any combination can be expressed by the sum of the numbers in the preceding table and changed with the Linux command **chmod** (change mode). However, you do not need to know exactly how this command is executed as every FTP browser lets you define the permissions intuitively.

Let's see and understand some examples for the permission sets:

- **777** (1+2+4 for each column) means that everybody (all three groups) is allowed to read, write, and execute the file.

- **755** means that the owner is allowed to do everything with the file, but group and public users are only allowed to read and execute the file. They are not allowed to change it.

- **644** means that the owner is allowed to execute and read the file, others are only allowed to read it.

There is a very important file in your installation that is worth securing with Linux permissions additionally. This file contains the database's connection data and is called config.php. It is like the heart of your installation.

While installing or upgrading, the file must be writable at least by the owner of the file, so its permissions must be set to at least **644**. As soon as the installation or upgrade is finished, you should lower the permissions of this file to **444** (everyone can read the file, but nobody can execute or change it).

In an FTP browser like FileZilla, you can right click on the file and select the option **File permissions**. The next dialog looks like the following screenshot:

Generally, avoid setting any files to **777** if it is not absolutely needed. This permission allows the reading, changing, and deleting of the file by every user on your server.

CMS Made Simple and server version

In the default template of CMS Made Simple, the version is shown in the footer area as follows:

 This site is powered by CMS Made Simple version 1.6.6

This information is provided in the template with the Smarty plugin {cms_version}. Delete it and do not use it in your templates at all. You should avoid revealing the exact CMS Made Simple version you use. The reason for this recommendation is the following scenario.

You use an actual version of CMS Made Simple. One day, a security issue is discovered in this version. The development team of CMS Made Simple reacts and publishes a security release. If you do not upgrade your system immediately, your website would be extremely vulnerable as everybody knows exactly what version you use on the website.

For the same reason, delete the doc folder from your installation. This folder contains the file changelog.txt which will reveal the actual version of CMS Made Simple as well. A malicious person just has to enter in the address bar of the browser the following line:

```
http://www.yourdomain.com/doc/changelog.txt
```

Backup all your files and your database again and again. If something is damaged or lost, then you can save your time and nerves by replacing the damaged version with the last backup.

Troubleshooting

While designing and configuring websites, you will surely encounter some issues. There is a solution for each problem if you know how and where to get help.

If you install CMS Made Simple with sample content and templates, then you will get the well documented content pages, templates, and stylesheets with a new installation of CMS Made Simple. They are an invaluable way of introducing yourself to the application and getting to know how it works. Read all these pages thoroughly and save them for future reference.

CMS Made Simple Wiki

The purpose of this Wiki is not only to allow the CMS Made Simple community to collaborate in the documentation process, but to also give you an appropriate and easy way to find information. This documentation is made by CMS Made Simple users and partly covers more languages than just English. However, a major part of the Wiki still remains in English. You will find the documentation on `http://wiki.cmsmadesimple.org`.

You can search this documentation to find answers to your questions. A search button is at the top-right of every page for your convenience. You can read this manual page-by-page or pick the pages you like. In the **Table of Contents** at the right-hand side, you can see where you are (the title of the page you are reading is black).

In the admin console of CMS Made Simple, you will see the **Community Help** link at the top-right of every page (below the main navigation). This link will take you directly to the Wiki page dealing with the function or the module you currently open in the admin console. However, there are still pages that are not written yet.

The more users participate in writing documentation, the more answers can be found in it. CMS Made Simple really needs everyone's assistance to make the documentation accurate, user friendly, and understandable. If you want to help, then please register as an editor on the Wiki site and start to help improving and enhancing the documentation for your own reference as well.

Help for modules

While trying to solve issues with the modules, you should differentiate between core modules of CMS Made Simple and third-party modules. The core modules are installed with CMS Made Simple, such as **News**, **Menu Manager**, **Printing**, **Search**, and so on. Third-party modules are installed manually. The help for third-party modules is not provided by the development team of CMS Made Simple but by the module's developer. Therefore, the quality of the third-party module's help depends on the developer of the module and cannot be managed by the official development team.

Built-in help

Each module installed in a CMS Made Simple website includes basic help and examples to assist you in utilizing the functionality. With CMS Made Simple, you get the built-in help in the admin console. Open any module, and find the link **Module Help** at the top right below the main navigation. The help sections of all modules look mostly similar and contain the following sections.

What does this do?

This section explains the purpose of the module and describes the available functionality. Read this section thoroughly before starting to use the module. Are all the functions you need covered? Will the module solve all your requirements? There are some third-party modules with very similar functionality. Read this section for each module in question, compare them, and decide which one to use. Also see the *Parameters* section (described as follows) for the advanced functionality.

How do I use it?

This section is aimed to introduce you to the module's usage. It is a wonderful possibility to quickly get the first impression of how the module works by following some simple instructions. Depending on the module, this section is more or less complete and sometimes contains sophisticated usage examples or useful hints as well.

Parameters

This section contains all the Smarty parameters you can use with the module. There are required parameters that you must use and some optional parameters. There is an explanation for each parameter with default value (value used if nothing is specified) and allowed values. The list of parameters will also give you a complete overview of what the module can do.

Forge (bugs and feature request)

If you use some third-party modules and encounter problems, then you can also check the bug tracker for the module. The bug tracker is a list of known issues with each module and is provided by CMS Made Simple in the developer section (http://dev.cmsmadesimple.org/). It includes not only a list of known problems but sometimes the solutions. Module developers are supposed to check the bug list regularly and to update their module with new versions.

If you encounter errors with third-party modules, then create a bug report to inform the developer of the module about the issue and use the support board to get help from the module's users. The bug tracker is a place where the developer can track the list of errors. However, it is not the place to raise support requests for the module.

How to get a quick answer in the forum

Using support forums is something that you probably do everyday. So, you may wonder why this section is so long. Well, there are some rules that you should follow while asking for free support in the forums. If you have ever had some questions unanswered in any forum, then you should go through the rules given below to see what the developers want from you to be able to help you.

If you do not follow these rules, then you are not going to get quick answers. Moreover, your questions may be completely ignored. Consider that the forum offers support for free. The developer team and many other volunteers on the forum really want to be helpful and make things work for you. But remember that they all have jobs, families, friends, and other responsibilities. None of them are getting paid for the work they do on the forum. You can buy their time with commercial support or help them to help you by giving them everything they need.

Using search

Search in the forum for your question before asking. Remember that a lot of questions are already answered and you will get the answer quicker. Use the search button in the forum and try different spellings, synonyms, and abbreviations. For example, if you search for any issue dealing with the module **FrontEndUsers** and login functionality, try:

- ◆ Front End Users login
- ◆ FrontEndUsers login
- ◆ FEU login
- ◆ Front End Users sign-in, and so on

Sometimes, it is advisable to search the entire CMS Made Simple project including the forum, bug tracker, and documentation with Google. Open the search engine and enter your search phrase followed by **site:cmsmadesimple.org**, as shown in the following screenshot:

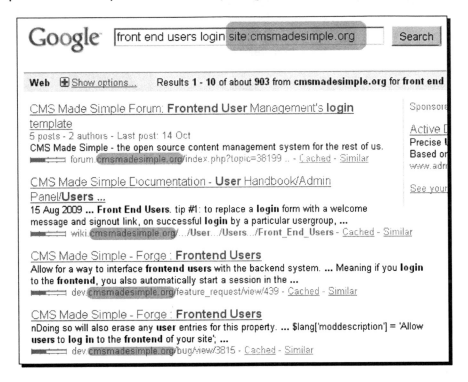

This would bring up search results from all sections of the CMS Made Simple website and not only the forum.

Finding the right board

If you did not find the answer by searching, then use community help. First of all, find the right board on the forum for your question. The important boards on the CMS Made Simple forum are:

♦ **Installation and Setup**: Offers help with getting the core CMS Made Simple up and running. Once you have successfully installed CMS Made Simple, you should choose another forum for your support request.

♦ **Product Support**: Offers help for questions and problems with the core CMS Made Simple after you have finished installing. This board is not for anything that has not been distributed with the CMS Made Simple package itself.

- **Layout and Design (CSS & HTML)**: Is intended for discussion and questions related to CMS Made Simple templates, stylesheets (CSS), and themes or layout issues.

- **Modules / Add-ons**: Is intended to assist if you have a question or problem with any third-party module or plugin that was not included in the standard package of CMS Made Simple.

- **Developers discussion**: Is for talking about programming with and for CMS Made Simple.

- **International Discussions**: Includes boards in other languages. If your problem is related to any language other than English, you can discuss it here.

Choosing the right board from the very beginning will ensure that you cover the widest group of users who are able to help you.

Topic subject

After you have figured out the correct board for the request, think about the right topic title or subject. Let's see some bad examples:

- Urgent help needed!
- Big issue
- Something goes wrong

Give a good summary of your problem as the topic title. If you encounter a problem with the login functionality in the module **FrontEndUsers**, then you should name your topic. **Login issues in Front End Users**. Although a lot of people do know the answer to your problem, they do not have time to look through each topic that is *urgent* or has a *big issue*. They would only pick up the topics with the subjects that they believe they know the answer to.

Provide as much information as possible

Make sure that you provide all the version information you can think of. It is better to include irrelevant data than to omit useful data. The easiest way to get the required information is to use the page **Site Admin | System Information** in the admin console of CMS Made Simple. This page includes everything you and someone who will help you should know. But do not just copy the entire page into the forum. There is a special text version of it. In the top-right corner of the page (below the main navigation), you will find the link **View Text Report (suitable for copying into forum posts)**. Click on it, copy it, and include it in your forum post.

Describe the problem step-by-step

Describe the problem, including as much detail as possible (especially including error messages exactly as they are presented to you). It is not enough to say "If I sign in with the module **FrontEndUsers** I get some weird errors."

If nobody knows what the errors are, then nobody will help you. There are no visionaries in the forum, just developers. Imagine you have a problem with your car. You call the garage and say "My car does not drive. Help!". If you do not provide more information on the exact behavior of your car, then the garage will not be able to help you. The same will happen in the support forum.

If the error can be reproduced, then detail the steps that one can follow to repeat the issue on their own installation. This is a very good method; sometimes by writing step-by-step what you are doing, you are able to figure out the issue yourself.

Be polite. Do not demand anything as there is no guarantee for a free product. Do not threaten to use another CMS if your problem is not solved instantly. If you do not like CMS Made Simple, then you are free to use any other system and claim free instant support there. However, I assume that you will not get free support this way anywhere. Do not insult the developers by saying the code of CMS Made Simple is bad or inefficient. You are not going to get any answers this way as in this case the developer team will assume that you are able to write your own beautiful and efficient code and do not need any help.

Be patient. If there is a solution to your issue, then you will get it. It does not make the process quicker if you hourly "bump" the topic to appear at the top of the board. On the contrary, this can be another reason for being ignored.

Help others if you have been helped

Once your question is answered and you have got your solution, open your first post for editing and add *[SOLVED]* in front of the topic subject. The developers can then concentrate on unsolved topics rather than looking into your topic again and again. If you feel that there is a bug and not a handling issue, then file a bug report for it in the development Forge (http://dev.cmsmadesimple.org) in addition to posting about it in the forum. This will help the developers to manage the process of tracking and fixing it.

If the question could not be answered in the forum, but you have found the solution yourself, or someone has given the solution to you by another way, then post it in the forum so that other people can benefit from it. Someday, you will be happy if someone posts his solution for an issue you have in your installation as well.

If you follow these steps, then you will save a great deal of time for yourself and the developers. Getting quick answers is simple.

Commercial support

So you've got CMS Made Simple up and running and you like what you see. However, your project requires some functionality that isn't yet available for the CMS or doesn't quite work the way you want it to. For that, the CMS Made Simple development team offers independent contracting services. Their in-depth knowledge of the tool and experience in building the package and additional modules can ensure that you get a working, well fitting, and quality tool.

Paid support is available to those people with an important project that are concerned about the turnaround time that may be related to getting an issue solved. Additionally, if you would like to have somebody to call for problems that you just can't fix, upgrade issues, backups, or any other concern, then commercial support may be an option for you.

The CMS Made Simple development team offers various professional services for the web developer that needs a bit more support or needs something a little bit different.

Support contracts

So, you are creating a new CMS Made Simple website for a very important customer, and you are concerned about "what if something goes wrong". For example, if the host changes something, or the site gets hacked, or some unexpected thing happens. You will need to fix it quickly and properly, and you are not sure how you can do this.

It is for such purposes that various members of the development team offer support contracts. A support contract assures your client that if something unexpected pops up, a professional and experienced programmer with intimate knowledge of CMS Made Simple will be available within a reasonable time to either take care of the problem personally, or to assist you via telephone, video chat, and so on in resolving the issue.

Support contracts are nominally priced, are usually on a per-site basis, for a fixed number of "tickets" and for a limited time period (like one year). Think of it like an insurance policy. If something goes wrong that you don't know how to fix, somebody is there for you.

Your clients will probably feel more secure knowing that there is ongoing technical support for their business-critical website.

Software development

So you have a number of websites running CMS Made simple already, and all of them are working well. However, this new site that you are working on is a bit different, and you're going to need some functionality that CMS Made Simple doesn't have yet. You may need some slight changes to the behavior of some of the existing functionality. Where can you go?

The CMS Made Simple development team can work with you to determine a solution to your problem, either by modifying some existing code, or by writing something new.

The developer team has a vast amount of experience working with CMS Made Simple and developing the CMS Made Simple Framework (after all, they wrote it).

Most of the development team members work on a pay for time mechanism. For a nominal fee, you can probably get one of the development team members to adjust their schedule to help you out.

What about larger projects?

The developer team can handle that too. Many of the modules that are available for CMS Made Simple were sponsored by members of the community who love CMS Made Simple and its flexibility, but needed some functionality that was not yet available. Maybe you can become another valued sponsor.

You can contact a development team member, and work with them to sponsor a project on a contract basis. Usually the fees for these contracts are based on a regular consulting rate.

Is the development team a corporation or company?

Actually, no; they are a loosely coupled group of independent contractors that work together. They collaborate and contribute to CMS Made Simple, to the various add-ons, and work on issues like support contracts.

They work independently because they are in many different locations spread around the world, and it is just easier that way. However, they are always ready to help each other, and spell off each other for various reasons, for example, if one of them is going on vacation, the other members are willing to cover for him/her for support contract issues. Similarly, if somebody is just too busy with other projects, they would be more than happy to recommend another appropriate development team member to help you.

How do I contact you?

Well, you can read more information about the development team on `http://www.cmsmadesimple.org/about-link/about-us/` and decide which member(s) you would like to contact. If you have further questions that you would like to ask, but don't want to contact anybody directly yet, then you can feel free to ask a question on the **Help Wanted (commercial)** board.

Pop quiz – administration and troubleshooting

1. What is included in the database backup?

    a. The entire website including page structure, languages, modules and templates.

    b. Only page structure, settings, and templates.

    c. Only page structure and design is saved in the files.

    d. Database does not include anything that is important to backup the website.

2. How often should you backup the website?

    a. Everyday.

    b. Depending on how often the changes are made to the content of the website.

    c. Depending on how often you would like to restore the website.

    d. You do not need to care about the backup. This will be done automatically.

3. Why should you regularly upgrade your websites that are run with CMS Made Simple?

    a. To keep the changes made during the whole lifecycle of the page.

    b. To inform visitors of your website that you use the newest version of CMS Made Simple.

    c. To keep the installation secure and avoid vulnerability.

    d. To be informed about the new features offered and be able to select those you need.

4. What name would be the best for the admin account?

    a. admin

    b. ro0t6i2go

    c. webmaster

    d. test

5. Where do you find free help when you encounter issues?

    a. Any HTML or CSS reference.

    b. Official help board of CMS Made Simple.

    c. Personal message to one of the CMS Made Simple developer.

    d. Comments in the installation files and database.

6. How can you stay informed about any updates of CMS Made Simple?

    a. You will be e-mailed automatically if an update is available.

    b. You have to look up in the official board daily.

    c. You will see the appropriate message in the admin console of CMS Made Simple.

    d. CMS Made Simple does not offer any updates for free.

Have a go hero – configure backup and stay up-to-date

Configure the backup for your website right now. If something goes wrong, you will not be able to recover the website without a backup. Double-check that your backup files include files and database as both of them are important. Play a recover scenario in case of emergency, so that you can be sure that backup is not corrupted or incomplete.

Stay up-to-date. Sign in with the official forum of CMS Made Simple and subscribe for new topics in the board **Announcements** (also RSS Feed is available for your convenience).

Summary

In this chapter, you have learned a lot of stuff concerning the administration of CMS Made Simple. As mentioned at the beginning of the chapter, you do not need to read all of the sections in this chapter. But I strongly recommend going through the sections on *How to secure your installation* and *Troubleshooting*.

Specifically, we covered:

- How to backup a CMS Made Simple website in case of an emergency. You have learned that the website consists of two parts, its files and the database. It is important to create backups for both the parts. Two ways of creating a backup were discussed, that is, third-party modules and manual backups for people who have hosting with restrictions.

- How to move the website from one hosting to the other. You have to move your website if you change the hosting provider.

- How to upgrade CMS Made Simple and its modules. We have learned why it is so important to upgrade the system regularly. You gain not only new features, but improved performance and security. It is your responsibility to upgrade the system and stay up-to-date with CMS Made Simple's development.

- How to secure the installation. There were some useful tips on how you can quickly secure your system and protect it from hacking, attack, and damage. Remember that if you spend some time learning how to secure the website from the very beginning, then it can save you days and weeks of getting your website backup and running, if it gets attacked.

- How to get a quick answer in the support forum. You got some tips on how to get the best answers from the free support forums of CMS Made Simple. Reading this section will save you a lot of time while solving issues with the installation.

Pop Quiz Answers

Chapter 3

Creating Pages and Navigation

1	c
2	b
3	a
4	c
5	c
6	b
7	b
8	a
9	b

Chapter 4

Design and Layout

1	a
2	a
3	b
4	d
5	a
6	d
7	c
8	d
9	a
10	b

Chapter 5

Using Core Modules

1	a
2	b
3	a
4	c
5	d
6	b

Chapter 6

Users and Permissions

1	a
2	d
3	c
4	c
5	a
6	d
7	b

Chapter 7

Using Third-party Modules

1	b
2	b
3	c
4	d
5	a
6	b
7	c

Chapter 8

Creating Your Own Functionality

1	a
2	b
3	b

Chapter 9

E-commerce Workshop

1	b
2	a
3	b
4	b
5	a

Chapter 10

Advanced Use of CMS Made Simple

1	b
2	d
3	a
4	a

Chapter 11

Administration and Troubleshooting

1	b
2	b
3	c
4	b
5	b
6	c

Index

Symbols

{breadcrumbs} 71
{cms_version} 71
{cms_versionname} 71
{created_date} 71
{current_date} 71
{last_modified_by} 71
{menu_text} 71
{modified_date} 71
{root_url} 71
{sitename} 71

A

additional content blocks
    about 275
    adding, for subtitles 275
additional editors 152, 153
additional modules
    installing 137-139
add to my cart template 246
AD Gallery 172
admin console, CMS Made Simple
    about 29-31, 300
    CMS menu 31
    content menu 31
    extensions menu 32
    layout menu 31
    logging in 30
    my preferences 32
    site admin menu 32
    system information 300
    users & groups menu 32
admin email template 249
administrator 146

admin log
    viewing 157
Archiver
    about 158
    installing 158

B

billing form template 249
breadcrumbs 54
browsecat parameter 121
built-in help, troubleshooting
    about 324
    functions 324
    parameters 324
    working 324

C

canonical URLs
    tags, using for 288
Captcha
    about 182
    activating 183
    adding, to forms 182
    installing 182
cart module
    about 245
    add to my cart template 246
    installing 245
    my cart template 246
    products and cart, connecting 245, 246
    product summary template 246
    view cart template 246
case study website
    about 10
    functional specifications 10

Cataloger 231
chmod 321
CMS
  about 8
  existing templates, working with 66
  structure 8
  versus, site builder 9
CMS Made Simple
  about 9
  additional content blocks 274
  additional modules, installing 137
  admin console 29
  advanced uses 296, 297
  advantages 9
  advantages, of upgrading 311
  case study website 10
  dates, configuring 266
  e-mails, sending 33
  FMS 231
  images, uploading 126
  installation, securing 316
  installing 20
  issues 35
  localization 265, 266
  Module Manager, using 136
  modules, adding to website 136
  modules, installing with XML file 139, 140
  modules, translating 273
  module upgrades 140
  moving to another hosting 309-311
  multilingual websites, making 267
  optimizing 314
  page alias 41
  requisites 11
  roles 146
  SEO 277
  Shootbox Made Simple 231
  SMS 231
  translation 272
  troubleshooting 323
  upgrading 311, 312, 313
  user-defined tags 289
CMS Made Simple, requisites
  browser 11
  CMS Made Simple files, uploading 12-17
  file archiver 12
  FTP browser 12

CMS Made Simple files
  uploading 12-17
CMS Made Simple installation
  about 20
  admin account, creating 26, 27
  database information, changing 27, 28
  file creation mask, testing 25
  file integrity, validating 21
  language, selecting 20
  requirements, checking 22-25
  sample content 28
  tables, creating 28
  templates 28
CMS Made Simple Wiki, troubleshooting
  about 323
  third-party modules help 324
CMSMS Forge 137
commercial support, troubleshooting
  about 329
  larger projects 330
  software development 330
  support contracts 329
confirmation email template 254
confirm order template 249
contact form
  adding, to website 174, 175
  Captcha, activating 183
  Captcha, adding 182
  customizing 176, 177
  fields, adding 178
  multiple choice selection field, adding with
    checkbox group 181
  pulldown field, adding 180
  salutation fields, adding 178, 179
  templates 177
content pages
  changes, archiving 158
  changes, restoring 158, 159
content permissions
  about 150
  additional editors 152
  add pages permission 153, 154
  editor account, creating 150-152
  new pages, creating 153
content types
  about 59
  content 59

error page 59
external link 59
internal page link 59
section header 59
separator 59
core modules
about 107
customization, applying 142
File Manager 125
Menu Manager 130
news module 110
printing module 133
search module 122
using 141
custom fields
adding, to news module 119
custom fields, products module
creating 234
defining 235
Is this a public field 235
name 234
prompt 235
type 235

D

database, back up
making, with module 306
dates
configuring 266
date format string 267
examples 267
format 267
default permissions
add global content blocks 160
add groups 160
add pages 160
add stylesheet associations 160
add stylesheets 160
add templates 160
add users 160
advanced usage of the File Manager module 162
allow usage of advanced profile in TinyMCE 160
approve news for frontend display 160
clear admin log 160

delete news articles 160
manage all content 160
manage menu 160
manage themes 161
modify any page 161
modify events 161
modify files 161
modify global content blocks 161
modify group assignments 161
modify groups 161
modify modules 161
modify news 161
modify permissions for groups 161
modify site preferences 161
modify stylesheet associations 161
modify stylesheets 161
modify templates 161
modify user defined tags 161
modify users 162
overview 160
remove global content blocks 162
remove groups 162
remove pages 162
remove stylesheet associations 162
remove stylesheets 162
remove templates 162
remove users 162
view tag help 162
description meta tags 279
designer 146
designer permissions
about 155
set of permissions 155
test area, creating 156, 157
detail templates
about 242
customizing 242-244
duplicate content
avoiding 286
preventing steps 286-288

E

e-commerce suite
optional modules 261
e-commerce workshop 262

e-mails, CMS
  sending 33
editor 146
email template 177
events
  about 293
  mails, sending after page update 293, 294
  triggering 293
existing templates
  ready-made template, importing 66, 67
  working with 66
extra page attribute
  about 276
  using 276

F

FFmpeg 191
fields
  adding, to forms 178
File Manager 125
files
  browsing, File Manager used 125
final message template 254
Forge, troubleshooting 325
FormBuilder
  about 174
  Captcha, adding to forms 182, 183
  contact form, adding to website 174, 175
  contact form, customizing 176, 177
  fields, adding to forms 178
  installing 174
form template 177

G

gallery
  creating 168
  images, uploading 168, 169
gallery module
  installing 168
gateway complete template 249
global content blocks
  about 108
  adding, to website 108-110
global meta tags
  adding 52

H

hierarchy report templates
  about 237
  customizing 237, 239
HTML template
  porting 84
  porting, to CMS Made Simple 85-90

I

IF code 94
IF structure 96
Image Manager 126
images
  uploading, image editor used 126, 128
  using, in content 128, 129
  using, in templates 128, 129
includetemplate parameter 134
installation security, CMS Made Simple
  admin directory, hiding 320
  file permissions 320, 321
  password, checking 319
  securing 316
  server version 322
  simple version 322
  system verification 317, 318
  username, checking 319
Instant Payment Notification. *See* **IPN**
invoice template 249
IPN 225

J

job 183
jQuery
  integrating, in navigation 294-296

K

keywords
  using, in image files 283
  using, in page alias 283

L

link template 134
localization 265, 266
lost email template 254

M

manual back up, website
about 307
database, backing up with phpMyAdmin
307-309
Mary 153, 154
Menu Manager 130
menu template
creating 97-99
message template 249
meta elements 50
meta tags
about 50, 279
adding, to pages 50, 51, 279, 280
description meta tags 279
keywords 280
mod_deflate 315
module FrontEndUsers settings
about 214
adjusting 215
preferences 215
Module Manager
about 136
using 136
module permissions 162
modules
custom translation 274
installing, with XML file 139, 140
removing 140
translating 273
uninstalling 140
multilingual websites
about 267
flags, adding as language menu 270
hierarchy solution 270
language entries, editing 269
making 267, 269
news articles, separating by language 271
multiple choice selection field
adding, to forms 181
mysql binaries 306
my cart template 246

N

navigation
adding, to template 79, 80

creating 63, 78
designing 80
designing, with pure CSS 80-82
sidebar navigation, adding 83
navigation control, website
about 57
content types, used 59
default page 58
pages, hiding 57, 58
navigation template
creating, with Smarty loop 96, 97
menu template, creating 97-99
neolao 191
new products catalog module
basic information 197
creating 196
final step 207, 208
first level (categories), creating 198-201
second level (products), creating 202-207
new products catalog module configuration
about 208
product list template, creating 209, 210
news
displaying, on website 111, 112
news categories
about 114
creating 114, 116
Newsletter Made Simple. *See* **NMS**
news module
about 110, 111
custom fields, adding 119
news, adding 112
news items, adding to page 112, 113
news articles, managing 110
news categories 114
news templates, customizing 116
news title, using as page title 122
news templates
browse category 116
customizing 116
detail 116
form 116
new summary template, creating 117-119
summary 116
NMS
about 183
installing 183

mails, sending to registered customers 184-186
templates 187

O

optimization, CMS Made Simple
  about 314
  compression 314
  CSS, in global settings 315, 316
  persistent connection 315
orders module
  about 247
  admin email template 249
  billing form template 249
  checkout step, adding 248
  confirm order template 249
  customer registration, integrating 252, 254
  gateway complete template 249
  invoice template 249
  login screen, integrating 250-252
  message template 249
  payment form template 249
  user email template 249
output, Smarty basics
  controlling, with IF function 94
  tags, hiding 94
override print stylesheet tab 134

P

page alias 41
page content
  formatting 43, 45
  formatting, WYSIWYG editor used 44
page hierarchy
  about 52
  breadcrumbs 54
  search engine friendly URLs 54
  search engine friendly URLs, enabling on
    website 55
  sub pages, adding to website 52-54
pages
  adding, to website 39, 40
  changes, previewing 43
  creating 39, 63
  deleting 43
  editing 42
  existing pages, editing 42

global meta tags, adding 52
meta tags, adding 50
multiple pages, changing 60
new page, creating as copy of existing page 60
page alias, changing 43
printing 133
parameters, news module
  browsecat 121
  showall 121
Payment Data Transfer. *See* **PDT**
payment form template 249
Paypal Gateway module
  about 255
  installing 256
  PayPal returns payment data methods 255
  test accounts, creating 256, 257
PayPal returns payment data methods
  about 255
  IPN 255
  PDT 255
PayPal seller account
  configuring 258
  instant payment notification 259
  language encoding 260, 261
  payment receiving preferences 258
  website payment preferences 259
PDF settings tab 134
PDT 255
photo gallery
  albums, adding 170
  creating 168
  custom gallery template, creating 172-174
  images, uploading 168, 169
  images, using on other pages 170
  random images, adding to template 170, 171
  resize methods 169
PHP code
  executing, in tags 293
phpMyAdmin 307
popup parameter 134
printed version, webpage
  customizing 135
printing module 133
print link
  adding 133
  customizing 135
  media type, adding to stylesheets 135

PDF version of page, generating 136
print template 134
print versions, pages
  avoiding 287
product catalog
  about 195
  creating 195, 196
  examples 196
  new catalog-like module, configuring 208
  new catalog-like module, creating 196
product hierarchy, products module
  categories 236
  creating 236
products module
  about 232
  advantages 232
  custom fields, creating 234
  first product, adding 233, 234
  product hierarchy, creating 236
  product templates, customizing 237
product summary template 246
product templates, products module
  customizing 237
  detail templates 242
  hierarchy report templates 237
  summary templates 239
protected pages
  creating 216
  service desk, protecting 217
pulldown field
  adding, to forms 180

Q

Qualifier 95
Qualifiers, Smarty
  eq 96
  gt 96
  gte 96
  lt 96
  lte 96
  mod 96
  neq 96
  not 96
question module
  installing 137, 139

R

reCaptcha
  about 183
  advantages 183
registration Template 1 254
registration template 2 254
resize methods, photo gallery
  crop 169
  scale 169
  zoom & crop 169
  zoom & scale 169
roles
  about 146
  administrator 146
  designer 146
  editor 146
Russian Translation Center example 272

S

salutation fields
  adding, to forms 178, 179
sample website 62
script parameter 134
search engine friendly URLs 284
search engine friendly URLs
  about 54, 284
  enabling, on website 55
  example 56
Search engine optimization. *See* **SEO**
search module
  about 122
  search form, adding 123-125
selfregistration module
  about 252
  confirmation email template 254
  final message template 254
  installing 252
  lost email template 254
  methods 253
  registration template 1 254
  registration template 2 254
SEO
  about 277
  duplicate content, avoiding 286
  keywords, using in image files 283

keywords, using in page alias 283
meta tags 279
page title 277, 278
search engine friendly URLs 284
SEO markup, using in pages 282, 283
SEO markup, using in templates 281
visitor statistics 289
XML sitemaps creating 288
SEO markup
using, in pages 282, 283
using, in templates 281
service desk functionality
custom functionality 229
implementing 211
module frontend users, settings 214, 215
protected pages, creating 216
support ticket system, creating 218
templates, FrontendUsers module 215
visitors logins, managing 211
Shop Made Simple (SMS) 231
showall parameter 121
showbutton parameter 134
sidebar navigation
adding 83
sitemap
creating 130-132
sitemaps 288
Smarty basics
learning 91
navigation template, creating with smarty loop
96, 97
output, controlling with IF function 94
Smarty variables, working with 91
Smarty parameters 72
Smarty plugins
about 73
using, in content 74
Smarty tags
about 67
adding, to templates 70
Smarty variables
about 91
getting 91-93
working with 91
Smarty web template system 67
Smarty plugins 73
Smarty tags

{breadcrumbs} 71
{created_date} 71
{last_modified_by} 71
{menu_text} 71
{modified_date} 71
adding, to templates 71
stylesheets
adding, to template 74
creating 75-77
media types 78
submission template 177
sub pages
adding, to website 52
summary templates
about 239
creating 117, 118
customizing 239-241
support forums, troubleshooting
helping others 328, 329
problem, describing 328
right board, finding 326, 327
search, using 325, 326
topic subject 327
version information, providing 327, 328
support ticket system
about 218
answer fields, adding 222, 223
creating 218
creating, CGFeedback module used 218-221
dialogue, enabling 226-229
summary template 223
ticket list, customizing 223-225
system information
CMS Install Information 300
PHP Information 300, 301
Server Information 300-303

T

tags output
controlling 72
Smarty tags, adding to template 72
template
creating 67-69
dynamic parts, adding 69
exporting 101
output, controlling 72

Smarty tags, adding 70
Smarty tags, adding 71
stylesheets, adding 74
Template Externalizer 157
templates, FrontendUsers module
change settings template 215
forgot password template 215
login template 215
logout template 215
lost username template 215
view user template 215
templates, NMS
archieve templates, 187
confirm subscribe, 187
subscribe, 187
unsubscribe, 187
user settings, 187
text parameter 134
third party modules 192, 193
TinyMCE
configuring 45, 46, 47
replace function, activating 48, 49
search function, activating 48, 49
translation 272
Translation Center
about 272
Russian Translation Center example 272, 273
troubleshooting, CMS Made Simple
about 323
built-in help 324
CMS Made Simple Wiki 323
commercial support 329
forge 325
support forums, using 325

U

upgrade, CMS Made Simple
about 311-313
advantages 311
user
assigning, to group 148, 149
creating 146, 147

user-defined tags
about 289
creating 290
custom user-defined tag, creating 290, 291
page information, getting in UDT 292
parameters, adding 291
user email template 249
user notifications 163

V

videos
displaying 188
own video player, adding 190, 191
view cart template 246
visitors login
managing 211, 212
user account, creating 212-214
visitor statisitcs 289

W

website, back up
database, backing up 306
manual backup 307
website files, backing up 304
website, CMS Made Simple
backing up 303, 304
files, backing up 304
website files, back up
making, with module 304, 305
WYSIWYG editor 44

X

XML sitemaps
creating 288

Y

YouTube videos
embedding 188-190

Packt Open Source Project Royalties

When we sell a book written on an Open Source project, we pay a royalty directly to that project. Therefore by purchasing CMS Made Simple 1.6: Beginner's Guide, Packt will have given some of the money received to the CMS Made Simple project.

In the long term, we see ourselves and you—customers and readers of our books—as part of the Open Source ecosystem, providing sustainable revenue for the projects we publish on. Our aim at Packt is to establish publishing royalties as an essential part of the service and support a business model that sustains Open Source.

If you're working with an Open Source project that you would like us to publish on, and subsequently pay royalties to, please get in touch with us.

Writing for Packt

We welcome all inquiries from people who are interested in authoring. Book proposals should be sent to author@packtpub.com. If your book idea is still at an early stage and you would like to discuss it first before writing a formal book proposal, contact us; one of our commissioning editors will get in touch with you.

We're not just looking for published authors; if you have strong technical skills but no writing experience, our experienced editors can help you develop a writing career, or simply get some additional reward for your expertise.

About Packt Publishing

Packt, pronounced 'packed', published its first book "Mastering phpMyAdmin for Effective MySQL Management" in April 2004 and subsequently continued to specialize in publishing highly focused books on specific technologies and solutions.

Our books and publications share the experiences of your fellow IT professionals in adapting and customizing today's systems, applications, and frameworks. Our solution-based books give you the knowledge and power to customize the software and technologies you're using to get the job done. Packt books are more specific and less general than the IT books you have seen in the past. Our unique business model allows us to bring you more focused information, giving you more of what you need to know, and less of what you don't.

Packt is a modern, yet unique publishing company, which focuses on producing quality, cutting-edge books for communities of developers, administrators, and newbies alike. For more information, please visit our website: www.PacktPub.com.

PUBLISHING

Building powerful and robust websites with
Drupal 6

Build your own professional blog, forum, portal or community
website with Drupal 6

David Mercer · PACKT

Building Powerful and Robust Websites with Drupal 6

ISBN: 978-1-847192-97-4   Paperback: 380 pages

Build your own professional blog, forum, portal or community website with Drupal 6

1. Set up, configure, and deploy Drupal 6

2. Harness Drupal's world-class Content Management System

3. Design and implement your website's look and feel

4. Easily add exciting and powerful features

5. Promote, manage, and maintain your live website

Alfresco 3
Enterprise Content Management Implementation

Install, use, customize, and administer this powerful, Open
Source Java-based Enterprise CMS

CIGNEX

Munwar Shariff   Vinita Choudhary
Amita Bhandari   Pallika Majmudar   PACKT

Alfresco 3 Enterprise Content Management Implementation

ISBN: 978-1-847197-36-8   Paperback: 600 pages

How to customize, use, and administer this powerful, Open Source Java-based Enterprise CMS

1. Manage your business documents with version control, library services, content organization, and advanced search

2. Create collaborative web sites using document libraries, wikis, blogs, forums, calendars, discussions, and social tagging

3. Integrate with external applications such as Liferay Portal, Adobe Flex, iPhone, iGoogle, and Facebook

4. Automate your business process with the advanced workflow concepts of Alfresco 3

Please check **www.PacktPub.com** for information on our titles

CPSIA information can be obtained at www.ICGtesting.com
226630LV00003B/71/P

9 781847 198204